INFORMATION MARKETING
A S S O C I A T I O N

The Information Marketing Association's Official Get Rich Guide to Information Marketing

Build a Million-Dollar Business in Just 12 Months

Dan Kennedy Bill Glazer Robert Skrob

With Audio CD

EP
Entrepreneur. Press

Editorial Director: Jere Calmes
Editorial Development and Production: CWL Publishing Enterprises, Inc., Madison, WI, www.cwlpub.com

This publication is designed to provide accurate and authoritative information in regard to the subject matter covered. It is sold with the understanding that the publisher is not engaged in rendering legal, accounting, or other professional services. If legal advice or other expert assistance is required, the services of a competent professional person should be sought.

—From a Declaration of Principles jointly adopted by
a Committee of the American Bar Association and
a Committee of Publishers and Associations

ISBN   13: 978-1-59918-140-0
          10: 1-59918-140-1

Library of Congress Cataloging-in-Publication Data
Kennedy, Dan S., 1954-
   The official get rich guide to information marketing : build a million dollar business in just 12 months / by Dan Kennedy, Bill Glazer, and Robert Skrob.
      p. cm.
Includes bibliographical references and index.
ISBN-13: 978-1-59918-140-0 (alk. paper)
ISBN-10: 1-59918-140-1 (alk. paper)
   1. Information services—Marketing. 2. Information services industry.
3. Information technology—Economic aspects. 4. Success in business.
I. Skrob, Robert. II. Glazer, Bill. III. Title.
HD9999.I492K46 2007
025.04068'8—dc22

2007025356

11 10 09 08 07   10 9 8 7 6 5 4 3

Contents

Contents

Info-Marketing Success Stories

Here is a *quick reference guide* to the individuals who shared the details of how they built successful info-marketing businesses. Look for the *Info-Marketer Profiles* in the chapters listed below.

Info-Marketing Success Stories

CHAPTER	INFO-MARKETER	STORY
Chapter 4	Greg Milner	Seminars, direct mail, newsletters, e-mail, ads, tele-seminars, Internet—this info-marketer uses them all to generate leads.
Chapter 4	Art Sobczak	How one info-marketer leveraged his business to create lucrative speaking opportunities.
Chapter 5	Ben Glass	Attorney produces marketing toolkit for lawyers
Chapter 5	Fabienne Fredrickson	It's 3:00 a.m., and Fabienne Fredrickson is sleeping like a baby.
Chapter 5	Brett Fogle	Building an info-marketing business with joint ventures: how one Internet marketer went from zero to 7 figures with zero advertising.
Chapter 5	Dave Dee	Making money by magic.
Chapter 7	Chris Mullins	Make your own news.
Chapter 8	Ed O'Keefe	Hard work and research pay off.
Chapter 8	Nigel Botterill	Selling "turnkey" marketing tools without creating work for the info-marketer.
Chapter 8	Matt Gillogly	Instead of selling how-to manuals an info-marketer sells automated lead-generation systems
Chapter 8	Reed Hoisington	Life at the beach with Reed Hoisington.
Chapter 8	Ted Thomas	Foreclosure can be a *good* thing—just ask Ted Thomas.
Chapter 8	Alexandra Brown	The "E-Zine Queen" rules.

CHAPTER	INFO-MARKETER	STORY
Chapter 9	Chris Pizzo	The most hated martial artist on the planet.
Chapter 9	Bob Serling	From computer manuals to "info millions."
Chapter 9	Troy White	From making corporate sales calls to making money in his sleep.
Chapter 11	Robert Bly	Running an info-business in only 27 minutes each day.
Chapter 11	Joe Polish	A different sort of ELF™.
Chapter 11	Daniel Levis	Man sheds his "monkey suit" and kisses the corporate world goodbye.
Chapter 11	Robin Robins	From zero to $1.4 million in two years: the story of a telemarketing "baby sitter" who cut her sales teeth by selling frozen meat.
Chapter 11	Scott Tucker	Creating a $3-million-a-year income in 18 months

Introduction

Welcome to the Most Profitable Business Ever Devised

by Dan Kennedy

Chairman Emeritus, Information Marketing Association

T HE OLD *NAKED CITY* TELEVISION SHOW USED TO OPEN WITH A statement about there being a million stories in the naked city. In the industry that I've played a large role in birthing, defining, and developing, the one we now call "information marketing," there may not yet be a million stories. But there certainly are tens of thousands. A few dozen of them are in this book, not for want of hundreds or thousands more, but in the interest of putting a book on the bookstore shelf that will fit there. The commonalities of these stories are important and fit into two categories.

One is proof. These stories feature ordinary people from all sorts of backgrounds, walks of life, businesses, and interests who have created extraordinary incomes, lifestyles, wealth, and positive influences on others, from scratch, in most cases very quickly, and in some cases with limited resources. They have little in common but having done that. I know personally almost everyone you will meet in this book. Some are highly educated, some are barely educated. Some are young, some old. Some brilliant. Some I won't identify are anything but. Some are pretty good writers, some can't write a grocery list. Some come from successful businesses. Others do not. There is a magician, a pest control guy, a lawyer. There is absolutely nothing "special" about them that you lack. Their stories are revealing of mindset, not of prerequisite qualifications. I think this is extremely important. In my experience of coaching countless people to million-dollar-a-year incomes and multimillion-dollar wealth by starting and developing these kinds of businesses, it's been my observation that, at the start, and as they progress, virtually all stumbling blocks are inside their own beliefs about what they can and cannot do, what people will and will not pay, how fast results can occur.

The other is mechanics. Within their stories and examples, you can find—and should diligently look for and list—the same basic steps repeated, the same strategies employed. Their products, their markets served, whom they sell to, and what they choose to sell in what order and at what price all differ. But the *structure* of their businesses is the same. You have in this book a collection of examples accurately representative of hundreds more just like them, all with the same structures. It is here for you to see. Here for you to copy.

The information marketing industry has become quite large but is almost entirely made up of small businesses, from the home-based solo operators or tiny teams generating a million to a few million dollars a year to entities doing 10 to 20 times that much, yet still "lean 'n mean" by traditional standards. At the time that I'm writing this, there are 34 of these information marketers in my private client group, and were they combined into one publishing conglomerate, it could boast of over $175 million of yearly revenue. Less directly, I've helped launch or have worked with well over 500 of these businesses, and were they all combined, we'd easily be accounting for over a billion dollars a year. Maybe as interesting is the incredible reach and influence of these businesses, individually and collectively. Through those who work in business niches, again combined, several million business owners a year are influenced and assisted. Also, in large part thanks to the Internet, these businesses are global. In Glazer/Kennedy, for example, roughly 20% of our members (customers) are from places other than the United States and Canada.

No other business offers you the kinds of fascinating and lucrative opportunities as information marketing does. You can pursue things that interest you; travel or not as you please—but if you please, legitimately make it tax-deductible; operate globally from your kitchen table; and place yourself in the top 1% income earners' club in as short a time as one year. You can become a celebrity or remain anonymous as you prefer. You can begin humbly or audaciously. One of the people I first studied when I was starting 30 years ago had begun selling a $5 booklet (about ridding your garden of gophers) via tiny classified ads in rural newspapers and farm magazines. One of the most recent info-businesses I helped launch started out selling a $40,000 coaching program. You can work when you please, where you please, as you please. You can have some employees, lots of employees, or no employees. You can outsource whatever you aren't good at or interested in. You can personally interact with your customers through tele-seminars, seminars, or coaching programs, or you can make millions without ever meeting a single one of your customers face to face. I could go on with this long list of flexibility. The point is this: You make the rules, you bend this business to your preferences, and you need sacrifice nothing for enormous financial success.

This brings me to one last comment, about the phrase "get rich quick" in this book's title. There's no virtue in getting rich slowly. There's nothing wrong with doing it quickly. When you make bank deposits, they don't add a bonus for "slow" nor deduct a penalty for "fast." You may have been conditioned and programmed to believe that there is something wrong with getting rich quick or that the very idea is "fool's gold," implausible, possibly even an outright lie. I ask you to ask yourself: Have any of the sources of that viewpoint gotten rich quick? Or at all? Quite frankly, if you spend any time with the people in this book and the thousands they represent, you'll get a very different perspective. As someone who repeatedly, consistently, and quite routinely works with people who accelerate from standing starts to giant incomes in info-marketing, "get rich quick" is my reality. With what you will discover here, it can be yours, too.

So step into a unique world virtually unknown to the general public, where entrepreneurs are alchemists, where ideas morph into thriving businesses at blinding speed free of the operational burdens and constraints of all other businesses, where people earn giant incomes immersed in their own interests and passions.

TERMINOLOGY: As you go through this book you will undoubtedly find industry terms that are unfamiliar to you. A handy glossary of these terms can be found on pages 251 to 260.

FREE IN-DEPTH INFORMATION: A free offer from the Information Marketing Association is on page 266. Additional information is also at www.InfoMarketingBook.com.

About the Authors

Dan Kennedy is widely acknowledged as the leader in developing the modern information marketing industry. Certainly more people have gone from zero to multimillion-dollar info-businesses under his guidance than by any other means or mentor, and virtually every significant breakthrough in this industry in the last decade has come from Dan and his clients, including the now common continuity and forced continuity approaches, the ascension model, every means of selling high-priced coaching, boot camp add-on days, contests to promote coaching, and on and on and on. To learn how to use Dan's most recent breakthrough, info-marketers each paid $12,000 to attend a three-day briefing. Four different info-marketers pioneering this newest business model each went from zero to over $1 million in income within 12 months. Dan is the author of nine business books, including *No B.S. Direct Marketing for Non-Direct Marketing Businesses* and his newest, *No B.S. Time Management for Entrepreneurs*, available in bookstores or from online booksellers. Additional information and free chapter previews are available at **www.NoBSBooks.com**. Included with the book is a coupon for a free kit of peak personal productivity tools. Kennedy is also a busy entrepreneur, consultant, speaker, and direct-response advertising copywriter. Info is available at **www.DanKennedy.com.**

Bill Glazer entered the information marketing field at Dan Kennedy's urging. As a famously successful owner of menswear stores, Bill began in that niche and quickly built his BGS MARKETING to a million-dollar-plus information business. Today, BGS provides "advertising tool kits," marketing, and training to 47 different retail niches, and its *Outside the Box Advertising* newsletter has over 3,700 subscribers throughout the United States, Canada, and 16 other nations. Bill so adeptly and thoroughly mastered every aspect of information marketing, and ran such a well managed info-business, that in 2004 Dan handpicked him as his successor and sold the *No B.S. Marketing Letter* and the membership business to him. Bill has multiplied its size; instituted the most progressive forced continuity marketing systems, online marketing, and affiliate programs; and now manages the original newsletter, a second newsletter—*Gold+ telecoaching*, Internet telecoaching, and this year, three coaching groups. There is also **DanKennedyWebstore.com**, itself generating revenues in the millions of dollars. Bill operates several coaching groups, one exclusively for info-marketers and three other groups serving multiple types of business owners.

Robert Skrob. For 13 years Robert has created and promoted trade associations and has consulted within that industry. His business, Membership Services Inc., is a successful association management company with dozens of associations serving different industries. His experience in multiple industries has given him unique insights into building info-marketing businesses, and he has created several info-businesses within different industries. In addition to running his businesses, he provides coaching, marketing, consulting, and copywriting services to info-marketers.

Chapter 1

Who Else Wants to Earn MORE Than They Are Worth?

by Bill Glazer
Chairman, Information Marketing Association

I N JUNE 1974 I GRADUATED FROM THE UNIVERSITY OF MARYLAND and decided to enter the family business. My father owned and operated a store that sold menswear in downtown Baltimore. I was young and worked hard, and our store grew slowly year after year.

Wanting to prove myself and create something of my own, I opened up our second store in March 1991 in Owings Mills, Maryland, an upscale suburb located in Baltimore County. As I said above, our stores continued to grow every year, but the growth was very incremental and largely due to hard work, quality products, more hard work, great service, and a whole lot of very hard work.

Then, in 1995, a friend of mine, Mark Rosenfeld, who owns one of the top big-and-tall menswear stores in Philadelphia, invited me to be his guest at a full-day Success Seminar that was coming to his city. It was one of those marathon rallies where they brought in motivational speakers, sports greats, business leaders, and politicians.

As the seminar was ending at 5:00 p.m., they announced there was going to be a BONUS speaker who was going to talk about marketing. Now, I was always attracted to marketing, but the extent of my education was watching what others in the menswear business were doing and attending seminars at industry trade shows. Unfortunately this was only exposing me to what others were doing within my own business, and by 1995 the industry was in serious trouble, with over half of the independents having already closed their doors.

As you might have guessed, the marketing guru who was presenting a bonus session was none other than the world famous Dan Kennedy. To be frank, I found what Dan had to say mesmerizing. For the first time in over 20 years I heard strategies that made a whole lot of sense and could actually put money in my pocket. This would be a welcome change from using conventional marketing media where the only ones getting rich were the media salespeople who were knocking on my door every day.

When Dan finished speaking, he offered his marquee product, called "Magnetic Marketing," and I was one of the first to run to the back of the big arena and invest in it. In fact, I was consumed by it while traveling on the train back from Philly to Baltimore and hated to be pulled away from it when I arrived at my destination.

I did two things immediately. I implemented several of Dan's strategies into my menswear retail business, and I also purchased more of whatever else Dan was making available as well as products from other marketing gurus. In short, I became what I now call a marketing junkie—I just couldn't get enough.

The results were staggering. The first year that I applied Dan's strategies, my business grew by 37%. The next year we experienced an additional 31% growth. It was exciting. I had finally discovered the "secret" I had been searching for.

Then, in 1998, as I was reading Dan's *No BS Marketing Newsletter* (available at **www.dankennedy.com**), I noticed that Dan and the

Success Seminar were coming to Baltimore. I got excited by the thought that I would have a chance to see my marketing mentor for a second time.

Now, I've never been known to be shy, so I figured I'd try to leverage Dan's visit as best I could. I wrote him a letter, introduced myself, and offered to take him out to dinner as my guest as a way of saying thank you for everything his information had done for my business.

You can imagine my excitement when my cashier who answered our phones said there was a Dan Kennedy calling me. When I answered the phone, Dan informed me he would be leaving right after the event was over but could squeeze me in for lunch before he spoke. I said great and told him I wasn't trying to "pick his brain" but just wanted to thank him for helping me.

Then Dan said something that would begin to change my life. He said, *"Bill, if you don't pick my brain ... you're crazy!"* Obviously, he didn't have to tell me twice, and on the day of our lunch I showed up with a pile of my ads, direct mail pieces, radio scripts, and a bunch of other marketing stuff that was over five inches thick. As we sat at the restaurant for over two hours going though all of my marketing examples, Dan said my stuff was so good that I should be teaching it to other menswear retailers. He then briefly explained to me how others in different industries were doing this and making a princely sum of money. This was my first exposure to the information marketing business.

I Was Hooked!

When the lunch was over, my wheels were spinning. After spending 25 years in the menswear industry working long hours, oftentimes seven days a week, the thought of becoming a marketing guru to the menswear industry was exciting and appealing to me.

Six month later I launched my first information marketing business called BGS Marketing (**B**ill **G**lazer **S**ystem), and eight years later it's still going strong, having branched out from just menswear retailers to all categories of retail in over 67 different business niches, including dentists, mortgage brokers, restaurant owners, auto repair shops, attorneys, etc., etc.

In 2004 I took over the day-to-day running of Dan Kennedy's Insider's Circle business, now called Glazer-Kennedy Insider's Circle. We have tens of thousands of newsletter subscribers, over 900 members in our coaching programs, and thousands of people who attend our two international yearly events.

There's Never Been a Better Time

The purpose of this book is to let you know about the opportunity to become what we call an info-marketer. I guess I should take a minute and give you my definition of information marketing. Although information marketing can mean a lot of things and can cross over to what a lot of people are doing, the definition I think best describes information marketing is:

> Identifying a responsive market with high interest in a particular group of topics and expertise, packaging information products and services matching that interest (written/assembled by you or by others or both), and devising ways to sell and deliver it.

Perhaps more important, you will be delighted to hear there has never been a better time to enter this very lucrative industry. There is a HUGE demand for information marketing products, fueled by the ever-increasing pressure on people's time to receive information in convenient ways that will shortcut their learning curve.

In addition, you do not have to look at this as a business where you must give up your current job or source of income. As it was for me from 1999–2003, it can be an interesting sideline business. Others look at it as a great retirement business that offers complete flexibility and portability while providing thousands of dollars a month in easy income. Or this can become your core business, providing a high six-figure or seven-figure income, and if desired—prominence, celebrity, and a saleable asset.

If You Can Name It, Somebody Is Packaging and Profitably Selling Information About It

Typically when people discover this business, they have a mental roadblock about what they can sell. That's because they take for granted the expertise they have developed. When Dan Kennedy first spoke to me about the information marketing business after seeing the marketing I had developed for my menswear business, I never dreamed I could take the expertise I had and turn it into a handsome seven-figure yearly income.

The fact is, if you take the expertise you have developed and package it in a way that systemizes your process, or if you know someone else who has developed an expertise and can package that person's information—YOU can be in the information marketing business.

For example, here's just a *brief sampling* of topics from people who are very successful info-marketers:

- Gardening
- Investing in Real Estate
- Yoga for Golfers
- Investing in Tax Lien Certificates
- Extreme Fitness
- Persuasive Voice Skills for Business
- How to Get Women to Approach You
- How to Make Money on eBay
- How to Learn Gunsmithing at Home, as a Hobby or Business
- Better Sex
- Teaching Parrots to Talk

- Business Niche Marketing Systems for:
  - Restaurant Owners
  - Dentists
  - Chiropractors
  - Auto Repair Shop Owners
  - Real Estate Agents
  - Insurance Agents
  - Menswear Retailers
  - Jewelry Store Owners
  - Pest Control Operators
  - Professional Magicians

Throughout this book you will read about dozens and dozens of successful info-marketers and what they have accomplished by leveraging what they know or what others know. While learning about their accomplishments, you will want to pay close attention to their lifestyle transformations.

This is the key to the attractiveness of the information marketing business, and I would be remiss if I didn't point out some of the most common advantages to you.

The Seven BIG Advantages of the Information Marketing Business

1. Replaces manual labor by "multiplying yourself" and leveraging what you know.
2. Buyers of information products buy more.
3. Small or low amount of interaction with buyers is possible.
4. Few staff required.
5. Small investment to operate the business.
6. Can be operated as a home-based business.
7. Large profit potential.

These advantages should be very exciting to you, so let's take a few minutes and talk about each of them.

1. Replaces Manual Labor by "Multiplying Yourself" and Leveraging What You Know

How does the information marketing business replace manual labor by "multiplying yourself" and leveraging what you know? ("Leveraging" is just a one-word way to say "makes what you know do the work for you.")

Whether you're working for someone else or you're a professional selling your services by the hour or by the job, you are being paid for what you produce. The moment you stop producing, you stop getting paid. This is true for everyone, even for professionals such as attorneys, doctors, CPAs, and businesspeople who have large incomes. Trying to "multiply yourself" by hiring employees to increase the amount of product you can sell is full of hassles. You have the employee who leaves and takes clients with him. You have training issues. You have liability issues even if the employee does a good job. There are hundreds of ways an employee can get the business owner into trouble. The work and the aggravation never end.

With an information marketing business, you create a product once and you're done. It takes a lot of work to create the product, but you can sell it many times, often over a period of several years, without having to do any additional work. Creating an information marketing business is a terrific way to multiply yourself. Few other businesses allow you to duplicate yourself in this way. With an information marketing business, you take information you already know and create a product.

You might think you have to be a genius and invent a newfangled device or identify a trend before it happens. You might worry that if you create a product, you won't know how to protect it through the trademark and patent process. You might not have any idea how to find a manufacturing and distribution company to put your product on the market.

With an information marketing business, everything you need to create a new product is already inside *you*. You don't need dozens of experts. You don't need newfangled distribution methods. An information marketing business allows you to take the information, the secrets, the techniques, *the things you already know* and leverage them. That's the easy way to "multiply yourself."

You may have a hobby and find yourself answering other people's questions about what you do in online chat rooms on Google or Yahoo. If that's true, you can be sure there are plenty of people who have not discovered those online discussion groups. You can package what you know into an information product and make money with your own information marketing business.

Or you may have developed great ways to perform services in a particular business. You can leverage that knowledge by creating a product to show others how to do what you do. By creating your product one time, you provide that business solution over and over again instead of performing the service yourself each time. That's how you multiply yourself and leverage what you know!

2. Buyers of Information Products Buy More

People ask me, "I'm already a consultant; if I create an information product that explains my entire process, won't people just do it themselves and stop hiring me to do work for them?" Absolutely not.

People who buy your information products are much more likely to hire you to perform services than any other customer you market to. Quite simply, having your own published information product makes you the obvious expert. It shows the customer the complexity of the services and the special ability you have to perform them. The only possible conclusion for the buyer is that he should hire you when he needs additional help with his business or hobby. Publishing your own information product will only increase the services you're currently providing and expand your businesses far beyond what you're doing now.

In addition, the people who buy your information product will buy other information products from you, whether they are products you create yourself or products you license from others. You can also partner with other information marketers to sell your products or pay them to create products for you. Once you find a customer who wants information about a particular subject, that customer will continue to buy information from you on that subject. In fact, in many cases he'll have a hunger to buy more than you can create.

Encouraging repeat business helps you further leverage yourself. You spend a certain amount upfront to identify potential customers and sell them your information product. That first product can then be used to sell them other information products. Once you've gotten a customer, you're going to be able to sell that customer many things in the future for as long as you continue to provide high quality information at a good price.

3. Small or Low Amount of Interaction With Buyers Is Possible

One of the best things about the information marketing business is that very few customers will insist on coming to your business location to buy your products. In addition, these businesses can be set up where you never have to speak to buyers if you don't want to.

Today, I never speak to a buyer of one of our products. This is mostly caused by the high demand for my time as a consultant, but many information marketing businesses require their buyers to either communicate by e-mail or snail mail, and this is perfectly acceptable as long as you set the rules upfront with your buyers.

4. Few Staff Required

The information marketing business is a terrific business because you don't need a lot of people to run it. Many info-marketers have no employees and instead pay an independent contractor to help maintain the customer database, ship products, and handle customers' questions. This is known as "outsourcing." You can literally operate a business that makes well over a million dollars a year with very little staff and very little operating overhead.

Once again let me relate this to my personal situation. When I operated my two menswear stores, we employed 65 staff during our peak seasons. My BGS Marketing company operates with just one part-time staff member and myself. If you hate managing staff, then this *is* the ideal business for you.

5. Small Investment to Operate the Business

The information marketing business does not require a lot of equipment. It doesn't require fancy offices, furniture, or multiple computers. It doesn't require special licenses (in most cases). And it doesn't require special education or degrees. You just need to leverage the information you already know.

That's why you can get into the information marketing business with a relatively low start-up budget. Just remember: you don't have to go to school for 12 years, you don't have to pass any exams, you don't have to buy special equipment, and you don't have to have huge facilities. But you must be willing to put *some* money on the table to find potential customers and to market your product to them. If you try to do this business without any investment at all, you're certain to fail.

Even the smallest franchise has an initial investment of $10,000 to $15,000, and there are continuing fees. You should not be fooled into thinking you can start an information marketing business with no investment. Some think the moment they create a product and put a sales page on a web site that people are going to suddenly flood that site and buy their products. That is a myth. Don't believe it.

But don't be discouraged! This is a very easy business. This is a business with a lot of profitability, but you will not create a business that generates over a million dollars a year by investing nothing. You must be willing to test a marketing strategy to find new customers (known in the business as a front-end marketing funnel) and test it until it produces positive results. When you get positive results, you must invest in expanding that marketing campaign and growing your customer base.

From personal experience, when I operated my two very success-ful menswear stores, I had at any one time no less than a million dol-lars of inventory on hand. Conversely, BGS Marketing, my original information marketing business, averages only $20,000 of inventory on hand and nets approximately the same as my two stores did.

What's worse, the menswear inventory was seasonal, so the longer I owned it the less it was worth because we had to liquidate it every six months. The price on your info-products is seldom reduced. In fact, prices are often increased over time.

One word of caution: Many info-marketers do not invest enough in their marketing and end up with a very slow start. Investing a little money in marketing upfront will increase revenue more quickly. You can take a "stair-step" approach by investing a small amount in your first campaign and reinvesting your sales revenues into the next cam-paign. You can increase your marketing investments as you continue to have success in selling your product. That way you can start with a very modest investment, but by continuing to reinvest profits into making new sales and getting new customers, you can build your business.

6. Can Be Operated as a Home-Based Business

This means you can work at home with your computer in a closet or build your information product on your kitchen table. You don't have to worry about customers showing up at your door to buy your new manuals and CDs. You can create products and sell them online from your beach home or as you vacation across the world. As long as you've got a way to create a product, you don't have to be in any particular location for people to buy it.

Not only is this exceptionally convenient, but it also helps you get into this business with very little overhead expense.

7. Large Profit Potential

Many info-marketers are making million-dollar incomes through their information marketing businesses. One day, without any products, without any customers, they went out and gave it a shot. They researched potential customers, they found out what those customers wanted the most, they offered it to them in a compelling way, and then they continued to sell their products until they were making a lot of money.

Some info-marketers have $50-million to $100-million businesses. Some info-marketers are making in the high single-digit millions and have 5 to 10 staff. Other info-marketers are making a half-million dollars with one or two staff people. This is a business that is completely scalable. That is, you can make it as small or as large as you want.

But don't think an information business doesn't require work. It does. You will have to work hard just like any other entrepreneur does. Just as you see entrepreneurs working hard in the mall, in a retail store, or in a new restaurant they've created, you should plan on working hard on your information marketing business. The good news is if you build an information marketing business and put in the necessary work, you can eventually replace your manual labor by multiplying yourself and leveraging what you know to create new products. Your customers are going to buy more from you in the future. You can run your business with little interaction with your customers. You can be successful using a very small staff. It takes a small investment, but the payoff can be huge—if you stick with it and continue to develop your business.

But Here's the *Really* Good News

The really good news is that although being successful in the information marketing business does require you to do some work, success does not come from doing things; *success comes from doing things in a certain way!*

As a matter of fact, after examining hundreds of information marketing businesses as well as working closely with over 60 of them every year, I have developed a formula for success that allows you to do things in a certain way. Here's the formula:

$$QP + QL + MF + RR + CI + WN = BIG\ \$\$\$$$

I know this formula might sound a bit intimidating and confusing when you first look at it, but it is really quite simple. Here's what each element of the formula stands for:

QP stands for **Quality Product**
QL stands for **Quality Lead**
MF stands for **Marketing Funnel**
RR stands for **Risk Reversal**
CI stands for **Continuity Income**
WN stands for **What's Next**

On the pages of this book that follow you will discover complete explanations of each element of the formula, plus you'll get to know a lot of very successful info-marketers who have used this formula in their businesses to achieve extraordinary incomes and lifestyles. If you're new to the information marketing business or just getting exposed to this outstanding industry, I hope you decide to join us.

Info-Marketer Resource

Info-Marketers' A–Z Blueprint Seminar
For Anyone Who Is in or Wants to Be in the HIGHLY PROFITABLE Business of Providing Information

Here's a partial list of topics discussed by Bill Glazer at the Information Marketing Business Development Blueprint Seminar:

1. Seven Decisions the New Info-Marketer Needs to Make
2. How to Evaluate a Niche or Subculture Market
3. How to Thoroughly Profile the Prospective Customer
4. How to Leverage the Affinity You Have With a Niche
5. How to Create a Relationship With a Niche You Have NO Affinity With
6. How to Get Testimonials When You Just Start Out in a Niche
7. How to Get GREAT Testimonials From Customers/Members
8. How to Use Your Lead Generation Strategies to Give You a Whole Lot More Information About Your Market Than JUST New Leads
9. A Close Look at a Beginning, Simple Marketing Funnel
10. An Inside Look at the Six-Year Evolution of Bill's Marketing Funnel
11. An Inside Look at Bill's 2004 Marketing Funnel
12. How to Create Joint Ventures That Produce Good Leads @ Bargain Cost
13. How to Work Effectively With Trade Journals and Associations
14. How to Systemize and Automate the Entire Marketing Funnel

15. How to Grow Rapidly With Minimum Staff
16. How to Find the Right Staff for an Info-Marketing Business (#1 headache I hear!)
17. When to Give Up the Front End and Concentrate on the Back End
18. The Easiest Ways to Create Back-End Products
19. Different Coaching Program Models to Consider
20. Outside-the-Box Lead Generation Strategies (Like "The Industry Survey")

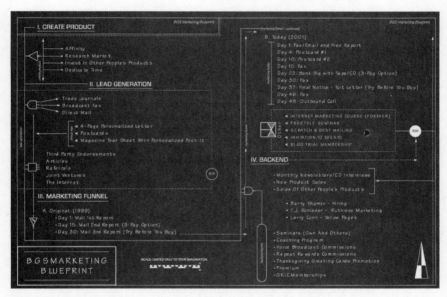

FIGURE 1-1. To help you on your journey, I thought you'd enjoy seeing the actual blueprint I created using the information marketing formula to sell my BGS Marketing System. As I said above, these can be very lucrative businesses when designed to do things in a systematized way.

21. Successful Uses of Audiotapes and CDs as Sales Tools
22. How to Sell via Trade Shows, Seminars, and Speaking Opportunities
23. How to (Legally) Use Broadcast FAX
24. How to Mine Unconverted Leads 12 to 36 Months After Acquisition
25. How to Build the Most Saleable Info-Products/Kits
26. How to Minimize Refunds
27. How to Maximize Referrals
28. THE COMPLETE BUSINESS BLUEPRINT—Used for Bill's BGS Marketing Business
29. How to Maximize Profits AND Customer Value With "Forced Continuity"
30. How to Front-End a Newsletter
31. How an "Offline Guy" Uses the Internet Painlessly and Profitably
32. An Inside Look at the Financial Truths of Info-Businesses: Actual Revenues, Costs, Profits, etc. (Real Case Histories)
33. How to Identify Missed Opportunities in Your Info-Business Plan
34. Seven Most Frequently Made Mistakes to Avoid
35. How to Expand From One Niche to Multiple Niches—How I'm Doing It Now
36. How to Negotiate With Media to Make Sure You Get the Best Deal—Even After They Already Said You've Got the Best Price
37. How to Analyze New Vendors to Avoid a Business Nightmare
38. Copywriting Formulas and Shortcuts—Bill will give you his own copywriting questionnaire that he personally uses before he writes any copy for a client or himself. Frank Discussion on Outsourcing vs. Doing It In-House (the Pros and Cons)
39. When Do You Give Up on a Niche?

For more details visit **www.InfoMarketingAtoZ.com** for a special limited time offer just for buyers of this book.

Chapter 2

Step 1: Identifying a Market That Will Support You in Style

by Robert Skrob
President, Information Marketing Association

I WENT THROUGH A SERIES OF TERRIFYING REVELATIONS. FRESH OUT OF college, I thought I knew everything. I soon discovered, however, that I knew nothing.

What a terrifying year or two that was. No matter how much I tried, how many magazines I read, and how many books I studied, I knew it was a small fraction of a percentage of everything there was to know.

That's when it occurred to me.

During conversations with my clients and co-workers, I figured out everyone else was an idiot, too. Even the professionals—the attorneys and the doctors—yep, they were guessing, too. What a quandary. Not only was I an idiot, but everyone else around me was one, too!

Even though I was an idiot, with a grasp of only a narrow bit of knowledge, my study had given me far more knowledge than anyone else around me, and they knew it. I've discovered that only a small number of people ever make this revelation. They are stuck in the stage where they realize they know nothing. Most people are constantly intimidated by everyone around them because they are searching for the person with all the knowledge.

Since then, I study before every meeting or sales presentation. I get myself familiar with the customer, I make sure I completely understand the details of the deal, and I learn everything I can about my competitors. That knowledge and confidence come through, and I consistently win the confidence of my customers. When someone gives you his confidence, it's 100 percent. If he trusts you on a $10 sale, he'll trust you on a $100,000 sale. And it's as easy as research, study, and a commitment to learning.

You don't have to be the world's foremost expert on all topics to be able to create and sell an information product. You simply need to know information that others want. And the best part is you don't even need to know it *before* you begin. Instead, you can figure out what people want, then go out and find the information second. You can begin this business right where you are, whether you have 30 years of experience or you are just starting out.

The Best Business Positioning

Marketing guru Gary Halbert once told a roomful of seminar participants, "I could operate a super-successful restaurant if I had only one thing." Then, Gary asked the participants what that one thing could be.

The meeting attendees threw out guesses like a great location, a bar, the best menu, or low prices. Because Gary is a great direct response copywriter, one guest said, "A great sales letter."

In the end, Gary told them the only thing he'd need to operate a successful restaurant is "a starving crowd." If there are starving people standing outside the restaurant, it's easy to get them inside and make money. And that's a lesson for all of us info-marketers.

The one thing your information marketing business needs to succeed is a crowd of potential customers starved for what you have to sell. If you do not have a starving crowd, quite likely you'll have a ton of frustration and an unprofitable business. Luckily, it's easy to identify plenty of markets where customers are clamoring for answers to their problems.

> The important factor in a successful info-business is identifying customers who eagerly desire information. **KEY CONCEPT**

The Key Is Identifying the Perfect Market

You must find a market of individuals who are aggravated, who need help, and who want to escape from everyday problems. Using Gary's restaurant example, it's a lot easier to sell food to hungry people than it is to convince people they are hungry and then try to sell them food. While "creating a need and then solving it" can be successful, it certainly is a much tougher thing to do.

Ed O'Keefe with Dentist Profits went from being a college student majoring in nursing to a motivational speaker to a book writer and has used the skills he picked up along the way to create an extremely profitable information marketing business that provides automatic implementation marketing for dentists.

Two years out of college, Ed was "dead broke" and tired of traveling from place to place trying to make a living from speaking to people at schools, businesses, and athletic groups. "Quite honestly, it was no fun fighting for gig after gig," Ed remembers.

Attending a Dan Kennedy Customer Appreciation Event helped put Ed on a new road to success. He bought Dan's "Magnetic Marketing" toolkit and put it to work. His first info-product was the "Ultimate Mental Toughness Training for Volleyball Players and Coaches," and he was able to tailor that product for a number of niches. Several years later, Ed was making "some money, but not much," so he started looking for another opportunity. This time he put some of his college skills to work and hit the library.

Ed believes it is important for anyone in the info business to "choose the market before you choose the product." How do you do that? In a word: RESEARCH.

Ed began his research with the Yellow Pages. He went through the entire book, noting the number of ads for each profession and niche industry. From this, he was able to gauge which industries were investing the most in their marketing.

"Some friends of mine thought I was absolutely nuts. They were like—'What are you doing?' And I said, 'I'm getting rich,'" Ed says, smiling and shaking his head. "I knew I needed a change. I remember seeing one guy selling software for 99 bucks a month, and it hit me right in the face. I did the math. There I was schlepping my $47 book and audiotapes to coaches who didn't have any money. That software guy wasn't any more intelligent than you or me or anyone else. He was just doing something right!"

Ed was determined to find his own "right thing," so he researched 47 different industries and professions. He called trade publications and requested media kits. He found out how many people were involved in each niche. He looked at the media already reaching each niche. As Ed says, "Everyone says to go find a target market and research it, but not too many people go into as much detail as I did. But it's so beneficial."

As part of his research, Ed also consulted the SRDS (Standard Rate and Data Service). This is a book you can find in most local libraries that includes lists of all mailing lists available for purchase. It can help an info-marketer discover the groups that might want to buy a particular product. The SRDS breaks down lists by state, demographics, the number of people who have bought a product, and so on.

With his research done, Ed was ready to choose his market. Now Ed does direct-mail lead-generation campaigns for dentists. Dentists can sign up for Ed's system, select the types of patients they want, and then Ed takes care of all of the marketing. The dentists are notified when the postcards go in the mail, and the next thing they know, they have new patients calling the office. Ed's customers don't have to learn anything. All they have to do is ask Ed to take care of the service, and he handles everything.

> Conduct the necessary research to completely understand your customer, so you can imagine yourself in his skin, going about his day and coming across your sales message.
>
> **KEY CONCEPT**

As you plan your information marketing venture, be sure you start with the market first. Find out what the market desperately wants before you create a product and a marketing campaign to sell it. Too many info-marketers create the product first and then try to find individuals to sell it to. It is a lot easier to identify potential buyers first, allow them to tell you what they want, and then simply offer it back to them in a compelling and exciting way.

Best Markets for Information Products

Business and Entrepreneurship

One of the best markets for information products is business owners or individuals who want to get into their own business. The reason: You can deliver a lot of value with your information to these markets.

If you are able to teach a business owner how to improve his marketing to generate a new customer each week, that could mean tens of thousands of dollars in new business for him. That piece of information has a lot of value to the business owner. Similarly, if you are able to teach a government employee how to buy a home as an investment, then sell that home in two months for a $20,000 profit, you've given him a tool to completely change his economic future. That's what makes business information products so profitable to sell; the information has such a large potential economic value to your customers that they are willing to pay higher prices for it.

Some of the most consistently successful topic areas include:

- Marketing systems for businesses
- How to obtain additional customers
- Getting more productivity from employees
- Saving money in your business
- Methods of selling at higher prices than your competitors
- Unique selling strategies that convert more prospects into customers
- Investing in real estate
- Starting in business
- Investing in franchise and business opportunities
- Communication skills, public speaking
- Tax reduction, tax strategy
- A successful person's plan for business success
- Business biographies

Self-Improvement

The psychology/self-help sections of bookstores have exploded in size over the last two decades. Successful individuals are always looking for that additional "slight edge" they can use to expand their productivity and achieve greater success in their lives.

In addition, Americans' desire for the next new system, diet, and exercise program is endless. These products have a large demand because of the positive impacts they have on your customers' lives. Customers are willing to buy information, strategies, and techniques within each of these categories:

- Dieting
- Exercise
- Better sex
- Goal-setting
- Time management and personal organization
- Sales skills
- Special personal development "philosophies"
- A hugely successful individual's own "plan" for success
- Self-esteem and self-confidence
- Relationships

Hobby-Oriented

Few people in the world are more aggressive customers than golfers. If you can teach a golfer how to lower his score from 80 strokes to 78 strokes, there's almost no amount he wouldn't pay. Not only that, how about the best golf courses to play, trip itineraries of golf courses in different parts of the world, or biographies of famous golfers? The fact is people are extremely interested in consuming information about their hobbies and interests.

Walk into a pet store. You'll always find a huge rack of magazines and books relating to animals. If you've never been, you'll be amazed at how many bird books there are. Can you imagine people getting in their cars, driving to a store, and buying bird books? If not, you need to do more research, because it's happening every day.

Look at the classified ads of any golfing, pet, or auto magazine. Chances are you'll find ads selling every sort of information about how to do that hobby better or differently. If you have a hobby or interest that occupies your time, you have the makings of a terrific information marketing business.

Business Opportunity

There are many business opportunities that are little more than information products. The business start-up guides sold by Entrepreneur

Press are some of the best examples of this genre. They publish dozens of start-up guides, each for a different, very specific business: restaurants, self-publishing, coin-operated laundry, etc. They also offer a "generic" guide that covers basics common to all businesses.

The entire entrepreneur business was started by Chase Revel, with little 1-inch display ads headlined:

HOW MUCH DOES JOE MAKE?

Chase wrote a book about the mail-order business that is well worth studying, and it includes the details of how he started and built this business.

Many information product marketers specialize in reaching out to the business opportunity market. You can find current copies of most of the magazines exclusively serving this market on the newsstand or at your public library. They include:

Black Enterprise
Business Franchise
Business Opportunities
Business Opportunities Guide
Business Opportunities Handbook
Entrepreneur
Franchise and Business Opportunities
Franchise Handbook
Franchise Times
Franchise World
Income Opportunities
Moneymaking Opportunities
New Business Opportunities
Opportunity World
Small Business Opportunities
Success Opportunities
Working Mother

One of the best features of this market is its stability. Many advertisers have been running the same or very similar ads for the same offer for 5, 10, 20, or even 30 years. Once you develop an offer that works, you can live on it for many years.

How to Find Out What Customers Want

There's an easy way to find out what customers want. Ask! And keep asking. Here are five easy market research steps to identify your markets and figure out the problems they want you to solve.

> Don't try to catch fish with broccoli. It may be what they need, but they don't want it. Instead, offer your customers what they want.
>
> KEY CONCEPT

Easy Market Research Step 1: Do extensive research to uncover the daily frustrations of your market. What everyday things aggravate them the most? What really drives them crazy? For businesspeople, quite often it's employee problems. Lack of new customers. Problems satisfying customers. Problems finding good suppliers. Worries about future trends or changes in the industry. Large companies luring business with low prices. Small companies stealing customers with false promises. Find out what frustrates your potential customers the most.

Easy Market Research Step 2: Make sure you have accurate information about the market. How large is it? How many customers are there? Are there regional distributions? How many potential customers do you have in each state? How easy is it to contact this market? Are magazines already being sold to the market? Are there multiple magazines for a particular market? Are there specialties or subniches, groups of people within the market that are interested in more specific programs and ideas? You need the answers to these questions before you can create a product that will sell. In addition, you might find out that this market isn't worth creating a product for!

Easy Market Research Step 3: Consider who else has tried to sell something to this market. Have other information marketers offered products to this market in the last two or three years? What products were they? Did they succeed? Are they still in business? Are established competitors aggressively selling to this market already? (While nobody likes a lot of competition, it can be a good sign that this market wants information products and services.) Don't ignore vendors that are not marketing information products. For example, are there equipment manufacturers? Vendors with services? How are they promoting themselves in the market? Who are the successful vendors in the industry, and who are the contact people? Are there ways to work with those individuals?

Easy Market Research Step 4: Go to the library. Seriously. Take some time to page through the SRDS (Standard Rate and Data Service). This is the great reference we mentioned on page 20. Contact the magazines that serve your market and ask for their media kits. This will give you advertising rates. Most magazines will send you an issue or two for free. Read them carefully! They are a huge source of information on what's going on within your market's industry.

Easy Market Research Step 5: Look through web sites. Research competitors. Research individuals within the market. Find out who the big companies are within this industry. Find out what trends are happening. Are there mergers and acquisitions? Have new products and services created a buzz? Are large economic factors impacting the market in a significant way? Or if you're researching a hobby-type niche, what new ideas, technology, and information are affecting this niche?

You need to carefully consider and extensively research your market before you jump into doing business as an info-marketer. This is not something you can short circuit. Even if you already believe you're an expert in the market, you must go through these steps, conduct this

---

Understand Your Market and Create Products Fast

Info-Marketer Resource

The Ask Database system helps info-marketers uncover quick-profit niches and discover what their prospects and customers want to buy most. With the Ask Database, you can create new products from scratch, effortlessly grab more testimonials from members, uncover new market niches, and quickly determine winning product content. Go to **www.InfoMarketersAsk.com**.

---

research, find out more information. You'll be glad you did. It can save you hours of time and thousands of wasted marketing dollars. You don't want to market a product that people don't want or aren't ready for. You don't want to repeat the mistakes others have made. Find out what has worked and what hasn't. Then you'll be ready to create your product.

> First, understand your market and create a product that people want. Don't create the product first and then try to find customers to buy it.
>
> **KEY CONCEPT**

Too many info-marketers create the "world's best information product" and then try to find a market to sell it to. That is absolutely backward. Your success depends on your understanding of the needs of your potential customers.

Info-Marketer Profile

How One Ex-Salesman, Ex-Law Enforcement Officer, Ex-Company Owner Turned Surplus Junk Into a Million-Dollar Info-Business

Sometimes life takes you down several dead-end streets before you get to where you want to go. That's the way it was for Gene Kelly.

Gene was a law enforcement officer turned salesman turned manufacturing company business owner who hit rock bottom in the early 1980s. He and his business partner ended up "dead broke," as Gene describes it. That's when he decided to try a completely new path.

"I took the last money we had, bought some surplus junk, and figured out how to make a kit—essentially an information product. It was a template with some instructions. We put a little classified ad in a trade magazine—my partner was really pissed off at me 'cause this was the rent money, seriously," Gene laughs.

Gene's partner didn't stay angry for long. "I experienced that 'kitchen table mail-order deal' where we literally went out there and the mailbox was full of checks. We went on to sell way over $1 million worth of that stock," Gene says. "All we did was to give customers some information they needed to make that 'junk' into what they wanted."

Selling Dreams

The way Gene explains it, he's not selling a product; he's selling dreams. "One of my friends in the surplus business told me, 'I don't sell surplus. I don't sell junk. I sell dreams.' That hooked me; what you're really selling in an information product is dreams."

As Gene went farther and farther long his new path of selling dreams, he discovered one "nightmarish" aspect of providing information to people—they ask questions—the same ones—over ➡

and over again. So he decided to add videos to his product that answered the questions he heard all the time. Ultimately he ended up with a $10,000 product all delivered on video. "I've always tried to take whatever product I was involved with and make it a non-commodity by adding information components to it," Gene explains.

Gene credits forced continuity for totally changing the dynamics of his business. "When a customer buys any one of our how-to videos, they don't have a choice. They're automatically given two free months of our monthly DVD gun magazine. It has some celebrity-type features in it. It has teaching, and there's a component to it where they're going to want to collect it," Gene says.

Gene's monthly DVD magazine becomes a library of reference material on gun assembly and disassembly. It comes with a four-color printed newsletter that supports the DVD, and the DVD fits in a little pocket on the newsletter. This is Gene's Silver level program. He is also working on a rollout of his Gold level, which will be an interview with the masters on audio CD each month.

Gene also offers an accelerated training institute, with this Unique Selling Proposition (USP): "Get certified in a high-paying trade in 90 days or less by watching one hour of video at home in your spare time, guaranteed." It's a state-certified distance education program with courses in locksmithing, gunsmithing, machine shop, welding, plumbing, and many others.

The next step for Gene is national certification and delivery of his training institute via the Internet. His target markets range from high-end hobbyists to disabled veterans in need of retraining for a new career to non-college-bound kids "or college-bound kids whose parents don't want them working at Mickey D's," Gene says. He is also looking into getting his programs onto college campuses around the country.

FIGURE 2-1. While many hobbyist info-marketers insist it is impossible to create a monthly continuity program, Gene Kelly has figured out how to do it. This continuity program has created a tremendous source of additional revenue and repeat business. This additional revenue helps to fund additional customer acquisition efforts that wouldn't have been possible without continuity.

FIGURE 2-2. Here is an ad from Gene Kelly's catalog. Gene has included several smart copywriting techniques: his program is a three-part series to maximize the revenue opportunity (note the Vol. 1 indicator in the top left corner); the speaker is an authority; and the ad includes a long list describing what's included, a testimonial, and a photo of a gun built by the lady who wrote the testimonial letter after she used the course.

"We give our students a trade," Gene explains. "They can learn quickly, and if it turns out they don't like the trade, they've got a skill set for life and can go on to the next trade."

For more information about Gene Kelly's products visit **www.AmericanGunSmith.com, www.atiTradeSchools.com**, and **www.GoldBuyingSecrets.com**. There is an expanded info-marketer profile with more information about Gene Kelly at **www.Info MarketingBook.com/Kelly**.

Jordan McAuley Started His First Business as a High Schooler

Info-Marketer Profile

Jordan McAuley has been an info-marketer for a long time—since high school, as a matter of fact. Jordan remembers, "In high school, I just wanted to make some extra money. I started paying attention to copywriting and ads I found in newspapers and magazines. I bought a celebrity address list from an ad on the back of one of those business opportunity rag magazines. That was the start of my database."

Jordan began offering his celebrity lists to people who wanted to send fan letters to request autographed photos of their favorite TV personalities and other famous people. He remembers getting a check in the mail for $300 and asking himself why he bothered working at a video store for only $5 an hour when there was so much more money to be made in his business. His mom wasn't so enthusiastic, though. Jordan remembers her saying, "What are you doing? It's illegal. You're probably going to go to jail." Not many high school kids were doing info-marketing, so it's not surprising that Jordan's mom was worried.

But Jordan was learning something very important in addition to making a ton of money for a kid his age. Jordan discovered he liked the marketing aspects of the information marketing business and found himself studying headlines and advertising content. So when it came time for college, he pursued something related to marketing. He studied the film and entertainment business—how to design posters for movies, issue press releases, conduct publicity, and set up press junkets.

Jordan recalls that his parents were a little disappointed about his choice of major, because they wanted him to become a director instead of focusing on the marketing aspects of the business. But Jordan took full advantage of the opportunities in the film and entertainment business, doing internships at CNN in the publicity department, for a modeling agency in South Beach, and with Turner Entertainment in Atlanta. These opportunities helped Jordan learn the business side of marketing and publicity. He also did some reading on the side. Books like Melvin Powers's *How to Get Rich in Mail Order*. Jordan thinks he got the best of both worlds that way—the business side from his college internship experiences and the grass roots "how the world really works" from the info-marketing books he read.

After settling in at college, Jordan started looking for ways to run his business through the Internet, which was just beginning to take off in the mid-1990s. Jordan soon realized there were ways to transform his business, like offering his lists to businesses, nonprofits, and people in the media working in Hollywood. So by redefining what his market was, Jordan was able to drastically expand the types of people who would buy his product.

Jordan began to study self-publishing, and his stapled pieces of paper with celebrity address lists became the *Celebrity Black Book* (**www.CelebrityBlackBook.com**). That led to a new product

➡️

called "How to Become a Number One Best Selling Author and Make Your Book Famous." Jordan began having authors ask him how he had published and distributed his book, so he knew there was another market he could tap (**www.MakeYourBookFamous.com**).

Jordan licensed an information product but added a couple of bonus reports on how to get testimonials from celebrities. In this way, he was able to take a product that was already created so he could begin selling immediately, but by adding his own special reports, he was able to differentiate his product from everything else being promoted by other product licensees.

One of his members, Jacqueline Marcel, used his service and, Jordan reports, "got 50 testimonials for one of her books from a whole bunch of famous people. She had never written a book before. She didn't know what she was doing. She didn't have any contacts. But because of the testimonials she was able to get, she ended up on the cover of AARP's magazine." Now Jacqueline is a full-time speaker, and she attributes her success to the celebrity endorsements that first drew attention to her book.

After attending a Dan Kennedy seminar, Jordan realized he needed to offer additional products and services to his past customers. He now offers a continuity program in which his members have access to a celebrity database that is updated daily (**www.IMACelebrityResource.com**). It contains celebrities' addresses as well as their managers' and agents' names, and everything is indexed. For example, if a charity such as the American Cancer Society is looking for a celebrity to work on a project, typing in the word "cancer" will show which celebrities have contributed their time to promote cancer research.

Another future project for Jordan is a book or other product for nonprofits. Jordan wants to do an information product for ➡

nonprofits to help them raise money. He has testimonials from non-profits that have used his lists to obtain autographed photos that they auction off. These organizations have found they can spend a few hours and a couple of hundred dollars and receive thousands of dollars' worth of celebrity photos and other items to auction.

For more information on Jordan McAuley and his products visit **www.IMACelebrityResource.com**. There is an expanded profile available at **www.InfoMarketingBook.com/McAuley**.

Info-Marketer Profile

A Direct Sales Process Expanded Into an Info-Business

Ari Galper's story begins and ends with education. He earned his master's degree in a specialized field called instructional design, the science of adult learning and education.

He applied his education in the corporate world, writing and designing sales training materials for large companies like UPS. "Whenever the company would roll out a new product or service, my job was to work with the marketing folks to design and develop the sales training skills and product training materials so the sales force could execute them in the field," Ari explains. "I was the 'knowledge transfer' guy. I was the guy they came to and said, 'O.K., here's what we're working on for next year. We need the salespeople to be selling this much, selling this to that customer. Help us design a vehicle to train them to do that.'"

Ari was a corporate trainer working with sales representatives who were calling prospects and new accounts, trying to close the sale. "They were hitting the same walls as everyone else," he says. Ari brought in gurus from the outside to help break through some

➡

of the problems his sales reps were experiencing, and that's when he realized there was a big hole in the methodology of training salespeople. "I realized that most of the training out there had this mindset that your only goal is to close a sale," Ari says. "When you take that approach with a new customer, they feel like all you care about is your commission, not really helping them."

Even the words a sales rep uses can make a difference, according to Ari. "There can be covert pressure in the words you use, like 'I was calling to follow up' or 'Did you get my stuff so far?' Any kind of momentum like that creates pressure on the customer."

So Ari invented a new way of thinking called the Unlock The Game™ mindset. Ari explains: "It essentially replaces the idea of trying to make the sale. It takes the pressure off the person selling (and the person potentially buying) and allows the prospect to say what he's really thinking. The funny thing is when you let go of trying to make the sale, you make more sales."

After seven or eight years working behind the scenes training sales reps in corporate America, Ari went into the field as a sales rep himself. He became a sales manager with 18 employees happily using his Unlock The Game mindset. Then a new boss came in who, in Ari's words, was "really old school." Ari decided to go out on his own, putting his theory of nonpressured sales to the test. He created his Unlock The Game program with a 20-page e-book.

"The book started selling like hotcakes," Ari exclaims, "so I added a video and a CD to it. Now I have my mastery program online (**www.UnlockTheGame.com**), which has video as well."

Ari's program includes coaching. "We have coaches that work with people over the phone to help them customize their language. The key to this is not only your way of thinking but also the words you use," Ari says. "If you use certain types of words, it sounds sales-y."

Ari helps his customers overcome the tendency to pressure their prospects by offering three hours of free coaching as part of his mastery program. Part one of his program sells for $597, and Ari offers a payment plan of $57/month over 12 months. Part two, advanced training, sells for $1,297 and includes more one-on-one video with Ari. He held a private seminar with 10 clients who had the mastery one program. "They got to pick my brain for a whole weekend," Ari says. The program includes six DVDs, a journal, and "action cards" (similar to flashcards) with reminders for reps to keep next to their phones.

For more information about Ari Galper, you can receive his Free Test Drive of his Unlock The Game program—a one-hour audio seminar called "7 Sales Secrets Even The Sales Gurus Don't Know!"—at **www.UnlockTheGame.com**. For the expanded profile about Ari Galper, visit www.UnlockTheGame.com or for the expanded profile **www.InfoMarketingBook.com/Galper**.

Chapter 3

Step 2: The Business of Selling Paper and Ink

by Robert Skrob
President, Information Marketing Association

I CANNOT GO ANYWHERE WITH MY SON, ROBERT WILLIAM SKROB, UNLESS he has his fans.

These are not electric fans. Robert manufactures his fans by pleating construction paper in small folds back and forth. The only motor is your hand as you wave it back and forth in front of your face. Any time we go to a restaurant, a baseball game, or even the grocery, we've got to wait while he runs to his room to manufacture and stuff his pockets with fans for the trip. Only then are we ready to go.

Robert's fan marketing program generally involves him approaching strangers, showing them the fans, and asking them, "Would you like to buy a fan?" There are usually three or four color choices. Most folks are pretty gracious, and for a while the fans sold well at 25¢ each.

Well, he has tested the price elasticity for construction paper fans and now charges $1 each, and he donates 25 cents of the proceeds to the Hurricane Katrina Fund. Sales haven't slowed a bit, and he makes three times the money. Now once a week we take every fourth dollar by the local Red Cross office for his donation.

FIGURE 3.1. Information marketing really is as easy as selling paper. My son, Robert William, proves that sometimes it is easy to create a lot of value for your customers.

His sister is furious because he is basically manufacturing money by folding up some construction paper and asking people to buy it.

That's not a lot different from what we do in the information marketing business. By taking inexpensive blank paper and blank CDs and packing them full of useful information, you deliver a lot of value to your customers and generate money for yourself.

There are many ways to package information for an info-marketing business. The key word here is *information*. You are not selling the packaging; you are selling the value of the content (the information) within your product. For example, if you package your information in a book, you need to promote your book as an information product. After all, the book itself is not valuable. It's just paper, ink, and a binding. It's the same if you offer your information as a speaker or a coach. The value to your customer is in the information you provide, so remember that your product is the information itself, not the way you're going to deliver it.

When you are creating a product, your goal is to create something that provides excellent value for the buyer, yet can be sold for 10 to 20 times what it costs you to produce. Information products are almost the only type of products that allows you to sell at 10 to 20 times your cost.

You don't need to have writing or speaking talent to create your own information products. There are plenty of individuals who have created audio series stuttering all the way through them. Or they wrote manuals by struggling through one page a day. Your buyers are not interested in perfect English; they are interested in buying the information you are imparting. It's critical that you understand you *can* create successful information products.

KEY CONCEPT The info-business does not require talent, just an understanding of your market and a little work.

It's also worth mentioning that most kinds of information products can be put together without investing a fortune. Many paper-and-ink products can be produced on an ordinary office photocopy machine or, in small quantities, at the local storefront print and copy shop. I know quite a few people in this business, each earning hundreds of thousands of dollars a year, who make up most of their products as they need them to fill orders.

This section of the book will jumpstart your thinking about what you know that can be converted into information products and what kinds of products might best fit your knowledge and markets.

Here is a quick partial list of the kinds of information products. You might start with one. You might develop a product line that includes all of them.

40 Types of Information Products

Paper and Ink

1. Reports—one to eight pages, addressing specialized topics
2. Tip sheets—one page, very specialized, very "how-to," no fluff
3. Manuals—usually published in loose-leaf notebook or spiral bound format
4. Books
5. Boxed sets of books
6. Home study courses—may include printed product with other types (e.g., audio, video)
7. Tests and quizzes—self-scoring or computer scoring
8. Seminar or speech transcripts
9. Newsletters
10. "Back issues" of newsletters or reports
11. Other continuity products, such as "Book a month"
12. Sets of cards (e.g., reminder cards, recipe cards)
13. Forms (e.g., time management systems, step-by-step processes)
14. Posters
15. Multi-author publications (several authors contribute to one product; each gets to sell it)

Audio and Video

16. Audiotapes—live recorded speeches, seminars, consultations
17. Audiotapes—how-to instructions, usually studio recorded
18. Audiotapes—interviews, conversations, roundtable discussions
19. Audiotapes—collections of radio broadcasts
20. Audiotapes—interactive, with a workbook
21. Audiotapes—subliminal, self-hypnosis, etc.
22. Videotapes—live recorded speeches, seminars, consultations
23. Videotapes—how-to instructions
24. Videotapes—interviews, conversations, roundtable discussions

25. Videotapes—interactive, with a workbook

Internet Products

26. E-book—book delivered electronically over the Internet
27. Download—customer downloads manuals and audio over Internet after purchase
28. Membership site—customers are allowed to access information on password-protected web site
29. Structured lessons—customers are led through a series of lessons, may include examinations

Miscellaneous

30. Trainer kits—multimedia, for use in conducting classes, workshops, etc.
31. Memberships
32. Devices (e.g., stress card)
33. Plaques
34. Computer software
35. "Packages"—of a variety of related information products, offered at a special price
36. Continuity programs involving multiple information products, multiple media
37. Services—tied to memberships or purchases or used as premiums
38. Customized—to different markets, different clients/users
39. Private-Labeled—for other marketers, users
40. Licensed—for republication

The more specifically tailored your products are for your target market, the better. By focusing on smaller niches, more individuals within those subniches will react, "That's for me." If after a while of marketing to the same small group you determine that you need to expand your market, you can do that, but you'll already have a base of customers supporting your new marketing efforts through their purchases and testimonials.

My son also applies this technique. When we go to the Florida State University games, he writes "FSU" on each of his fans. In addition, he tries to bring red, yellow, and black fans to those games. He's not shy; he even brings the appropriate color fans for the visitor's team. Now he has products appropriate for any team you are rooting for.

Keys to Effective Product Pricing

One of the biggest mistakes made by mail-order beginners is selecting or creating products to market that provide inadequate markups from cost to retail. The small mail-order business needs big gross profits to succeed.

The rule-of-thumb is that your markup should be at least 8 to 10 times from your cost to retail. That means that a product that costs you $1 should sell for at least $8 to $10. Any markup less than this will not be economically feasible, in most cases.

And this is a conservative figure. What we *prefer* to see is a markup that's twice that high, i.e., 15 to 20 times. Ideally, an item that costs you $1 will sell for $15 to $20.

Defining Cost

Robert used to walk up to people and speak too softly or take no too easily. However, selling construction paper fans isn't as easy as you might expect. Yes, of course, you have to follow all of the principles of getting attention and using persuasion, but there is a lot of competition out there as well as some sales resistance. It is a big task to sell a fan, and you cannot take it lightly.

It's the same thing for info-marketers. A lot of research and work go into pricing your product properly; you can't shortcut that process.

Before you can use the above markup objective to figure out what an item's selling price should be, you have to accurately calculate what the item actually costs you—which is not quite as simple as you might think.

An item's cost is a total of:

1. The manufactured or wholesale cost of the item
2. The inbound freight you pay to get the item or the component parts that make the item shipped to you
3. Some factor for any miscellaneous costs you incur in getting the item made or delivered, such as auto expense in driving to the supplier's place of business, long-distance telephone communication with vendors, etc.
4. Packaging for the item to prepare it for safe shipment from you to the customer
5. Shipping cost to deliver the item to the customer

And there may be other factors particular to a given product or business that need to be added into the total cost. You have to carefully analyze your product and every step of your business process to identify each one of these factors.

Determining the Selling Price

Once you've established an accurate cost, you should multiply it:

A. by 8
B. by 10
C. by 15
D. by 20

and consider each of those possible prices. How does the possible price compare to competitive or similar products already being marketed to your prospective customer? How does the price compare to the value the customer will receive from the product? Can the customer see that the price is a good value?

Many times, the impracticality of the price will rule out the product. Don't ignore this warning signal. If an eight-times markup creates a price that is too high to be saleable, the product is simply not suitable for your first information product.

Sometimes, a product may warrant a price that is even higher than that created by multiplying cost times 20. When this occurs, you've got a number of great options. You can sell the product for the higher price and enjoy a superior markup, you can afford more expensive advertising and marketing, or you can market your product at the 20-times price and offer the consumer a superior value.

Look For the Upcoming Guide
Information Marketing Association Official Guide to Creating Info-Products Quickly

In this book, we'll outline the easy ways anyone can create products from their existing knowledge, easily acquire knowledge from others, or actually get your customers to create products for you. This book will detail the easy ways info-marketers create million-dollar products that sell for 10 times their production costs. Coming soon from the Information Marketing Association and Entrepreneur Press.

Publish on Demand

You do not need to create large inventories of product before you sell them. As long as you ship promptly, you don't need to manufacture the product until after you receive an order. In many cases info-marketers promote a particular book, manual, or workbook. When they receive an order, they send somebody to the copy machine to produce it. They may have a few blank binders or a few blank tape holders, but when they receive the order, that's when they actually produce the materials, the books, or the audio CDs.

Publishing on demand is especially important when you're starting out. You should not take your initial investment and use it to purchase inventory. You need that money to market. Instead, get ready to ship your product but then manufacture and deliver the product after you've received the order. That's especially important if your marketing campaign happens to be unsuccessful. You don't want to have 600 copies of your book lying around unsold! You should only publish as much as you need when you need it.

Automatic Implementation Products

There has been an evolution over the last several years in how customers want to receive information products. While books, guides, and audio CDs still sell very well, one of the secrets of the info-marketing business is to provide as much as possible of the system already implemented for the customer.

A number of years ago info-products were detailed manuals that taught a process on how somebody should do something. Then that started to change. People wanted more workbooks to lead them step-by-step through a process. Then people started asking for ready-to-go samples and fill-in-the blank examples of the things they needed to do. Most recently people have decided they want everything completely done for them—and they're willing to pay a premium for it. Now info-marketers are able to create products that are completely turnkey for their customers, literally "done for them."

Let me give you an example of the evolution related to client newsletters. It is well documented that everyday businesses that publish a monthly newsletter, print it, and mail it to their customers experience tremendous increases in customer value over businesses that don't publish newsletters. This monthly communication increases the frequency with which customers come back to the business to make purchases, it increases the amount of money they spend with each visit, and it increases the referrals a business receives, an extremely cost-efficient means of acquiring new customers. This rule applies to all businesses, from service businesses like plumbers, carpet cleaners, and auto repair to retail stores to restaurants and even to medical services such as physicians, dentists, and chiropractors. All experience a significant increase from publishing newsletters.

Teaching business leaders that newsletters are important is nothing new. Info-marketers have been teaching this for many decades. However, the ways info-marketers teach this strategy have changed, and it's illustrative of the transition many info-marketers are making to help their customers.

Popular Product in 1975. Info-marketers created guides on publishing customer newsletters for businesses. These products detailed the benefits of customer newsletters; provided information on where to obtain or how to write articles; and gave tips for the printing, mailing, and distribution.

Popular Product in 1985. Even though the results of businesses that published newsletters were remarkably good, many business owners never found the time to go through the monthly process of creating one. They just couldn't seem to ever get the first one out. Or if they did get one out, often there wouldn't be a second issue. A significant innovation for info-marketers was the workbook. Info-marketers created a couple of dozen fill-in-the-blank newsletter templates. This way, the business owner could adapt one to his needs and then publish his own newsletter to his customers. The increase in ease of implementation helped a lot of business owners get better results.

Popular Product in 1995. For many business owners, the templates were not enough. Info-marketers began providing actual newsletters each month, ready to mail. All the business owner needed to do was drop in his own name, print it, and mail it out to his customers. This was a huge innovation because business owners no longer had to go through the creation process at all. In fact, the task became something any administrative person within the office could implement.

Popular Product in 2007. Now customers don't even want to touch the monthly newsletter. In response, info-marketers create monthly programs in which the customer gives the info-marketer the customer list and the info-marketer creates content, prints customized newsletters with the business owner's information, and mails them out for the business owner. The business owner never has to think about the newsletter. If someone is ambitious and wants to significantly customize a newsletter, this can be done in just a few minutes a month.

While this example was about client newsletters, this trend has occurred throughout the info-marketing business. A classic example is Matt Gillogly's "Mega-Marketing Machine." While Matt previously sold the sales letters and the list resources to his members, he wasn't able to get the mailings out to generate the leads his members needed for their real estate investment businesses. Now Matt offers a web site that pulls together everything his members need in one place, in one web screen dialog in which several months of marketing can be implemented within five minutes. And because it's so easy, his members are willing to pay a premium for that service.

For more about Matt Gillogly's automated system, visit **www. InfoMarketingBook.com/Gillogly**.

There is a trend away from giving individuals information for them to implement new processes and marketing programs within their businesses to creating monthly products that do all of the work for the customer. This is good for the info-marketer because these products create customers who pay every month for a service, rather than customers who pay every few years for new manuals and audio programs.

Here is an example of an "automatically implemented" service that you may be familiar with. While the weight-loss company Weight

Watchers gives you a points system and a log book to track the amount of food you eat with each meal, NutriSystem delivers prepackaged food to your door; all you have to do is eat. NutriSystem is implementing the weight loss program for the customer by creating menu options, creating meals, and delivering them in ready-to-heat-up packages.

> Your customers don't want to have to learn or to work harder to implement new strategies; as much as you can, remove the work from your products.
>
> **KEY CONCEPT**

I'm not saying one of these companies is better than the other. Some customers will be attracted to the flexibility of the Weight Watchers program while others will love the structure that NutriSystem offers. As an info-marketer, it is important that you offer both.

Some examples of automatically implemented products that info-marketers often sell include monthly newsletters created, published, and shipped for customers; and online staff training systems so managers can let an online computer program train, test, and evaluate their employees.

Specialize, Specialize, Specialize!

When you create your product, the information should appear as specialized as possible. It's critical for your potential customer to look at your product and say, "Oh, that's for me. I need that!" You must understand your market and then design your product to be exactly what your customers want. Basically tell them: "Here are the four things you asked for. Here are the four things we delivered." Then they'll say, "That's for me" and buy your product.

Don't Fall in Love With a Product

One of the things that trips up beginning information marketers the most is that they fall in love with a product and then want to perfect it. There is no perfect product, and no amount of time you can spend on a product will make it perfect. The definition of perfect is always changing. There's no reason to delay your marketing implementation so you can create the perfect product. Today's perfect product will probably be less than perfect 30 days from now. So there's no reason to wait, slow up, change, edit, or try to make it perfect. You must make it *done*.

You Must Deliver to Make Money

The most important product, the only product you can sell in the information marketing business, is one you can deliver. Even if it's not the perfect product, even if it's just Phase 1, you must execute it and deliver it. A good product is good enough. Don't try to make it perfect. Don't try to make it the be-all and end-all of information products. The most important feature your product can have is to be done and ready to ship. Once you're selling your product, that's a great time to start tweaking it. Take your customers' feedback and add their ideas to your product to improve it a little. (That's another reason you should publish on demand.) Now, many people plan to go back and improve their product, but then it starts selling and they don't see any point in improving it. Customers like it. It's getting sold. No one's returning it. There's no real reason to change it. I agree! That's all the

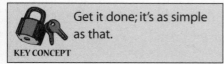

more reason why you need to be done with your product. Don't worry about making it perfect. Don't fret over every little detail. Instead, get it done, get it out the door, and move on to the next project.

Get it done; it's as simple as that.

KEY CONCEPT

Simple Changes Multiplied Product Price 4 Times

Info-Marketer Profile

Persuasive-speaking expert Susan Berkley revised her product to create something that supported a higher price point. A former radio personality and well-known voice on TV and radio commercials, Susan is one of the voices that says, "Thank you for using AT&T," and she is the voice of Citiphone Banking.

Susan originally sold her audio product *Voiceshaping: How to Find Your Million Dollar Voice*—seven audio CDs and a manual along with a copy of her book *Speak to Influence*—for $195. She thought this product was so comprehensive that it never occurred to her that she could add on to it and make even more money.

Then she discovered Dan Kennedy and realized that selling a $195 product was not going to allow her to maximize her information marketing opportunities. One of those opportunities was to take advantage of her speaking skills to become a platform salesperson. Because platform sales often require a higher-priced product, she needed to add components to raise her price significantly.

Susan renamed her product *The Magnetic Speaking Power System,* adding a new product, *Magnetic Self-Confidence,* which includes four CDs. She created this product by interviewing experts about the psychological causes of a lack of confidence and the fear of public speaking. These interviews give her program more depth because the psychological component makes it unique.

Then she created a two-session vocal makeover, which was recorded as tele-classes. After that, she added *Vocal Vitality*, two CDs created with a top speech pathologist about voice care with demonstrations of vocal warm-up exercises.

➥

To enhance the selling component, she interviewed Art Sobczak of Business by Phone to create *Magnetic Telephone Selling Power*, which is a 60-minute CD about selling by phone.

Then she added three bonuses. They include: (1) a certificate for a personal 30-minute, one-on-one tele-consultation with Susan and a written critique of the customer's outgoing voicemail message; (2) a three-month trial membership in a continuity program, which includes a monthly CD of an interview with an expert on persuasion, communication skills, or voice; and (3) a certificate good for a quarterly review of the customer's voice or presentation.

The package, if purchased separately, would cost $1,894. Online, it is available for $795 or four monthly installments of $205.

Susan has sold this program through several joint venture relationships, often adding a special bonus for each group. For "Loan Officer Success" she interviewed seven industry superstars to create "Billion Dollar Secrets of the World's Most Successful Mortgage Brokers." For Mike Crow's Millionaire Inspector Community she created "Speak to Influence for Young Adults" as a relationship-building tool and included a reprint license with a private branding opportunity.

After getting coached by Dan Kennedy on her platform selling presentation, she was excited to sell over $100,000 worth of product in 90 minutes.

In Susan's words, "It was probably the best 90 minutes I ever had in my life. But the best news is I met many wonderful people who will hopefully remain customers for life."

For more information about Susan's products, visit **www.GreatVoice.com**. An expanded profile of Susan Berkley is available at **www.InfoMarketingBook.com/Berkley**.

The Story of a Frequent Flier Who Turned in Her Wings—Taking "Bank on Yourself" to the Bank

Info-Marketer Profile

The life of a professional speaker is glamorous, right? Here's how Pamela Yellen describes it:

"I did the dog and pony show, you know, doing 100-plus gigs a year, going from city to city to city .... "

O.K., so maybe the lifestyle *isn't* all that glamorous. But Pamela continues:

"I really have to say I did enjoy it for the first few years. It was exciting, and I did kind of bask in the glory of getting up in front of the room and all these people showing adulation and all that stuff."

In addition, Pamela remembers, the travel was fun, getting to see places she had never seen before: "If a meeting was in a really great place, I'd extend my stay and write the whole thing off. I even had speaking engagements in Asia, so I got to visit great places, basically for free, and even make some money doing it. So it was exciting and glamorous and adventurous for the first few years."

Pamela Yellen started out as a motivational speaker, teaching insurance agents and financial advisors how to do their prospecting and marketing. She tried her hand at selling products at the back of the room but says, "I definitely didn't know what I was doing. I sold them for like nothing, and I hardly sold any of them."

Pamela went from meeting to meeting, with her husband trying to sell products for her, because she "wasn't making enough money to justify bringing staff along." Things needed to change. Enter Dan Kennedy.

Pamela remembers, "Dan sent me these sales letters saying that professional speaking is the easiest and fastest way to make $25,000 or $30,000 or more in an hour without using a gun. And I thought, 'Hmm, well I've certainly never made that kind of money ➡

Bank On Yourself™

How to Pocket the Interest You Now Pay to Banks, Credit Card and Finance Companies... and Turn it into Personal Wealth and a Tax-Free Income for Life

By Pamela G. Yellen

Discover how to...

Finance a car, home, credit card debt, home theater, boat or RV, vacation of a lifetime, business equipment or a college education— and pocket the interest you would otherwise give to banks and finance companies

Recapture the *entire* purchase price of your cars and other big-ticket items, over a reasonably short period of time

Benefit from this strategy *even if you typically pay cash* for major purchases

Increase your monthly cash flow by an average of 20-30%, simply by changing the way you buy and pay for things (this applies to both personal and business cash flow, if you own a business... and does not necessarily require you to "give up" anything)

Make your money literally work twice as hard for you

Create a tax-free stream of income with no government limits on how much you can contribute... and no restrictions on when or how much you can take out penalty-free (you control your money... not the government)

FIGURE 3-2. For a free copy of Pamela Yellen's report, "Bank On Yourself™ How to Pocket the Interest You Now Pay to Banks, Credit Card and Finance Companies ... and Turn it into Personal Wealth and a Tax-Free Income for Life," visit **www.FindOutMoreNow.com** and enter pass code 4646.

WARNING: Do Not Finance a Car, Home, College Education, Business Equipment or *Any* Other Major Purchase Until You Read This FREE Special Report!

Discover How to Pocket Every Penny of Interest You Now Pay to Banks, Finance, Leasing and Credit Card Companies... and Get Back the *Entire* Purchase Price of Big-Ticket Items!

If you're financing any major purchase the ordinary way – by using a bank, credit union, dealer financing, or putting it on a credit card – I have one word of advice for you: **STOP!** You see, you could actually be putting all the interest and finance charges in your **own** pocket and use it to pay yourself a tax-free income for life.

This proven strategy has existed for more than 100 years, but the public—and even most financial advisors and CPA's—know nothing about it. And your banker desperately hopes you never hear about it.

You can get all the details in a **FREE** Report that ***also*** reveals...

How to get back the entire purchase price of your cars and other big-ticket items over a reasonably short period of time

How to grow wealthier each and every year—*no matter what happens in the stock or real estate markets*

How to **profit** from this strategy ***even if you typically pay cash for major purchases***

How to grow your wealth both **risk-free** *and* **tax-free**

How to protect yourself from the pension crisis gripping our country

How to ***spend*** your money and ***still*** have it working for you!

How to gain control over your finances and win the money game

The author of this Report has charged as much as $295.00 for this ground-breaking information. But, for a **limited-time-only**, you can download this Report FREE on-line at:

www.FindOutMoreNow.com
Enter Passcode: 4646

© 2006 Pamela Yellen

FIGURE 3-3. Pamela Yellen's lead generation ads identify financial advisors and life insurance agents interested in a new system for finding prospects eager to do business.

Iron-Clad Money-Back Risk-Free
Infinite Banking Concept Course on Audio-CDs
Trial Acceptance Form

"Okay, Pamela – send me the Nelson Nash **Infinite Banking Concept Course** on Audio-CDs. I want to discover how to finance a car, home, credit card debt or college education – FREE, how to get back the entire purchase price of big-ticket items, grow wealth risk-free **and** tax-free, and how to become a hero to my prospects and clients! Please rush the 12 Audio-CDs, book and handout to me. My investment is only US$412, which includes $15 shipping and handling. If I'm not convinced this is the most powerful financial advice I've ever received, I can return the Course Materials and Bonus Audios to your office any time within the first 90 days, and receive a full refund, less shipping & handling. On that basis, sign me up…"

Name _____ Title _____

Company _____

Address (**Must be physical address for UPS delivery**) _____

_____

Phone _____ Fax _____

Email Address (your personal email address, if you have one): _____

☐ **Rapid-Response Bonus:** I'm responding **within 3 days** – please include the Prospecting and Marketing Magic Audio Collection for FREE (a $397.00 Value)

☐ I would also like to participate in the "live" Course-By-Phone, **at no extra cost**, the next time it is offered (Value: $297.00)

☐ Please charge my check card or credit card:

    __AMEX ___VISA __MC __ Discover __Optima ___Diners Club

    Card # _____ Exp. Date _____

    Signature: _____

☐ My check or money order for US$412 is enclosed
    Note: Orders paid by check will not be shipped until payment has cleared.

How to Order:

1. FAX this form to **(505) 466-2167** anytime. No cover sheet necessary.
2. Call **(505) 466-1167** to enroll by phone. (After hours you can leave order information on our secure voice mail. Be sure to leave all the information requested above.)
3. Return this order form by mail to: PMI, Inc. 39 Vista Estrella South, Lamy, NM 87540 USA

Iron-Clad Risk-Free Money-Back Guarantee

When you order the **Infinite Banking Concept Course**, you'll be rushed a copy of the book, **Becoming Your Own Banker**, the Course handout and 12 Audio-CD album. If you aren't thrilled, or if you're unhappy with it for *any* reason, simply send all of your Course materials back, along with your Bonus Audios, for a full refund of your tuition, less shipping and handling. (Must be postmarked no later than 90 days after the purchase date.)

Prospecting & Marketing Institute, Inc. * 39 Vista Estrella South * Lamy, NM 87540 USA
Phone: 505-466-1167 * FAX 505-466-2167 [IBC Course on CDs – DM]

FIGURE 3-4. This product gives agents a comprehensive introduction to "Bank On Yourself" as well as Pamela Yellen's services that generate leads for insurance agents and financial advisors.

in an hour. Maybe I can learn something from him.'" So Pamela bought Dan's program and got started.

One of Dan's key concepts is that you don't have to wait to sell your product from the back of the room. If you're in a niche industry, you can sell the products using industry media and direct mail all the time. Pamela took Dan's advice and created her first sales letter. She ran an ad in one of the trade journals and tested her letter. "Maybe it was beginner's luck," Pamela says, "but that thing just worked right from the get-go." Within three months, she was selling $20,000 a month "without even working at it."

Pamela continued her full schedule as a public speaker but knew she was on the verge of something better. She happened to live in the same city as Dan Kennedy, so she called him up and said, "All right, whatever your consulting fee is, charge it to me. I'm coming in, and I'm getting your help. You're onto something, and I want to figure out how to do more of it."

The next step for Pamela was a joint venture with insurance agency managers. As she became more and more immersed in "Planet Dan," Pamela found more and more ways that would take her away from having to get on a plane, which she was fast losing interest in. (Pamela's final answer on whether the life of a speaker is glamorous? NO!) As Pamela puts it, "I was beginning to dread getting on a plane." Her new info-marketing business was going to give her a brand-new lifestyle—on the ground.

Today Pamela focuses her business on a broad audience: anyone and everyone; but she converts leads into sales using a very targeted niche: about 500 financial advisors and insurance agents. Her "Bank On Yourself" product helps average people become their own bankers. This means getting back the interest otherwise paid to banks, finance companies, and credit card companies and turning ➡

it into tax-free income. Even better than that, using Pamela's system allows everyday people to get back the entire purchase price of cars and other big-ticket items. "My last three cars have all been free," Pamela says, "and the last one was a 650i BMW worth $80,000. I really don't care what a car costs, because I'm getting it free."

The promise of free cars and other big-ticket items easily generates leads, and these leads are distributed among the financial advisors and insurance agents in Pamela's customer base. "The advisors are just blown away because they're getting a quality of leads they have never seen before. My automatically implemented lead generation basically pre-sells the product; people are so well educated, it's basically 'Where do I sign?'"

Pamela enjoys a very loyal following because the financial advisors and insurance agents are getting leads they could never get on their own. It's what Dan Kennedy refers to as "iron cage retention." The pain of disconnect is too great; Pamela's customers don't want to do anything to stop the lead flow, so they are committed to the program.

Pamela uses lead generation ads and free tele-seminars to educate insurance agents and financial advisors on what her program does. The first product is a course on CD that sells for $397. Pamela actually limits membership in the program, accepting about 50 new members at a time so she can thoroughly train them. Once advisors and agents are trained on the "Bank On Yourself" strategy, Pamela offers them coaching and mastermind groups where they get access to other moneymaking tools and automatically implemented marketing. Her continuity coaching program is $5,000 per year. From there, customers go into the automatically implemented lead-generating program.

An expanded profile and additional exhibits are available at **www.InfoMarketingBook.com/Yellen**.

Info-Marketer Taps Personal Experiences to Help Others Overcome Illness, Disability

Life Skills Inc. was born out of Marc Lerner's personal struggle with multiple sclerosis. Since there is no cure for MS yet, Marc decided he needed to take responsibility for how he dealt with his condition. He soon found that every struggle in life demands the same life skills: a positive self-image, self-trust, and an ability to connect to the wisdom of one's own body. He also discovered that others could benefit from his Life Skills approach to managing intellectual, emotional, spiritual, and physical needs to achieve a sense of wellness, and so he began conducting seminars about his approach.

According to Marc, everyone has these qualities of positive self-image, self-trust, and an ability to connect to the wisdom of one's own body within them already, but conditioning has created habits that block them from manifesting. Since we have the power to consciously condition our minds, we have the power to unleash these qualities and make them a part of our character, especially when we face a health crisis.

"Death is an amazing motivator, but so is life. If you really want to better your life and how you deal with your health challenge, develop these life skills and you will naturally develop a conscious perspective that will serve you," says Marc.

Life Skills Inc.'s first product was seminars presented to three main groups: (1) combat veterans with post-traumatic stress disorder; (2) people facing life-threatening illnesses like cancer or AIDS; and (3) the mentally ill homeless. Marc's info-business grew out of these seminars as he developed handouts for his techniques and began writing e-books to increase the reach of his life-changing approaches to dealing with illness and other struggles like disabilities. ➡

Marc has grown his business by connecting with people in their individual struggles. "By not over-explaining my techniques, but giving the participants an experience they can identify with, it is hard for them to deny what I share. People in a health crisis demand practical experiences that help them in their struggles. If what I share with a person in a health crisis doesn't connect to them on that level, they just walk away from it," explains Marc. "I also saw that by empowering patients to connect to their inner resources they can better participate in healing with a positive effect. People appreciate being empowered; and it is also good for their work, their health insurance company, and their family life. You could say the nature of peace is that both sides win. We need to find that peace in a health crisis and make it work for us."

Marc is legally blind and has several other handicaps, so performing functions like computer programming on his web site is difficult. He needs to create partnerships with others who can keep his web site up-to-date and market his books. This allows Marc to concentrate on giving seminars, creating new products, and adapting the Life Skills approach to different companies and struggles. Through it all, Marc has relied on what he calls the "Wisdom of the Body." This is the part of a person that operates every function of the body with incredible precision. "From the complex functions of digesting one's dinner, healing, and spiritual experience to the simple act of being creative, we need the Wisdom of the Body," says Marc. "Being able to connect to that part of you directly is an amazing tool to better the quality of one's life."

Marc is distributing his Life Skills approach through e-books that are downloaded from his web site and Amazon.com. He has adapted these e-books to HMOs, health insurance companies, corporations, and large businesses that empower people to take an ➡

active role in healing. The life skills that empower patients to be active in healing are the same skills required to be effective in the business world. "Imagine empowering the workers of a company so they can better deal with their health challenges and at the same time those skills help employees be more effective in their work; that company benefits on two levels, and the employees improve the quality of their lives in the process," Marc explains.

In addition to his e-books, Marc conducts seminars for those who work with people in a health crisis or who have disabilities. He uses the appropriate e-book as a handout for each seminar and believes every group will have a person who can be trained to lead people through the e-book to empower them to better deal with their struggles. These seminars can also be geared to staff development, where employees learn to become active in healing and develop skills to improve their work.

"I have had MS for over 25 years. Relating to my illness from a negative perspective is very easy and doesn't create any positive benefits. When I look at how I was forced to deal with poor vision, memory problems, and several other handicaps, I can see I have been on a journey that has taught me incredible lessons. Our awareness is like watering plants to a gardener; what we are aware of grows. I want to be aware of the benefits of MS instead of only my complaints. I believe this helps me switch to a positive perspective and helps others in a struggle to do the same," comments Marc.

You can download a free e-book that describes Marc Lerner's Life Skills approach from his web site at **http://LifeSkillsInc.com**. His blog at **http://LifeSkillsApproach.com** can also give you a good understanding of this effective approach to healthcare. Visit **www.InfoMarketingBook.com/Lerner** to find out more about Marc's approach to information marketing.

Easy Veterinary Marketing Techniques
Create Profitable Business

Info-Marketer Profile

The veterinary profession grosses in the neighborhood of $40 billion annually and has an estimated potential of over $100 billion a year. Yet the vast majority of veterinary professionals are clueless about how to create the careers they want. In fact, they run their practices like they were a hobby. Most of them are oblivious to the huge potential the profession offers. This is where Steve Kornfeld, DVM, CPCC, comes in.

Steve, who is both a veterinarian and a certified business coach, literally grew from within the profession and was subject to the same frustrations and lack of business acumen as 95 percent of its members. Then, in 2000 he stumbled upon a book that brought about a dramatic change in his career. The book was called the *E-myth*, and it put in focus the need to work *on* one's practice even more than *in* one's practice. From there the road was short to discover Dan Kennedy, Bill Glazer, and their materials and teaching. Steve signed up for Dan Kennedy's program, read all of his books, and developed a direct marketing plan using many of the tools he learned. Once Steve saw the potential of information marketing, the decision was easy—he became the guru of information marketing in veterinary medicine.

The average veterinary professional grosses around $350,000 a year. Yet many studies have shown that these professionals can easily increase that to over $1 million a year. In other words, almost every veterinarian around the country leaves $650,000 of easy business on the table. That's where Steve found his niche.

Steve says, "Most veterinarians are stuck in a lack mentality, and this gives me an amazing opportunity." Indeed, he quickly generated speaking engagements to veterinarians on coaching and ➡

information marketing issues. On many occasions, Steve was able to convert members of his audience directly into his coaching groups and continuity programs. Many of the practices associated with him have seen their revenues grow by 70 percent or more in less than a year. These were all established practices that had seen only 3 to 5 percent growth a year in previous years. With success came invitations to coach other practices and a fast-growing information marketing business. In fact, Steve has seen his own income grow by almost 300 percent in the last six months. "And this is just the beginning," says Steve. With his increasing recognition, invitations to speak to large groups are pouring in. An important lesson Steve learned from Dan was that every speaking engagement is the beginning of a relationship with the audience, not the end of it. Steve has developed systems that make many of those who listen to his presentations sign up for his free newsletters and from there join the folds of his growing information marketing customer base.

Another important lesson Steve learned from Bill and Dan is to keep going back to those who have signed up with him, offering new programs and campaigns, strengthening the bond, improving their bottom lines, and sharing their financial success.

Last year Steve self-published a book on veterinary coaching called *Leading the Way to Your Dream Practice*, which crystallizes three years of coaching in the profession. The book is loaded with powerful questions that allow veterinary professionals to chart the paths they want. Steve says, "Reactions to this book have been outstanding so far. I am working on the audio version of the book, which will be a standalone or an addendum to the book." Steve was invited to submit his book to be published and marketed by the largest veterinary publishing company in the country. Steve realized that although he would be giving up some control of the book, ➡

on the other hand he would get unbelievable marketing channels to many of the 25,000 veterinary hospitals in the United States. Indeed, Steve recently came back from his first book tour with many sales under his belt and many more speaking engagements.

What is amazing to Steve is that it doesn't take a genius to become successful in information marketing. The formulas are out there, and what works in one profession can easily work in another. If you know more than the general public about your subject, you can become an information marketer.

Steve is a believer in "You learn one, you do one, and you teach one." According to Steve, the best way to learn is to teach. He is not averse to teach subjects he has not totally mastered because he knows he will learn quickly by teaching them.

According to Steve, "The cardinal concept of coaching is that we all have all the answers we need to live a fulfilling life. What I do is help people find these answers and then create a plan to achieve what they want."

You can read more about Steve Kornfeld's training programs at **www.VeterinaryCoaching.com**, and the complete profile is available at **www.InfoMarketingBook.com/Kornfeld**.

Chapter 4

Step 3: Separating Your Customers From the Rest of the Market

by Robert Skrob
President, Information Marketing Association

W E GO TO A LOT OF THE FLORIDA STATE UNIVERSITY BASEBALL games, and we go to almost all of them here in Tallahassee. My daughter, Samantha, enjoys the outdoors, the players, and the action. My son, Robert William, enjoys the popcorn, the Cracker Jack, the Cokes, and the boiled peanuts.

As you know, there is a lot of downtime during a baseball game. Batter changes, pitcher changes, and inning changes all create breaks where there isn't much for the fans to do. Well, Samantha takes it upon herself to get the crowd into the game.

She seizes the opportunity to put herself in front of an audience and leads everyone in a cheer. This cheer involves her raising her arms to get everyone's attention. As more and more people notice her they yell out, "AHHHHHHHHH." (Sometimes this process can go on for a while, and you need to grab a quick breath to keep from passing out.) Then, when the time is right, she waves her arms and contorts her

FIGURE 4-1. Not everyone at the Seminoles games wants to cheer; Samantha has to invite everyone to cheer along, and then she works with the ones who want to work with her.

body to roughly form the letters, N-O-L-E-S, and as she does the crowd yells, "N-O-L-E-S, Noles!"

You should know that it is never sufficient to do this cheer one time, or so Samantha tells me. She gives every single person a chance by repeating this process six to eight times by going around to each section of the grandstand.

We didn't think much of this by the eighth or tenth time. Sure, her mother started out embarrassed, but there was no way she was going to teach Samantha to be embarrassed in front of a crowd.

There are 4,000 to 6,000 people, all out to see the Noles play baseball. But believe it or not, not all of them came to cheer for the game. So Samantha offers the cheer to everyone, and in the end the committed fans self-select and cheer.

When you are offering information products to a market, you have to separate the individuals who are interested in you and your products from the individuals who aren't interested. While it's easy enough for Samantha to stand up in front of everyone at the game, in your info-business your marketing costs would be too high if you tried to deliver a marketing campaign to every single one of your potential customers within your market.

No matter what your market is, no matter what product you're offering, there's no way you're going to create something that everybody wants to buy. Quite frankly, that's completely impossible. So how do you separate the potential buyers from the ones who will never buy? That process is called lead generation.

Lead generation stems from the idea that you should invest the majority of your marketing dollars in individuals who are most likely to say yes to your offer.

Most lead generation starts with an ad designed to get people who have problems you can solve to con-

> Send inexpensive marketing to the entire market. When individuals indicate KEY CONCEPT they want more information, then you invest in extensive marketing sequences to them.

tact you for more information. The ad can get people to call a toll-free number for a recorded message. It can direct them to a web site. It can get them to call or even visit your retail location. When they contact you for additional information, you should invest the majority of your marketing dollars into selling them your product and services.

Don't try to make your entire sales presentation within your lead generation advertising. The purpose of any lead generation advertising is to get prospects to ask about your product or service. You're simply trying to identify individuals who are interested in hearing more about your sales message and weeding out those who aren't. Do not try to make your lead generation advertising sell your product. You don't want to give them lots of detail about your product or service or your company's history or benefits. Your one goal is to show them they've got a problem *you can solve*.

Info-Marketer Resource

Easy Follow-Up Messages and E-Zines

A lot of info-marketers build web sites that invite web visitors to enter their names and e-mail addresses for additional information. One of the best systems to capture e-mail addresses and to follow up with them using e-mails or e-zines is AWeber. With AWeber, info-marketers can configure follow-up and newsletter messages with name personalization click-through and open rate tracking, attachments, RSS, and split testing at no additional cost. Messages can include HTML using our 51-plus predesigned templates, or create your own with the integrated easy editor and images or plain text. Visit **www.AWeberEmail.com** for more information.

When a customer calls your message line, visits your web site, or comes to your retail store, you will ask the prospect for his name, address, telephone number, fax number, and e-mail address. The goal is to get complete contact information.

Once you have the complete contact information of an individual who has read your lead generation ad and asks for more information about how you can solve his problem, then you will be ready to invest your marketing dollars. This system is very common throughout the direct marketing world. Individuals who have shown interest in your solution to their problems are more likely to purchase your product than your market as a whole.

There are two main ways to conduct lead generation advertising: (1) the free offer; and (2) self-liquidating leads.

The Free Offer: Most info-marketers start their businesses by offering a free offer to their lead generation lists. Prospects can call a number or visit a web site, give their contact information, and with no charge receive additional information about the product and service offered. This is a good method because the info-marketer receives the maximum number of leads and has the maximum opportunity to convert those leads into customers. It is extremely expensive, however, because the info-marketer will also receive a number of leads from people who are not really interested in the product being offered. Some people will ask for the information just because it's free. Still, most beginning info-marketers use the free offer and are happy to have customers to market to even if some of those customers are not qualified prospects.

Self-Liquidating Leads: Another lead generation technique is called self-liquidating leads. The info-marketer asks the customer to pay a small amount of money to receive a "special report" or access to a tele-seminar that has some of the information the prospect wants. The info-marketer then uses the special report or tele-seminar to sell his products and services.

Info-marketers who use self-liquidating leads receive substantially fewer leads than those using the free offer method. However, the leads they do receive are more qualified because these potential customers have invested some money to receive the information. These prospects are a lot more interested in carefully reading through the information. Often, these leads are more likely to buy the product than a lead who has responded to a free offer. Self-liquidating leads have two main benefits: (1) the info-marketer gets some money to help fund his advertising budget; and (2) each lead has a lower marketing cost because fewer marketing pieces are sent out and each lead is better qualified and more likely to buy.

There are many ways to generate leads for your business. For instance, you can advertise in publications, use direct mail, write articles for trade journals, publish books or newsletters, do radio talk shows, obtain press coverage in newspapers and magazines, and speak at events that feature you as an expert.

It's critical to do a lot of testing with all of your lead generation pieces. For each one of the media you're using, you should test different lead generation techniques and pieces. For example, if you're generating leads for your business by speaking at events, you should test ways to make your presentation better. If one day you get 30 leads and then you change one feature of your presentation and get 35 leads, you know to keep that change in your speech. If the number of leads goes down, you know to take that change out. The point is to continually test different lead generation techniques and different lead generation media so you will always have the lowest cost per lead. That's how you maximize your marketing dollars.

There are a number of ways that info-marketers generate leads; here is a quick summary:

Direct Mail: Information marketers will create a postcard, letter, or large direct mail sequence to generate leads for their products or services. Once you have created a direct mail lead generation system that works, it is one of the most stable systems you can have. Several info-marketers have used the same sales letters for many years. Few of the other lead generation techniques can deliver as many leads over such an extended period of time as direct mail can.

Display Advertising: Paid advertising in magazines, trade journals, television, or radio. These ads are extremely common. Now, you'll find that a lot of companies will offer a free report or other information in one of these ads, and it turns out that they are not selling an information product. All types of businesses use reports and other items to generate leads. It is a powerful technique for information marketers, too.

Speaking: Many information marketers have built large businesses through speaking. You allow an association or a for-profit promoter to fill the room with individuals within your target market, and then you conduct a presentation and offer your product to the group. Essentially, the lead generation was done by the promoter who filled the room. The promoter identified individuals within the market that were interested in more information about a subject. Those individuals identified themselves by attending the meeting. Then you were there to present your information and offer your product. Many speakers get paid a speaking fee in addition to the products they are able to sell, so they win three ways; they are paid for their appearance, they generate revenue through their product sales, and they obtain new customers.

Internet Advertising: Info-marketers will often purchase placement on search results (one example is Google Adwords: **www.Google. com/ads**) or through banners on web sites. Through these methods you are reaching millions of individuals who have gone to a web site and entered terms into a search engine; this tells you that they are actively searching for a piece of information. If you can put your products in front of these individuals as they search, you can frequently obtain new customers.

Internet Search Marketing: While advertising offers you an opportunity to pay to have your ad listed within a web user's search results, there is an entire process called "Search Engine Optimization" (often referred to as SEO). SEO is the process of creating a web site that search engines will index and list within their search results. SEO attempts to create web sites that are the first or second site returned when a user searches for a particular product.

Preview Seminars: Info-markers often travel throughout the country to offer seminars of their own within a local area. The info-marketer conducts a marketing campaign for several weeks leading up to the program, trying to get potential customers into the seminar room. Then, at the seminar, the info-marketer offers his products to the attendees through a detailed presentation. This is a lot of work; however, it often generates customers that wouldn't have been obtained through any other technique.

Articles: Many trade publications are constantly searching for articles. If you write an article that is suitable for their publications, they will happily publish it along with your two to three sentence biography at the end. This biography is your chance to include your lead generation offer. You'll see many info-marketers writing articles for printed publications, web sites, and e-zines to generate leads.

> **KEY CONCEPT** The most successful info-marketers use a combination of several lead generation strategies.

Publicity: Television, radio, newspaper, and magazine reporters are constantly hunting for information to publish. If you are able to create an interesting story, very often they'll happily publish it for you. They publish these stories without charging you. Best of all, you have increased credibility with the individuals who read the story, and you can use the story as a clipping in your future marketing efforts.

There's "No Place Like Home" for Making Millions
A Small-Town Info-Marketer From Kansas Tells His Story

Info Marketer Profile

T. J. Rohleder's story is pretty simple: "Small town boy makes good." But a simple story doesn't mean life was always easy for T. J.

➡

His story begins in Goessel, a small town in Central Kansas. Small is the key word: at the 2000 census, Goessel had a population of 565—T. J.'s prospects for striking it rich in his hometown weren't all that good. Still, in the 1980s, he began to dream about making his first million, so he started sending away for get-rich programs and multilevel programs. "I never made a single dime from any of those things, but I did learn goal setting. I became a self-development 'junkie,'" T. J. says.

Armed with self confidence and a strong work ethic, T. J. began his own business, got married, and settled down. But he was still sending away for money-making plans, hoping to find the one that would make him a millionaire. His wife, Eileen, made a simple observation: "The only people making any money with those plans are the ones selling those plans." Well, T. J. had had some success with a couple of the programs he had bought, so he combined two business opportunities, added a few insights from his experience, and created his own proprietary business opportunity. He and Eileen started their info-business with a $300 ad—now, 20 years later, they have sold over $100 million in products.

Getting your program to stand out over all the others in the marketplace is the key, according to T. J. "It should have the *appearance* of being new without necessarily *being* new. Actually, if you tell people you've discovered a new twist on something that's more established, they will feel more secure about buying your product. Nobody wants to be the guinea pig," T. J. says.

Image is also important. Back in the 1980s, when T. J. was scouring magazines for his next get-rich plan, all of the ads showed people dressed up in tuxedos, standing next to their limousines or mansions, looking the part of a millionaire. T. J. and Eileen took a

FIGURE 4-2. Every month T. J. Rohleder invests thousands of dollars in lead generation advertising to identify new customers. While the majority of any info-marketer's profits come from sales to existing customers, these sales decline if an info-marketer stops generating new customers.

different approach, one they credit Dan Kennedy for teaching them. T. J. and Eileen are average people, just like their customers. Their customers identify with them—and they trust them. T. J. explains, "We're just like our customers who have identified with our story. We have built bonds with our customers, and the same people who have done business with us almost since day one just keep re-buying our stuff again and again because they like us, they trust us, they believe in our story. They see themselves in our story, and they're hoping things are gonna turn around for them just like they turned around for us."

Twenty years later, T. J. and Eileen's business is going strong, more successful than ever. T. J. credits their longevity to the fact that he and his wife worked together. "Eileen is very conservative," T. J. explains." She insisted we break even on every new customer, acquisition, or promotion, always using self-liquidating leads." Over the years, the couple has found that recouping their acquisition costs as quickly as they can provides stability for their business.

Today T. J. enjoys his work as much as he enjoys his life. He's always working on his ideas, but he leaves day-to-day operations to a good general manager. He uses seminars and tele-seminars for new product development. He has found recorded tele-seminars work well; he comes in live for a few minutes at the end to answer questions. His continuity programs include web site hosting and maintenance fees—the tools his customers need to implement his products.

For T. J.'s book, *How to Make $900.00 a Day Without Doing Any Work*, visit **www.FreeWealthEducationBook.com**. For an expanded profile about what the good life is like for T. J. Rohleder in small-town Kansas, visit **www.InfoMarketingBook.com/Rohleder**.

Info-Marketer Profile

An Info-Marketer Integrates Online and OfflineMarketing for Maximum Stability and Profitability

John Alanis, "The King of Let 'Em Come to You" (**www.JohnAlanis. com**), is a veteran information marketer whose 10-plus years of experience include a variety of businesses as well as a variety of marketing approaches. His story begins in the mid-1990s when he purchased a chain letter because, as John recalls, "I was desperate for revenue. Reading the letter, I thought, 'Hey, maybe this'll work.' Then I went to the library to look up chain letters because the letter said it *wasn't* a chain letter. Well, I found the exact letter in a book called *Building a Mail Order Business* by William Cole. And I said, 'This letter's no good, but this mail order stuff is really interesting.'"

John started reading about mail order and discovered Ted Nicholas. He bought several of Nicholas's products, and then in December 1996 he purchased the Jeff Paul course, "How You Can Make $4,000 a Day, Sitting at Your Kitchen Table, in Your Underwear!" (**www.JeffPaul.tv**)."I still use almost verbatim what's in that course," John says, "and it still works just as well today as it did in 1996."

In his info-business, **www.WomenApproachYou.com**, John teaches men how to get women to approach them first for a date, regardless of a man's looks, age, or income. "You might say I serve the market of men who have issues attracting women or who want to make their relationships better," John says.

John began his info-business back in 1996, when there was no online marketing, so he knows the value of using offline techniques. "The Internet works well," John says, "but after using it exclusively for a while, I very quickly came to the conclusion there was a lot of bad stuff happening online. E-mails were being blocked, and it's a ➡

FIGURE 4-3. Lead generation display ads generate customers with a higher lifetime value than customers generated from e-mail opt-ins. The additional profits and business stability make the investment in display ads and direct mail well worth it for John Alanis.

single media business—a dangerous business to be in. So I went through the time, energy, and effort to reinvent my business to be primarily an offline-based business with an online component. And it'll always be that way."

For his offline marketing, John continues to use the lead generating methods he learned from the Jeff Paul course. He places space ads, including some full page ads. In addition, he mails lead generation postcards to rented direct mail lists. Within those pieces he offers free information and directs the reader to a free recorded message. The customer then receives a four- or five-step direct mail follow-up.

When John was going from a purely online business to offline, he was contacted by a joint venture partner who had a list of people who in the past had purchased materials on how to attract women. Since this partner already had a relationship with the customers on this list, John had a good environment in which to test his lead generation mailing. "We did an endorsed mailing," John says. "It was only 500 pieces, so it was probably the least risky environment there was to test this thing. I wrote up a postcard, put my JV partner's endorsement on it, and sent it out to the list. As leads came in, I sent a sales letter to them with a cover letter and an endorsement. It was a very good environment to test in, and it worked phenomenally well."

Once John had tested his program, he went on to using rented lists. "Things went from there, and it continues to work very well," John says. "I'm always coming up with new direct mail pieces for my products, and I send them to my best buyers. If one works then I do a test mailing to the leads. And if it works there, and I've been pleasantly surprised to find a lot of them do, then I'll put it in my sequence to leads as part of the back-end sequence that people have bought. I like to test these things in a pretty permissive environment."

John recommends the value of direct mail to info-marketers who would like to add an offline component to their business. John comments, "A lot of online-only marketers are fighting direct mail. They think it costs too much and you have to lick stamps and all that. (There are people who will do that for you.) The thing to keep in mind is you want to test in the least risky way possible so you can get the control right and become familiar with offline marketing. I recommend—and I've done this myself—going back to your e-mail list and sending an e-mail advertising that you have this wonderful free report that is too controversial to put on the web. You don't want the public to see it. You send it to them in the mail, but they pay for the shipping. So what you're doing is getting a self-liquidating lead. You just pay a little money to get your direct mail produced."

John also recommends going back to the old Jeff Paul model (JPDK business model detailed in Chapter 11) of placing a small lead generation ad in an industry publication, leading readers to a web site or a recorded message with a multistep sequence of reports. "You may spend a couple hundred bucks on that ad," John says. "You may get 20 or 30 leads, and you follow up those leads with direct mail. If it doesn't work, at most you're out a couple hundred bucks. Once you achieve success, then you can go to the riskier rented direct mail lists."

The main benefit of offline marketing? According to John, it's stability: "Space ads and direct mail, those media are as predictable and stable as the day is long. E-mail's changing while we speak."

John also finds that direct mail has brought him a significantly better customer. "The online source customers are not proven buyers, and they tend to buy much lower priced items," John says. "I start with the lower priced product and once we have a relationship I can up sell them by e-mail, but not at the rate I can with a direct mail customer who has come from a buyer's list and knows how to get out his credit card and buy. I can start my direct mail customers out with a product for hundreds of dollars—because they're used to buy-ing—so they're a much better customer than the online source. Their lifetime value is significantly higher. They'll buy more from me, they know how to buy, and I get a better customer and more stability."

Another benefit of direct mail is its durability. John calls e-mail a "horribly inefficient medium," saying, "Once they read it, it's gone, and most of it's blocked, so you've got just one shot with them using e-mail. When you do an e-mail campaign, after three days it's done. And you get most of your responses the first day.

"Direct mail tends to stick around a lot longer. It's a much more effective media. The way people go through the buying process, particularly on an expensive product, is that they don't read some-thing once and then buy. They read it, they put it aside, they look at it again, they scratch their head, they go back, they re-read it, they underline, and then, finally, they make a decision to buy.

"Direct mail is a media that stays around," John says. "E-mail and web sites are a perishable medium. When you start using these offline methods of marketing that tend to stay around, they're much more effective. That's why you get the higher response rates and better customers, new people who know how to buy."

Take a look at John's available resources at **www.Women ApproachYou.com.** You can read more about John Alanis's market-ing techniques at **www.InfoMarketingBook.com/ Alanis.**

Greg Milner and Salon Owner

Greg Milner's quarterly magazine, *Salon Owner*, is a magalog sent to beauty salons and day spas in Australia and New Zealand (see example on next page). Rather than send his magalog only to individuals who request it, he sends it to all 8,000 salons on his mailing list. This is one of Greg's best new client acquisition tools. If you would like to see the rest of Greg's magalog, visit **www.InfoMarketing.org/Milner**.

FIGURE 4-4. Beauty salon and day spa marketing guru Greg Milner takes time out to ride his Harley-Davidson Softail Deuce. While dating a salon owner, Greg got the idea to create a marketing system for the industry. Although he was a successful marketing consultant for many years, his current business creates residual income and equity value.

Seminars, Direct Mail, Newsletters, E-mail, Ads, Tele-Seminars, Internet—This Info-Marketer Uses Them All to Generate Leads

From Perth, on the west coast of Australia, Worldwide Salon Marketing (**www.Salon-Marketing-Secrets.com**) now has a global reach, selling big-ticket marketing and sales toolkits; web site memberships; and coaching to beauty salons, day spas, and hair salons in 14 countries.

Using a combination of seminars, direct mail, newsletters, e-mail, magazine advertising, tele-seminars, Internet lead generation, and automated multistep sequences—both online and offline—the company markets to a narrow-but-deep niche of salon and spa owners who don't have the time, skill, or desire to write their own marketing materials.

"Early in 2004, I was pretty much dead broke," says Greg Milner. "I'd been a top producer in TV news for 20-odd years, got bored, and bailed out suddenly in the mid-90s, with absolutely no idea of what I was going to do and no planning."

Greg knew that to succeed in the info-marketing business, he needed a starving crowd and a great product to market to them. His girlfriend at the time was a beauty salon owner who complained there were no marketing materials written just for her industry. Greg offered to teach her how to write ads and sales letter that work, but she said, "I don't have the time or the skill or the interest. I just want it done for me … so I can simply *turn a key*."

"That was my big 'Aha!' moment," Greg says.

Inventing the Product

Greg didn't want to reinvent the wheel, so he started researching. He Googled till his eyes fell out, looking all over the world for ➡

FIGURE 4-5. Some sample pages from Greg Milner's catalog

somebody, somewhere, who had already done what he wanted to do. Maybe he could find something and simply license it.

"Nothing. Nada. Zip. Sure, there were bits and pieces, elements of what I wanted, but no complete system, nothing that 'gave 'em the fish on a plate,' rather than taught them how to fish. There were hundreds of those," Greg remembers.

Right about then, Greg got a call from his friend Jill Groves, a hot-shot tele-saleswoman who had made a name for herself in a big trade exchange company. She wanted out. Within a week, they'd cleared some space in a spare room in Greg's house and started writing.

"We injected artificial scarcity, limiting the toolkit to only one per postcode (ZIP code). And we decided on a strong guarantee—12 months unconditional money back. We created two versions, a Bronze pack at $2,200 and a Silver pack at $6,000, the Silver coming with 12 months of one-on-one phone coaching," Greg says.

In September 2004 they took a booth at the Sydney International Beauty Expo and launched the Essential Salon Owner's Marketing Toolkit®. They sold 10 of them at $2,500 apiece. They were on a roll and decided to try selling at seminars. They bought a mailing list, booked conference rooms in hotels all over Australia, and used direct mail to fill the rooms.

How They Sold It

Greg remembers, "We'd get maybe 20 or 30 people in a room. I'd do a pitch for 90 minutes. I'd hand over to Jill for a 20-minute talk on selling. Then I'd come back for the close. The one-per-postcode rule was a clincher. Soon as I'd say that, you could see people all over the room furiously filling in order forms lest their competition got hold of it."

Greg and Jill discovered they were selling their products too inexpensively and decided to double their prices. They kept flying coast to coast, doing seminars. The higher price made no difference to sales.

But they were still selling more of the basic toolkit at $2,500 rather than the deluxe version. At a seminar in Sydney in November 2004, Bill Glazer said they should bring the pricing together, so the deluxe pack was about 50 percent more than the basic version, and pitch the deluxe version first, with the basic kit as a down-sell. They tested it immediately and experienced a stunning turnaround.

"From that day on, we almost never sold the basic pack. It was 95 percent deluxe version at $4,500, and we put a payment plan in place, spreading payments over six months," Greg says.

Greg says that in the first year he would have been "happy if we'd managed to do $200,000 in sales." (This was in a market 20 times smaller than the United States.) Greg and Jill tripled that forecast in the first 12 months, and they were "only scratching the surface."

Fast Fax ACTION FORM - fax to 08 9388 4722

☐ "YES! I Want the **Essential Salon Owners Marketing Toolkit** - the Toolkit That Salon Owners Featured in SALON OWNER magazine *Raved About!*

I'd like to INSTANTLY acquire AMAZING marketing and sales training tools so I can instantly and easily attract a FLOOD of clients eager to give me their cash—NOW. I want to legally, morally and ethically extract every available dollar from my clients, while providing them with the absolute best services and products imaginable. I want these 'done-for-you' tools NOW so I don't waste another second struggling to write ads and flyers myself—in fact I want to get these tools working for me TOMORROW and start attracting more wealth, with less work and less stress than I have ever experienced in my life before. I understand that the **Essential Salon Owner's Marketing Toolkit®** contains totally unique, cutting-edge material, is unavailable anywhere else. I also understand that the Toolkit comes with a truly AMAZING 12-month, 100% Money Back Guarantee. On that basis, please accept my application!" (IF my Postcode/Zipcode is available)

Your 12 Month 100% 'No Profit-No Pay' Money Back Guarantee:
"If anytime up to 12 months you are not absolutely *delighted* with your Toolkit, just say so, send it back in re-saleable condition, and your entire investment will be refunded!"

The *Essential* Salon Owner's Marketing Toolkit	IF PURCHASED SEPARATELY	BRONZE VERSION	SILVER VERSION
86-Page "Selling with Energy" - The Amazing, Easy-to-Read 'How-To' sales manual by sales guru Jill Groves. Guaranteed to double your sales!	$1975	INCLUDED	INCLUDED
140-page Marketing Manual including "Done-for-You" Sales Letters, Ads and Flyers Guaranteed to Create a Flood of New Clients, get them back over and over again, and Double Your Average Client Spend!	$6,485	INCLUDED	INCLUDED
Ads, Flyers & Letters on CD—you don't even have to type out your own letters & flyers, they're all here on CD—just insert, change your details and hit 'print'!	$2,115	INCLUDED	INCLUDED
TWO 'Getting Started' Action Sessions—right away, we'll take you by the hand and advise you on **exactly** where to start!	$800	INCLUDED	INCLUDED
Salon Masterminds One-on-One Coaching and Advising Program—a course of 12 personal sessions where you can 'pick our brains' every month about **any** marketing or sales issue	$4,500	N/A	INCLUDED
DVD: "How to Create an Offer so Powerful Your Competition will Think You're Crazy—and your clients will LOVE you!" with Greg Milner, CEO Worldwide Salon Marketing	$187	INCLUDED	INCLUDED
CD: "How I Used Simple Marketing Strategies to build a $1.4m a Year Day Spa" with Silver Toolkit owner David Pryor, *of A Touch of Health Day Spa*, Memphis TN. Listen and be amazed—YES, I *can do this too!*	$147	INCLUDED	INCLUDED
CD: "The 5 Secrets to Finding, Hiring & Keeping Great Staff" with Andrew Finkelstein, President of *The Beauty Resource*, New York. If you've ever wished for a 'magic wand' to solve staff problems, this CD is *dynamite!*	$147	INCLUDED	INCLUDED
CD: "How I built my one-room salon at the back of a hair-dressers into a 13-staff cash-machine inside 5 years" with Silver Toolkit Owner Tracey Orr, of Absolute Beauty. (And how you can too!)	$147	INCLUDED	INCLUDED
CD: "Queen of Referrals—How to Get Your Best Clients Referring their Friends Like Mad" with Jill Groves, author of 'Selling with Energy' and 'Selling Like Crazy'. Listen to this and you will be *inspired*	$147	INCLUDED	INCLUDED
Two Critique Certificates—send us any TWO of your existing ads, flyers or sales letters and we'll give you a detailed, written review and improvement suggestions	$800	N/A	INCLUDED
	TOTAL VALUE $12,150	$17,450	
	YOUR PRICE $ 4,887	$ 7,228	
	YOU SAVE $ 7,263	$10,222	

WARNING!
The Toolkit is Strictly Limited to ONE per Postcode or Zipcode. No exceptions. If YOU don't get the world's only complete salon/spa marketing and sales training system, one of your nearby competitors will. (And may have it already)

Subscription to our exclusive online update Membership is compulsory with Toolkit ownership. Monthly subscription is $US24.95.

While you maintain your membership, no other beauty salon or day spa in your area may purchase the Toolkit.

Call us NOW to check if your postcode is free.

Enrol NOW and get this FREE GIFT:
Your Bonus SMS Marketing Pack—use these proven text messages to fill your appointment book instantly! *Valued at $355!*

Amazing Upgrade! "Selling Like Crazy"
Jill Groves' brand new 12-module, best-selling sales training system, as featured in Salon Owner Magazine. *Retails for $1,117.* Upgrade Your Toolkit and get this manual for just $297!

Please tick your choice of Toolkit & payment option

☐ Yes! I want to **upgrade** my Toolkit and get the brilliant in-salon sales training manual 'Selling Like Crazy' for just **$297**. *I'll save $820!*

☐ **Silver Toolkit** Please debit my credit card 1 payment of **$AUD7,228** OR

☐ **Interest Free Easy Payment Plan:** (Includes small book-keeping fee) Please debit my credit card a deposit of **$AUD1,397** and then 9 easy payments of $AUD**659** for a total of **$AUD7,328** over 10 months, plus $US24.95/month Membership. Membership is compulsory with Toolkit purchase.

☐ **Bronze Toolkit** Please debit my credit card 1 payment of **$AUD4,887** OR

☐ **Interest Free Easy Payment Plan:** (Includes small book-keeping fee) Please debit my credit card a deposit of **$AUD1,397** and then 5 easy payments of $AUD**718** for a total of **$AUD4,987** over 6 months plus $US24.95/month Membership. Membership is compulsory with Toolkit purchase.

Worldwide Salon Marketing Pty Ltd ACN 112 848 978 ATF the Greg Milner Family Trust ABN 71 962 537 699 Suite 7, 144 Northwood St, Leederville WA 6007

Card type: Visa/MC/Amex/Bartercard only (please circle)

Card No: _ _ _ _ / _ _ _ _ / _ _ _ _ / _ _ _ _   Exp _ _/_ _

Name on Card: _____

Signature: _____ Date: _ _/_ _/_ _

Salon Name: _____

Address: _____

_____ P/code: _____

Email: _____

Business Phone: _____ Mob _____

Got any BURNING questions? Call us at Worldwide Salon Marketing on 08 9388 4727

FIGURE 4-6. Greg Milner markets his "Essential Salon Owners Marketing Toolkit" across Australia and New Zealand. His order form positions his guest contributors into celebrities with exciting descriptions of them and their accomplishments.

***Lip GOSS* Newsletter Action Form - Fast Fax** to **08 9388 4722**

Salon Owners—If You Want To Turn Your Clients Into Paying *Customers For Life* You Need to Use This AUTOMATIC PROFIT SYSTEM.

YES! I want to *recognise* and *reward* my customers NOW by sending out the *outstanding* 'Lip GOSS' newsletter. I want to get them spending—and *referring* to my salon like crazy! I want to turn my customers into my BIGGEST sales people! **It's the EASY, INSPIRED SOLUTION.**

Every month, without ANY hard work on my part, I will be sent:
1. **'Lip GOSS'**: a full colour, double sided, tri-fold newsletter PACKED with tips, tidbits, and interesting articles on EVERYTHING your customers will be interested in. Lifestyle, fitness, health, reviews, recipes, kids and parenting, pets, gardens, celebrity news...*they'll look forward to receiving it!*
2. **Personalised Ad Insert**: a page *dedicated* to selling more services to your existing clients. Get them trying more and spending more! You choose a treatment or special for every newsletter and we SELL SELL SELL. Similar to any newspaper advertisement or leaflet but you *save on advertising!*
3. **Referral coupons**: for your customers to give to their favourite family members and friends. Designed to get them into YOUR salon with $10 off any treatment—you're basically buying customers at an *unbeatable price.*
I'll be sent the files for EVERYTHING ready to be sent *straight* to the printers—*it couldn't be any easier for me!*

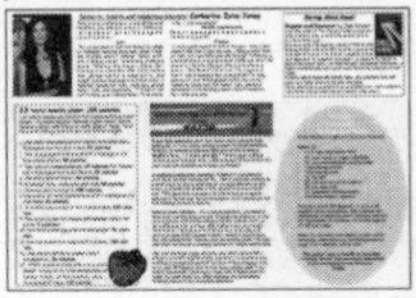

To get started on SAVING TIME and MAKING MONEY *RIGHT AWAY* I need to:

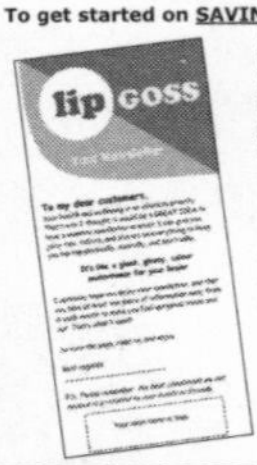

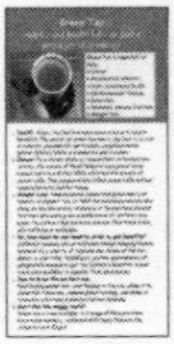

1. Decide if I would like to delight and excite my customers without ANY big effort on my part for **6 months** or **12 months.**
2. Decide if I would like to write the advertising content in the personalised sections of the Ad Insert **myself,**
OR if I would like to supply all the information to write the advert and have an **advertising professional do if for me.**

Personalised Ad Insert completed by YOU.		Personalised Ad Insert completed by EXPERT.	
6 MONTHS	12 MONTHS	6 MONTHS	12 MONTHS
Per month **$389**	Per month **$350** (save $39)	Per month **$589**	Per month **$542** (save $47)

3. Fax this Lip GOSS newsletter Action Form to Worldwide Salon Marketing, fax number **08 9388 4722.** If I have any questions I can contact Worldwide Salon Marketing on **08 9388 4727.**

OUR IRON-CLAD GUARANTEE—If after 3 months of mailing the Lip Goss newsletter and insert to at least 300 of your customers you haven't seen a *traceable increase* in profits or customer referrals compared to the same months in the previous year, **We'll refund EVERY CENT you gave us!**

Please **tick** the Lip GOSS newsletter plan that will be charged MONTHLY to your nominated credit card:

Ad Insert personalised by YOU
☐ 6 months at $389 p/month
☐ 12 months at $350 p/month (save $39 per issue)

Ad Insert personalised by Advertising Expert
☐ 6 months at $589 p/month
☐ 12 months at $542 p/month (save $47 per issue)

Please bill my nominated card with my chosen payment plan
Card Type: (Visa/Mastercard/Amex only) :__________
Card No: ____/____/____/____
Exp__/__ Name on Card: __________
Signature: __________
Date: ____/____

Salon Name: __________ Owner Name: __________
Address: __________ City/Suburb: __________ P/code: ______
Email: __________ Phone No: __________

FIGURE 4-7. While his "Essential Salon Owners Marketing Toolkit" includes training on producing newsletters for salons, many of Greg Milner's customers aren't able to produce a newsletter for themselves every month. Therefore, Greg allows his clients to enroll in an automatic service that publishes a newsletter automatically for his clients' customers. This program is a large profit center for Greg, and it benefits his clients because their customers return more frequently and buy more products. To review complete samples of Greg's marketing materials visit **www.InfoMarketingBook.com/ Milner**.

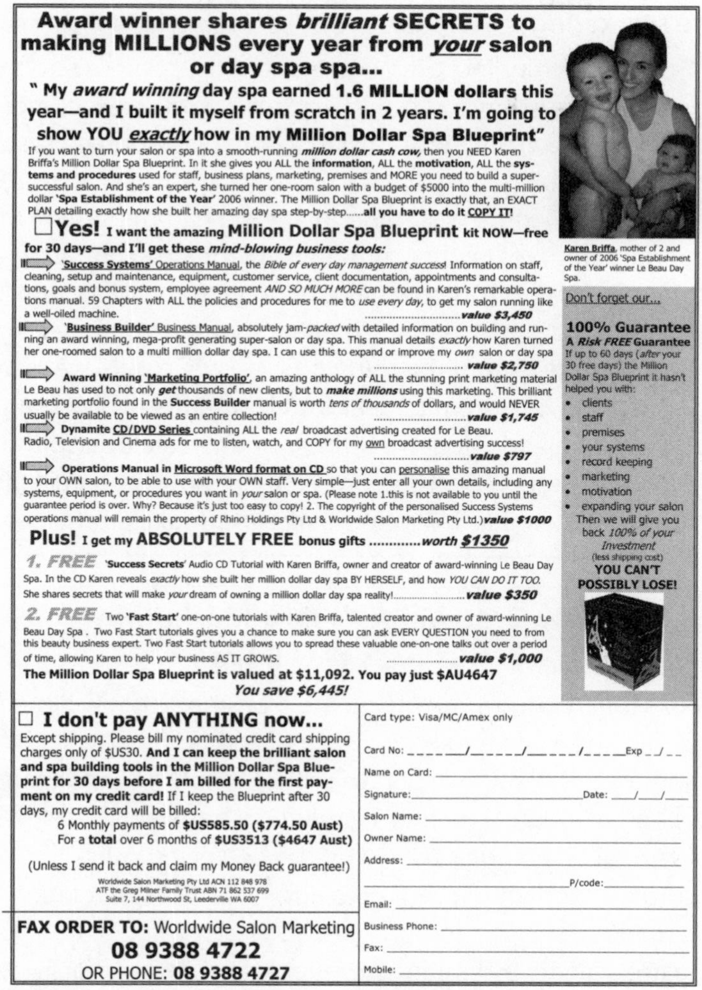

Award winner shares *brilliant* SECRETS to making MILLIONS every year from *your* salon or day spa spa...

" My *award winning* day spa earned 1.6 MILLION dollars this year—and I built it myself from scratch in 2 years. I'm going to show YOU *exactly* how in my Million Dollar Spa Blueprint"

If you want to turn your salon or spa into a smooth-running ***million dollar cash cow,*** then you NEED Karen Briffa's Million Dollar Spa Blueprint. In it she gives you ALL the **information**, ALL the **motivation**, ALL the **systems and procedures** used for staff, business plans, marketing, premises and MORE you need to build a super-successful salon. And she's an expert, she turned her one-room salon with a budget of $5000 into the multi-million dollar **'Spa Establishment of the Year'** 2006 winner. The Million Dollar Spa Blueprint is exactly that, an EXACT PLAN detailing exactly how she built her amazing day spa step-by-step......**all you have to do it COPY IT!**

☐ **Yes! I want the amazing Million Dollar Spa Blueprint kit NOW—free for 30 days—and I'll get these *mind-blowing business tools:***

- **'Success Systems'** Operations Manual, the *Bible of every day management success*! Information on staff, cleaning, setup and maintenance, equipment, customer service, client documentation, appointments and consultations, goals and bonus system, employee agreement *AND SO MUCH MORE* can be found in Karen's remarkable operations manual. 59 Chapters with ALL the policies and procedures for me to *use every day*, to get my salon running like a well-oiled machine. ....***value $3,450***
- **'Business Builder'** Business Manual, absolutely jam-*packed* with detailed information on building and running an award winning, mega-profit generating super-salon or day spa. This manual details *exactly* how Karen turned her one-roomed salon to a multi million dollar day spa. I can use this to expand or improve my *own* salon or day spa .... ***value $2,750***
- **Award Winning 'Marketing Portfolio'**, an amazing anthology of ALL the stunning print marketing material Le Beau has used to not only ***get*** thousands of new clients, but to ***make millions*** using this marketing. This brilliant marketing portfolio found in the **Success Builder** manual is worth *tens of thousands* of dollars, and would NEVER usually be available to be viewed as an entire collection! ....***value $1,745***
- **Dynamite CD/DVD Series** containing ALL the *real* broadcast advertising created for Le Beau. Radio, Television and Cinema ads for me to listen, watch, and COPY for my own broadcast advertising success! ....***value $797***
- **Operations Manual in Microsoft Word format on CD** so that you can personalise this amazing manual to your OWN salon, to be able to use with your OWN staff. Very simple—just enter all your own details, including any systems, equipment, or procedures you want in *your* salon or spa. (Please note 1.this is not available to you until the guarantee period is over. Why? Because it's just too easy to copy! 2. The copyright of the personalised Success Systems operations manual will remain the property of Rhino Holdings Pty Ltd & Worldwide Salon Marketing Pty Ltd.)***value $1000***

Plus! I get my ABSOLUTELY FREE bonus gifts ....*worth $1350*

1. FREE **'Success Secrets'** Audio CD Tutorial with Karen Briffa, owner and creator of award-winning Le Beau Day Spa. In the CD Karen reveals *exactly* how she built her million dollar day spa BY HERSELF, and how *YOU CAN DO IT TOO.* She shares secrets that will make *your* dream of owning a million dollar day spa reality!........................***value $350***

2. FREE Two **'Fast Start'** one-on-one tutorials with Karen Briffa, talented creator and owner of award-winning Le Beau Day Spa . Two Fast Start tutorials gives you a chance to make sure you can ask EVERY QUESTION you need to from this beauty business expert. Two Fast Start tutorials allows you to spread these valuable one-on-one talks out over a period of time, allowing Karen to help your business AS IT GROWS. ....***value $1,000***

The Million Dollar Spa Blueprint is valued at $11,092. You pay just $AU4647

You save $6,445!

Karen Briffa, mother of 2 and owner of 2006 'Spa Establishment of the Year' winner Le Beau Day Spa.

Don't forget our...

100% Guarantee

A *Risk FREE* Guarantee

If up to 60 days (*after* your 30 free days) the Million Dollar Spa Blueprint it hasn't helped you with:

- clients
- staff
- premises
- your systems
- record keeping
- marketing
- motivation
- expanding your salon

Then we will give you back *100% of your Investment*

(less shipping cost)

YOU CAN'T POSSIBLY LOSE!

☐ **I don't pay ANYTHING now...**

Except shipping. Please bill my nominated credit card shipping charges only of $US30. **And I can keep the brilliant salon and spa building tools in the Million Dollar Spa Blueprint for 30 days before I am billed for the first payment on my credit card!** If I keep the Blueprint after 30 days, my credit card will be billed:

6 Monthly payments of **$US585.50 ($774.50 Aust)**
For a **total** over 6 months of **$US3513 ($4647 Aust)**

(Unless I send it back and claim my Money Back guarantee!)

Worldwide Salon Marketing Pty Ltd ACN 112 848 978
ATF the Greg Milner Family Trust ABN 71 862 537 699
Suite 7, 144 Northwood St, Leederville WA 6007

FAX ORDER TO: Worldwide Salon Marketing
08 9388 4722
OR PHONE: **08 9388 4727**

Card type: Visa/MC/Amex only

Card No: ____/____/____/____ Exp __/__

Name on Card: ____________

Signature: ____________ Date: __/__/__

Salon Name: ____________

Owner Name: ____________

Address: ____________

____________ P/code: ______

Email: ____________

Business Phone: ____________

Fax: ____________

Mobile: ____________

FIGURE 4-8. Greg Milner began marketing a product with a lower price point called "Million Dollar Spa Blueprint." This ad is successfully marketing a one-step sale (directly soliciting the sale without a long form sales letter marketing sequence) using a 30-day free trial offer.

Online Marketing

Right from the beginning, Greg had insisted they have a strong web lead generation system and turned to former Oracle exec George Slater to build the first web site, using a Canadian-sourced system called Site Build It.

"Trouble was, George was so good at it, he had the site up and generating a storm of leads ... hundreds in the first couple of months ... we just didn't know what to do with them. We had little or no follow-up systems in place; it was a shambles. At one stage I had to ask George to turn the thing off for a while until we established some kind of system to deal with leads effectively," Greg says.

Greg's web site and salon marketing resources are available at **www.Salon-Marketing-Secrets.com.** Find out how Greg built his system to deal with leads at **www.InfoMarketingBook.com/Milner.**

How Greg Milner's Info-Marketing Business Was Born

1. Looks for an opportunity to create a business that will produce income and build equity.
2. Brings in a marketing expert to create sample ads and materials.
3. Decides to create a manual instead of a book; books sell for $19.95, while manuals have a higher perceived value.
4. Improves product packaging to appeal to the expectations of his market.
5. Creates scarcity by limiting product availability and provides a strong guarantee.
6. Test markets product at a tradeshow booth; good opportunity for customer interaction, marketing feedback, and sales opportunities.

7. Markets product with in-person, community seminars throughout the country; the seminars are filled by using direct mail marketing.
8. Creates a deluxe version of the product to increase margins and profits by making the same number of sales, but with more sales at higher prices.
9. Creates additional revenue opportunities, including forced continuity programs such as a monthly newsletter and an automatic newsletter for his customers.
10. Expands marketing to include web sites and direct mail.

How One Info-Marketer Leveraged His Business to Create Lucrative Speaking Opportunities

Info-Marketer Profile

Successful info-marketers make a lot of money. They work hard. Some live well. Art Sobczak has managed to do all three, with no regrets.

"I've always been all about balance," Art says, "Even when I was speaking and traveling, I made a commitment never to be gone more than two days in a row and never more than four days in a month when my kids were growing up and still in grade school and high school. I coached their sports teams and was always there. I've got no regrets about that."

Art remembers his colleagues in professional speaking poking fun at him because of how little he worked and how much he made. The key, according to Art, is creating a business with a passive income. Here is how he did it.

Art's story begins in the early 1980s when he left the corporate world and started a consulting business. He had learned a lot about training people on telephone sales (aka telemarketing, but Art doesn't like to use that term), and he was ready to put his knowledge to work for himself.

Young and somewhat naïve, but also cocky and smart, the budding entrepreneur soon recognized a major downfall of the consulting business: unless he has recurring revenue, a good consultant will put himself out of business. So Art created a newsletter, *Telephone Selling Report*, and started out by offering it for free for one year. At the end of that first year, Art had about 500 people on his mailing list. That's when he decided to begin charging for his newsletter.

He sent a renewal notice and began charging $79 per year. With about 60 percent converting to paid subscriptions, Art had the beginnings of a passive income stream. Now he was in the information marketing business. In addition, the subscribers were repeat customers for the products he created as well as specialty seminars, and many became consulting clients.

With his background in training, Art created some booklets and audio programs and soon realized he could transform his business even more by getting into the speaking and training business. It was a natural segue for Art, who says he's not just a speaker; he's in the information dissemination business, providing information through a variety of ways.

Art's info-business had a major breakthrough when he was asked to write a monthly column for the trade publication *Teleprofessional*. This gave him a high profile in the field of inside sales. During this time Art produced his first audio product, using Dartnell, which at the time was the premier sales training publisher. Using Dartnell instead of self-publishing made a lot of potential clients take notice of Art because of the credibility and exposure that comes from being a published author with a known publishing house.　➡

How To Sell More and Cold Call Without Rejection By Phone

The Telesales College Two-Day Training Seminar

By Art Sobczak

Business Inc. **By Phone**

What is the Telesales College?

The Telesales College is a complete step-by-step training workshop for professional business-to-business sales representatives who use the phone as an integral or primary method of communication for their prospecting and/or sales calls.

Participants are led through the logical sequence of the sales call, using a consultative (question-based) sales approach, learning step-by-step, what-to-say and how-to-say it ideas, strategies, and techniques which help them become more confident, effective, and productive on their very next call.

Customers tell us, and graduates affirm, that in no other seminar will sales pros find such an abundance of real-world, proven, no-baloney telesales ideas and methods that work. And learning is made fun and motivating, presented by telesales expert Art Sobczak

As a result of this two-day learning and self-discovery process, participants hit the ground running upon arriving back at the office. Attendees tell us they have a new sense of confidence as they prospect for new business, follow-up with existing contacts and customers delivering real value, and handle inquiries and turn them into sales.

Bottom line, this is the program that demystifies professional sales and prospecting using the phone, and provides real how-to information–not blue sky theory or goofy, salesy garbage–that participants use and show results from right away!

Who Attends the College?

The Telesales Rep College is designed for professional business-to-business salespeople who use the phone as their primary method of communication with prospects and customers. Titles for this function include Inside Sales, Telesales, Account Management, Customer Service (if they're proactive) and Telemarketing (if they use a consultative, needs-based approach). Outside sales reps who want to be more effective and use their time more efficiently also show great results from the College.

The instruction is at the hands-on level, for the person who is on the phone. However, we find about 30% of attendees are managers, supervisors, and trainers who are able to take the hundreds of how-to ideas, word-for-word tips and strategies and use them in their own in-house training.

For Both the New and Experienced Sales Professionals

Sales reps who have never had sales training walk away with a methodical system and process for placing successful calls, and are confident in doing so. (Our experience shows it pays to correctly train new reps before bad habits are entrenched.) And experienced sales pros leave energized, armed with new ideas, old bad habits corrected, and being reminded of the tried and true (yet sometimes neglected) fundamentals which were rescued from the recesses of their memory. We've even had individuals attend the College a second time a year or so after their first experience, and get as much or more from it. Ultimately, the results shown from the College aren't a function of an attendee's years of sales experience, but rather his or her attitude toward self-improvement.

"I have become one of Dell's top acquisition reps and, using your techniques, have had tremendous success selling into non-Dell accounts. The people here at Dell are truly amazed at my cold calling skills. Your sales techniques really do work, and I am most appreciative to have taken your class." –Ryan Quarles, Dell, Inc.

"Before your course my sales here and there averaged $1500-$3000, while working very hard. When I got back from your class I brought in two big deals for $11,440 and $13,800 almost immediately! Now I'm working very smart, no longer hard." –Dara Bills, Thompson, NETg

2006 Sessions Fall/Winter Schedule

Atlanta, September 19-20
Amerisuites Airport

Chicago, October 10-11
Doubletree O'Hare -Rosemont

Seattle, November 15-16
Homewood Suites Downtown

To Enroll, Call
800-326-7721
Only 30 Students Accepted Per Session

FIGURE 4-8. In addition to his paid appearances, Art Sobczak has his own speaking engagements every other month through his Tele-Sales College program. This way he creates ongoing revenue in his business and doesn't have to compete with other speakers for those opportunities.

With a building reputation, Art was ready to create more of his own products, including books and audio programs. He also found that his status of being an expert in the field opened doors for speaking and training opportunities. Even though he "hated the thought of public speaking," Art decided that if he was going to do it, he needed to be the best there was at it. He turned to the National Speakers Association, "devouring all the materials" and taking speaking programs. He used what he learned to put together a topnotch training program based on his own real world experience.

With many of his newsletter subscribers requesting him to conduct in-house training or to speak at meetings, Art decided to build up the speaking and training side of his business. He conducts seminars (Telesales College) six to eight times a year and earns $10,000-plus per day of training. The wealth from his business has created a lifestyle that allows him to spend his time on what he really values: his family.

Art has the luxury of deciding how often he accepts speaking engagements because over the years he has built a business that provides significant passive income. He has about 40 products that he markets on the Internet, has published eight books for other authors, and distributes an e-mail newsletter to over 35,000 subscribers. This e-letter creates a monthly revenue stream from four endorsed sponsors who pay Art every month for exclusively recommending them within their niches to his subscribers. For a time, Art focused almost exclusively on electronic marketing and products (Internet and e-mail), but influenced by Dan Kennedy and his own observations about spam and the growing difficulty in getting e-mail delivered, Art has recently gone back to producing a paper newsletter. He also uses Amazon.com and his own web site as well as a printed magalog to sell his information products. By using ➡️ different mediums to sell his products, Art creates high volume and a continuous stream of income.

For more information about Art Sobczak visit **www.BusinessBy Phone.com** or **www.InfoMarketingBook.com/Sobczak.**

Chapter 5

Step 4: The Sales Process to Convert Shoppers Into Buyers

by Robert Skrob
President, Information Marketing Association

ANY YEARS AGO, KORY AND I WERE SITTING AT OUR TABLE eating dinner. The dining room was immediately adjacent to the living room in the small yellow house we were renting at the time, so sometimes we watched TV while we ate.

The news anchor was excitedly reading the news stories when an image of the house across the street from us flashed across the screen. "Police officers shoot dog at Eddie Road home."

"What? That was across the street! The police are shooting across the street from our home?"

We tuned in and found out the police were serving an arrest warrant and a dog had attacked them. To defend themselves, one of the officers had shot the dog and killed it. But the police didn't get the guy they had come to arrest.

There I sat. Living across the street from someone who was getting arrested, in a terrible neighborhood with my family. We had a swing set in our backyard where I played with my 18-month-old daughter all the time. The only comfort I had was at least there was one less killer dog in the neighborhood.

My wife and I lived there because we had no choice. We were married young, and my wife was pregnant before our first anniversary. We had to grow up quickly. That meant we had to put off home ownership and rent while we saved money for a down payment.

That evening I noticed a letter in my mail for a "No Money Down" real estate course. Several months before I had called in response to an infomercial I saw on television, but I didn't buy. The operator took my name and address and I'd been receiving mail every week since. That night I pulled out my credit card and bought the product.

Within a month of receiving the product my family was in a new home in a better neighborhood. I really owe that information marketer a lot because he repeatedly followed up with me. He was there, on the night I was ready, to provide me with the exact information I needed to solve my problem. And solve it he did.

When I originally called in response to the infomercial, I became a lead. That info-marketer had a follow-up process that continued to keep in contact with me. He sent me sales letters, post cards, and information about upcoming seminars in my area. Each week I received more information that allowed me to become more familiar with the info-marketer and grow to like him. Then, when I was ready to change my circumstances, his sales material was there.

I learned later that everything I received was part of a structured sales sequence. Each item was written from the beginning to build on the one before it. In fact, each step was continuously tested against other possible marketing pieces.

Too many marketers respond to a lead with a single sales step, and then they don't send additional materials. Once you've obtained a lead, you need a process for turning that lead into a customer.

This process could involve a web site the customer visits. It could be a sales letter. It could be a telephone call. It could be a sales presentation given in person, either from the stage or in a one-on-one environment. Whatever process you use, you need a way to put all of your leads into a "marketing machine" or funnel so leads go in and customers pop out. The nice thing is, once you create your marketing funnel, you will have it forever. You'll need to make changes as you go along, but it's a lot easier to tweak an existing marketing funnel than it is to create one from scratch each time you develop a new product. Creating your own marketing funnel will give you a marketing advantage.

Ways to Sell

There are several ways to sell your product. The first way is a one-step sales process. Instead of advertising to generate leads, you advertise to sell your product and service, so there's no free offer option for customers. They see your ad, and they either buy or don't buy.

Next is direct mail. These can be long letters or short letters. Many are 60 pages long, and 112 pages isn't unheard of. These longer letters are detailed stories that talk the customer through the problems you are promising to solve, the solutions you're proposing, and the proof that your solutions will work for your customer.

A lot of info-marketers ask me how long a sales letter should be. My answer is as long as it takes to communicate your message. If you need 40 pages to tell your customers you understand their situation, to tell why your product is the best product they can buy, to give your proof, to explain all the ways your product is going to benefit them, to present the price in a compelling way that makes it sound like a terrific deal, to add bonuses that entice them to take immediate action, and to ask for the sale, then you write it in 40 pages. If you can get it done in eight pages, then eight pages is long enough.

You should not have a long sales letter just for the sake of having a long sales letter. Every paragraph, every word should be pushing the

---

Software System That Puts Your Small Business on Autopilot by Automating Your Marketing, Sales, and More

Info-Marketer Resource

The largest obstacle to implementing marketing sequences is keeping track of which customers are within which marketing step. As leads arrive over the course of a few months, each week you are dealing with leads that are in every step of your marketing sequence. It's extremely confusing to keep track of the marketing pieces that each lead should receive. Finally someone created a web-based software that, among a lot of other features, tracks which leads are in which step of multiple marketing sequences.

ManagePro CRM lets you *supercharge* your follow-up sequences. In addition to sending follow-up e-mails, ManagePro CRM will send direct mail pieces, faxes, voice broadcasts, and more—automatically.

For a free product tour, auto responder test drive, and online demonstration visit **www.InfoMarketingCRM.com**.

---

customer toward the sale. However, you should not invest your money in generating and following up on leads without giving yourself the best possible opportunity to sell to a prospect. The only time you have the best possible opportunity to sell to a prospect is when you're able to tell your entire story. Sometimes that means a long sales letter!

A lot of folks tell me that people won't read a long letter. "I'm not going to send that; it's too much." Well, sending a one-page letter is like sending a sales rep into the field and telling him he only has two minutes to talk to the customer. Delivering one page when 40 pages is necessary is like pulling your salesperson out of the customer's office without giving him a chance to make the sale.

Your letter is your sales rep. Let your letter give the complete marketing message, and make sure it does it in a compelling way. If a salesperson is boring, then the prospect is not going to buy. If your sales letter is boring, then your prospects are going to throw it away without reading the entire thing. They're not going to buy from you. But if your letter is enticing, if it meets their needs, if it offers them a solution to their problems in a compelling way, then they will read 50 pages or even 400 to solve their problem!

Another way to deliver sales messages is online, either on web sites or via e-mail. Your web site should be an information-packed page that sells only one product. I've seen too many sites that try to get fancy with this. They market many different products, or they try to sell one product but at the same time also offer consulting services or registration for their meeting. You must take the lead through just one sales message for a particular product or service.

> **KEY CONCEPT** Your sales sequence should repeat your entire sales story several times in different formats. These can include sales letters, faxes, e-mails, tele-seminars, and telemarketing.

Don't try to offer multiple things at one time, unless they are within one package. If you are going to package several products to sell all together, you need to explain everything that's in the package. Just don't tell your customers you are selling a package and then allow them to cafeteria-choose what they want out of the package. Everything from start to finish must lead prospects to only one option: to buy your product or service. Offering four or five different products and asking them to choose creates confusion. Confusion will keep your customers from making the decision to buy.

Another very popular method of selling information products is via tele-seminars. The telephone is a much more interactive medium than advertising, direct mail, or even the Internet. The customers hear the info-marketer's voice. They hear what you have to offer, and they hear testimonials about your product and service. Even though a tele-seminar provides a more personal connection than you get with a sales letter, the process is much the same. You bring in prospects using a lead generation ad. Once they're on the phone, you go through your complete marketing message and give your prospects a reason to act immediately.

Prove It!

Whatever sales method you use, one of the most important parts of your message is *proof*. Use every way you can think of to prove to your customers that your product will do exactly what you say it will do. You can do this through product demonstrations. You can do it through piece examples. You can do it through testimonials. Nothing is more powerful than personal testimonials from your customers who have succeeded because of your product. Always include glowing testimonials in your marketing to maximize your sales.

Attorney Produces Marketing Toolkit for Lawyers

Info-Marketer Profile

Lawyer Ben Glass with Ben Glass Law (**www.BenGlass Law.com**) has taken what he has learned from the Glazer-Kennedy Insider's Circle seminar and turned it into a toolkit for personal injury attorneys.

As he sat listening to Dan Kennedy's presentation, Ben remembers thinking, "Someone else must have already taken these concepts and niched them for lawyers." So Ben bought what was available and began talking with people in his profession. He soon found the available materials fell short of what lawyers needed to promote their practices. And the reason was simple: Most of the information was written by people who are not lawyers. So Ben set out to tailor for personal injury attorneys what he had learned from Glazer-Kennedy Insider's Circle.

Following advice from Kennedy and fellow attorney Bill Hammond, ➥

Ben focuses his efforts on communicating the authentic nature of his program, that is, his ideas work—and he knows they work—because he is a practicing attorney successfully marketing his services in the real world. When Ben says he can show lawyers how to do effective, ethical, outside-the-box marketing, he has the day-to-day experience of running a law practice to back him up.

Ben targeted solo practitioner and smaller law firms whose lawyers often feel at a disadvantage when trying to compete with the marketing dollars of large, high-volume firms that specialize in personal injury law. Following the concepts he learned from Glazer-Kennedy, Ben built his marketing list by giving away marketing advice in an electronic newsletter. He also wrote a series of articles and mailed them to all of the state trial lawyer associations to give them content for their newsletters and journals. When Ben knew in advance that a state association was going to print one of his articles, he purchased lists and mailed postcards to lawyers in the state telling them to "watch for the next issue of *Trial Lawyer* because it has an information-packed article. And, by the way, if you want to know more about effective, ethical, outside-the-box marketing, go to my web site." All of this helped brand Ben as an expert in marketing lawyers' services.

Then Ben attended Dan Kennedy's Renegade Millionaire Conference (**http://www.RenegadeMillionaire.com**), where he learned he needed to develop his sales letter even before completing his product. He set up his **GreatLegalMarketing.com** web site, posting a long sales letter with the proposition that he could teach any lawyer how to market himself. He includes topnotch guarantees, including money-back any time up to five years if a client hasn't made $50,000 or isn't satisfied with the product. Ben drives clients to his web site via direct mail postcards and advertisements in state trial lawyer associations' journals. For an expanded profile about Ben Glass, visit **www.InfoMarketingBook.com/Glass**.

Info-Marketer Profile

It's 3:00 a.m., and Fabienne Fredrickson Is Sleeping Like a Baby

It's 3:00 a.m. But Fabienne Fredrickson doesn't wake up in a cold sweat, wondering where her next client is coming from. At least not anymore.

Fabienne is an info-marketer who has used her past experiences to create a client-generating program for herself and her customers.

After eight years in the corporate world of advertising, marketing, and sales, Fabienne knew she didn't want "anybody else breathing down her neck," so she quit her job, became her own boss, and opened a private nutrition practice in her home.

You might think a seasoned advertising professional would have no trouble attracting clients, but at first Fabienne had the same struggles most entrepreneurs have with identifying and marketing to their potential customers. So she put her skills to work and created a system for herself, "something that was going to be repeatable and verifiable so I didn't have the '3:00 a.m. I-don't-have- enough-clients sweats' anymore," Fabienne explains. She talked with coaches, read books, and took courses, but noticed that no one had all of the information about getting clients in one place. "There were the networking gurus, the people who knew how to close the sale, and then others who knew how to do mailings; everything was there, but just not all in one place," Fabienne recalls. "So I decided to put everything together in one package for self-employed people." Fabienne later named her creation "The Client Attraction System" when she began marketing it to others.

"About a year after I created my system, the door of opportunity just kept knocking. People were saying, 'You need to show other people how to do this,'" Fabienne says. (*continued on page 107*)

Announcing, for the FIRST TIME EVER, My "Client Attraction VIP Total Access Mentoring Program"

If you qualify to become a Client Attraction
VIP Total Access *member, here's what you get:*

One-hour Quick Start Phone Consultation.

During this call, we'll conduct an in-depth analysis of your business, your marketing, and your goals and objectives. Then we'll lay out a detailed action plan to guide you toward them.

Weekly Coaching and Mentoring Calls.

The first three weeks of each month, we'll meet via phone to review your progress, keep you moving forward, give you next-steps to tackle, and adjust your plans, if necessary. I'll coach and guide you to take the exact steps you need to succeed. You can also ask me questions and get advice on your marketing and/or business decisions.

Unlimited Access to me via phone and e-mail.

When you're stuck on an assignment or an issue, it's easy to give up or lose momentum. But not when you can have access to me as often as you like to get moving forward, get answers to your questions, or get feedback. I do not offer this in any other program I offer. In my opinion, immediate feedback on marketing is not only priceless; it can make or break certain situations. You can call me anytime with a quick question, and I'll do my best to help you on

FIGURE 5-1. In this example of one her ads, Fabienne Fredrickson builds the value of her program by explaining all of the business areas in which she helps her clients. This copy, which outline's Fabienne's coaching program, highlights the benefits of working with her. While it would be natural to end the sales copy after explaining the one-hour quick-start call, the weekly coaching, and the unlimited access, Fabienne provides a lot of details on her areas of experience. This builds the value of "what you get" from her coaching program.

the spot. Or schedule a phone appointment with me if you need to talk longer. You can also send me your questions via e-mail, and I'll send you answers—usually within one business day and many times much sooner than that.

Your own personal Marketing Success coach.
We'll examine your current position in the marketplace, what you offer, what results you provide, who your ideal clients are, and ways to reach them in large numbers and inexpensively. We'll also look at your current marketing materials, whether they "speak" to your ideal clients, and then create new ones or tweak the old ones. We'll put together a plan for reaching your clients in large numbers and inexpensively, ways of getting you out there in a big way, and create packages and programs that really get them to buy. Finally, we'll teach you how to put your marketing on autopilot so you never have to struggle again to fill your practice.

Your own personal Networking Success coach.
The reason most people don't like to network is they're simply not doing it right. I'll personally coach you on all the techniques and scripts that have made me a master networker for the last six years. I've used each and every technique, and we'll transform your networking efforts from ones that don't work to ones that really attract clients to you.

Your own personal Closing the Sale coach.
You've spent weeks, if not months attracting that one client, but if you don't know how to close the sale like a master, none of your hard work so far will have been worth it. Sadly, most self-employed professionals, especially those in private practice, don't know how to close the sale without feeling sales-y or sleazy. It's time to change that. I'll coach you on exactly how I have developed the script to

close 97 to 99 percent of my prospects into paying clients. It's actually easy when you know how.

Your own personal Passive Revenue coach.

Our goal will not only be to get you more clients, but also to make you more money, and that means *not* always being chained to your desk or your phone. In the last six months, I've made over $25,000 in info-product sales, without having to be there. I'll teach you exactly how I did it and how you can, too. There's nothing like the feeling of seeing money go directly into your bank account and not having to be there for it to happen.

Your own personal Time Management coach.

If you're like most self-employed people, you're always putting out fires (or so it seems) and always have too much on your plate. At the end of the day, that means you have no time left to market yourself and attract clients. We're going to change all that by making big changes in how you handle your time. That way, you'll start getting the results you've always wanted from your marketing, while being able to close down your laptop at the end of the day (at a reasonable hour!).

My own personal Ideas and Brainstorms for you.

One great idea can mean the difference between attracting one client here or there and attracting a whole lot of clients, consistently. Together, we'll brainstorm and come up with ideas to grow your business quickly. Sometimes, having someone (successful) to bounce ideas off of and kick an idea around with is just what we need!

Free Admission to any and all of my Tele-seminars during your membership.

While you are an active VIP Total Access member, I'll give you free admission to any tele-seminar that I host during that time. These events can range from one-shot calls to entire series of marketing training tele-classes. I'll be sure to let you know when they are and how to access them during our time together.

WEEKLY Coaching and Group Mentoring Calls

Every week for 10 weeks, you'll meet with me and up to 19 other high-achieving peers looking to attract more clients. Via phone, we'll spend 60 minutes per week going in depth into one step of the Client Attraction System™ per week, give you assignments and worksheets, review your progress, keep you moving forward, give you next steps to tackle, and adjust your plans, if necessary. I'll coach and guide you to take the exact steps you need to succeed. You can also ask me questions and get advice on your marketing and/or business decisions. That's 15 hours of time on the phone with me coaching you. (A $7,500 value.)

Your own personal Coaching Success Buddy.
You will be assigned a coaching success buddy to speak with once a week, a peer of yours from the Boot Camp. We recommend that you spend one hour speaking to each other each week, but some past participants chose to speak more than once a week for added results. Many of them found this to be one of their favorite parts of the Boot Camp and loved being paired with a likeminded individual, to keep moving forward on the assignments each week, brainstorming and giving each other feedback. (A $1,200 value.)

FIGURE 5-2. As an introductory product, Fabienne Fredrickson offers her Client Attraction Boot Camp. Priced at $1,095, she provides the lessons over a 10-week period.

Access to your peers through an Online Forum.

In addition to your weekly Group Mentoring calls and your weekly Coaching Success Buddy calls, you'll have access to all the other peers in your Boot Camp via a collaborative online forum. Using your group of peers, you'll get even more feedback, accountability, brainstorming, and resources. You are encouraged to send your completed assignments to the group, ask questions as often as you like, and get guidance and support. Trust me, there's nothing like a fast-paced class and a group of peers to get your butt in gear, keep you accountable, and stay disciplined to create results! Most of all, you'll find the camaraderie and encouragement very rewarding. (A $450 value.)

Your own Client Attraction System™ Workbook.

Before the start of the Boot Camp intensive, you'll receive the entire Client Attraction Boot Camp Intensive workbook, including all the worksheets we'll be discussing during the 10-week class. You are encouraged to start reading and get familiar with what we'll be covering during the 10 weeks. (A $65 value.)

Weekly Open Office Hours to ask me anything you want.

Each Friday, between 8:30 a.m. and 11:30 a.m. Eastern, you have permission to call me and ask me anything you want about your assignments, marketing materials, or anything that you need help with to attract more clients. Anything. The only thing I ask is that you keep the calls to 15 minutes so that I have time to be able to help everyone. (A $1,250 value.)

Weekly Progress Reports to keep you on track.

You'll be given a Weekly Progress Form to fill out and send to me the day before each and every coaching call. You can save this in your files and fill in the answers throughout the week or the day before our Boot Camp call to help you track your progress and improve the efficiency of our time together. It will serve as a road map for our work that day. The more you tell me what you want to work on with this form, the more I will be able to help you. It works. (A $10 value.)

Recordings of each and every class.
If, for whatever reason, you aren't able to make a particular class, no worries, you'll be able to listen to the recording of it on the web site as many times as you like. We record each and every one of the 10 classes and post it on the web site, sometimes within minutes of the call, but usually within 24 hours. This way, you will never miss any information, but it also gives you access to the material as often as you like. (A $695 value.)

My own personal Ideas and Brainstorms for you.
One great idea can mean the difference between attracting one client here or there and attracting a whole lot of clients, consistently. Together on the calls, we'll brainstorm and come up with ideas to grow your business quickly. Sometimes, having someone (successful) to bounce ideas off of and kick an idea around with is just what we need! (A $1,000 value.)

(*continued from page 101*) For the last seven years, Fabienne has been coaching one-on-one and also in groups. At first Fabienne did individual telephone coaching, providing each client three 30-minute calls per month. Her six-month program was $2,400. "It was so cheap at the time that I was always at full capacity," Fabienne says.

During that time she also worked to put what she knew down on paper. "It took me three years to put together what I call my 'Home Study System,'" Fabienne says, "and then I began selling it online." ➡

Now she was an info-marketer, but Fabienne didn't know very much about what that meant. "I didn't know what a sales letter was. I didn't know about shopping carts and auto responders or anything like that. The second manual I wrote in three weekends, and I'm slowly starting to crank out more stuff," Fabienne laughs.

Today, Fabienne's main business is still coaching on the telephone, but by creating a VIP program and tripling her rates, she has been able to reduce her client list from 30 to 15, giving her more time to devote to sales of her "Client Attraction Home Study System" and the "Secrets of Master Networkers." Now her info-business is growing to become a larger percentage of her overall operations.

Most of Fabienne's clients are women (97 percent!), and most of them are what she calls "solo-preneurs" or one-person entrepreneurs. In her VIP total access program, a group of 10 people get hour-long calls with Fabienne along with unlimited access via e-mail, chat, and additional 15-minute calls. "The program is really just lots and lots of access to me, which is what most people kept saying they wanted," Fabienne explains. "In addition to all of the proven client attraction marketing systems in my written materials, they can have me 'hand hold' and come up with their tag lines, their entire campaigns right on the phone with them over a five- or eight-month period. They also get recordings of all of our calls."

Fabienne charges $9,700 for her eight-month program and $6,700 for her five-month program. It was a huge price jump from her $2,400 six-month program, but after testing three spots and having them sell in a week and a half, Fabienne knew she was meeting a demand in her marketplace. "People were saying, 'Fabienne, I want a lot of you, and I'll pay what it takes to get it,'" she marvels.

Fabienne markets her coaching program via her web site and e-zine. "When people are ready to raise their hand and say, 'O.K., ➡

Fabienne, I'm ready for you to work with me,' they call my virtual assistant through the 800 number on the web site or they e-mail me directly to set up a get acquainted session, which is a 15-minute call," Fabienne explains. During that call, Fabienne explains the various options. She has a sales letter but has found talking it through over the phone is more effective, and it allows her to use the system she developed to attract clients.

"The first 15 minutes of my get acquainted talk is me asking the client questions," Fabienne says. (She advertises the call as 15 minutes, but it usually runs up to 10 minutes longer.) "In my 'Client Attraction System,' I teach about becoming a master of the soft close, because most of my clients are women. Women who learn how to close the sale from men feel inauthentic and ineffective. I teach them to ask questions instead."

Fabienne describes a typical get-acquainted call: "I ask a whole bunch of questions, and then I'll be quiet for a while. Then the client will say, 'Tell me about your program' and then for five or seven minutes I'll describe all the juicy details of the program, and then I'll just say to her, 'So, if you were to do this, ideally which program would you want?' And she'll tell me, and then I'll say, 'Well, hypothetically, if you were going to do the VIP eight-month program, which day would you want to start? Monday? Great. Let's do it.' And then I get her credit card number, and my assistant takes care of the rest."

Fabienne finds this approach works well across all industry niches, and so her client list varies from financial planners to consultants to nutritionists to even a corporate magician. The thing most of her clients have in common is being a single-person business.

For more information about Fabienne Fredrickson and her products visit **www.ClientAttraction.com**. For the complete profile visit **www.InfoMarketingBook.com/Fredrickson**.

Info-Marketer Profile

Building an Info-Marketing Business With Joint Ventures
How One Internet Marketer Went From Zero to 7 Figures With Zero Advertising

We often hear about information marketers taking their direct mail businesses and transitioning them to work on the Internet. Brett Fogle with OptionsUniversity is doing just the opposite, going from selling e-books online to using direct mail, other media, and joint ventures (JVs) to build his business into a full-scale information marketing business.

Brett's primary market is people who have identified themselves as being interested in stock market trading or options trading. "Options are hot right now," says Brett. "I started an advisory service three years ago for options, and it didn't really take off. So I temporarily walked away from trading and delved into Internet marketing."

Brett established two criteria for his info-marketing business:

1. He would sell an information product.
2. The market would be people with a large amount of disposable income.

"At that point the only two markets I could think of were Internet marketing and stock trading," Brett remembers, "and the Internet marketing field was pretty well saturated. Long story short, I went back to my contact list and found the best options guy I could. I got really lucky because he's probably the best in the country."

Brett connected with Ron Ianieri, who was a floor trader for 15 years, including four years as the lead market maker in Dell computer options. In addition to being a leading expert in options trading, Ianieri turned out to be an excellent teacher and the perfect match for Brett's business.　➡

In just two years, Brett has been able to grow his business from zero to over seven figures in sales per year. "That's with zero advertising!" Brett exclaims. "I've done it exclusively through joint ventures."

Brett approached a well known Internet marketer, Steven Pierce, who was also in the stock arena. He had a very successful product called "FibonacciSecrets™." Pierce turned down Brett's initial proposal, so Brett tried his promotion with a lesser-known info-marketer who was happy to do a joint venture deal.

Once he had results to show Pierce, the two were able to launch a joint venture that did very well. Brett leveraged the success of his first two JVs to land more deals. "Joint ventures are a very effective way to get started," Brett says. "For anybody who is getting started in information marketing, and specifically online, I would recommend JVs as the easiest and best way to do it."

For example, Brett has an exclusive marketing deal with a brokerage company that pays a five-figure fee every quarter for referring all of his leads to the firm. He also taps businesses that want access to his customers to sponsor seminars and events.

Brett continues to use JVs as his primary business builder because he thinks they are the biggest and fastest way to grow a business. He hired an affiliate manager last year to go out and find JVs for his business. They structure the partnerships so the JV partner gets 35 percent of sales and the affiliate manager gets 10 percent. Using JVs has worked so well that Brett has expanded his business internationally.

One of the ways Brett promotes his product is through Google ads. By hiring an experienced copywriter and tinkering with his web site, Brett has cut his costs per lead in half.

"We used to have several different ads that sent leads to one landing page for a free report to get the opt in," Brett explains.

"Now we have very specific ad campaigns targeted to either beginners or to more advance traders. Each ad goes to a separate landing page that's slightly different. This has boosted our conversions."

Brett is also using direct marketing to promote his products. He started with a sales letter that he tested to five different lists. He also split tested using a third-class stamp versus a first-class stamp to see if the more expensive postage would get his mail into the "A" pile instead of "straight into the trash." Even though the first-class postage cost Brett more upfront, his results have been significantly better.

You can contact Brett at his web site by visiting **www.Options University.com**. To learn more about how Brett Fogle uses joint ventures to build his business, visit **www.InfoMarketingBook. com/Fogle**.

Joint Venture Sources

Brett Fogle launched his info-business, OptionsUniversity, through joint ventures with other businesses. Here are his sources for finding potential partners:

- Searched Google for sites serving his target market and then contacted the ones that looked the best.
- Hired a JV manager to conduct research, locate, contact, and create agreements with partners for a 10-percent commission on any JV sales he found.
- Received referrals from existing JVs.
- Pooled names with other marketers with a list broker who controls how many times each partner can use the list.

Making Money by Magic

Info-Marketer Profile

Dave Dee is a real-life professional magician. That's magical in and of itself. Many little boys dream of becoming a magician (or a pro baseball player or an astronaut or ...), but few follow their dreams into adulthood and make them happen. Dave Dee is exceptional, and so is his story.

Dave begins, "I always had the dream of being a professional magician, ever since I was 8 years old, but everyone told me I couldn't do it, that it wasn't practical. You know, when people say that kind of stuff, it really gets into your head. You begin to believe it. So I took the traditional route. I went to college. I got a job in radio advertising sales after college. But I still dreamed of being a professional magician."

Dave's dream didn't take off until he learned a little something about marketing. As Dave tells it, "I was a good magician, but I wasn't very good at booking magic shows. I was doing about three shows a month. But then I learned direct marketing, and I went from doing three shows a month to averaging 30 shows a month in less than three months!"

It turns out that Dave had a mentor named Dan Kennedy. Dave purchased Dan's "Magnetic Marketing" and ended up booking 57 shows in his fourth month of direct marketing. This got him to thinking. "I realized that what I had actually done was trade time for dollars," Dave says. "I was living my dream, but I was limited by what I could do. I couldn't really do more than 57 shows in a month, nor did I want to. And then the other thing that got me thinking was what if something happened to me—what happens if I break my leg or get sick—if I can't go out and do the shows, I'm not making any money whatsoever."

➥

"7 Steps For Making More Money With Your Magic"

****

This report reveals how you can make more money and even have more fun as a magician.

PLUS DISCOVER HOW YOU CAN GET THE BOOK YOU JUST BOUGHT FOR FREE, RECEIVE MORE FREE BONUSES, AND DISCOVER HOW YOU CAN MAKE YOUR MAGIC CAREER SOAR – GUARANTEED.

I urge you to get comfortable, ask not to be disturbed, and STUDY this letter - it IS that significant! It introduces something THAT amazing!

****

Dear Fellow Performer,

If you are a **Children's Performer**: how would you like to <u>get a steady stream of phone calls everyday</u> from parents interested in your service? How would you like to close over 70% of the people who call? Put an end to the "I'm just calling around for prices" objection? Have a list of names, phone numbers, addresses and birthdays of kids months before their party? <u>How about if this list cost you nothing</u>?

If you are a **School Show Performer**: how would you like to <u>dominate your market</u> even if someone else has been performing in the schools for years? Learn how to get booked over and over at schools, even when they tell you they don't have time for assemblies?

If you are a **Corporate or Trade Show Performer**: how would you like to attract prospects who are interested in using a magician for their event and are pre-disposed to hiring *you* ? <u>Have qualified prospects calling *you* and asking for your help</u>?

If you are a **Performer of *any* kind**: how would you like to <u>stop wasting money on advertising</u> ? Finally have a proven, systematic way to get quick results from every dollar you invest in ANY kind of advertising, marketing or promotion? Develop a constant stream of <u>new prospects</u>?

FIGURE 5-1. Here are the first pages of each letter of Dave Dee's three-step sales letter sequence selling his magician marketing tool kit. Notice how each letter is slightly different; however, they are almost the same. On the second sequence he starts off with a list of reasons why the reader wouldn't have responded to the first step. Later in the letter he continues

Should I Send Out The Search Party?

Dear Friend:

Just kidding about the search party - but I am wondering why I haven't heard from you.

Ten days ago, you asked me to send you a copy of the Special Report which explains how to book more shows and make more money with your magic. Since I haven't heard from you, I thought I'd write to you again.

My name is Dave Dee. I'm the magician who went from doing three shows a month, with $14,000 in debt, to performing over 30 shows a months, increasing my income 1000%, and becoming debt free.

I have put all my marketing secrets into a comprehensive, easy to use, 100% guaranteed System called, "The Ultimate Insider Secrets Marketing Program For Magicians". This is the same program that changed my life and my income and it can change yours too! Before we get started, let me ask you a question: Have you ever said this to yourself or your spouse?:

"I'm really good. If I could only book more shows,
I'd be happy."

Guess what? I know exactly this feeling of frustration you have. It stinks to feel this way. But you know what?

EVEN THE GREATEST MAGICIAN IN THE WORLD WILL
NOT MAKE IT WITHOUT A CONSTANT STREAM OF SHOWS

Here is a super important fact you need to drill into your head if you want to survive in the magic business.....

THE ABSOLUTELY, POSITIVELY, WITHOUT A DOUBT, MOST IMPORTANT
THING YOU MUST KNOW IS NOT ABOUT TRICKS.
IT'S ABOUT MARKETING THAT WORKS!

I know this probably bothers you. I used to think that all I had to do was practice, practice, practice - get really good - and I would be successful. Then I discovered an undeniable truth:

Being a marketing pro is significantly more important
than being a master magician.

Hold on now. I'm NOT saying that having a great show isn't important. It is SUPREMELY important but if you don't know how to book yourself it does not matter. Do you agree? I hope so because it's the truth. So, let me ask you this:

with the same copy as in Steps 1 and 3. Notice how Step 3 is almost identical to Step 1; the headline and the first few paragraphs are different, but the rest is the same. These are smart and easy ways to add to the life of a marketing campaign by making small changes to the initial letter. For the complete sales letters visit **www.InfoMarketingBook.com/Dee.**

If You've Wanted To Get My Marketing Program For Magicians But Simply Couldn't Afford It, Here's Some Exciting News.

Dear Friend,

You've received information from me three times, gently encouraging you to take advantage of my special offer to invest in the "Ultimate Insider Secrets Marketing Program For Magicians".

I suspect the only reason you've NOT responded before now has to do with the amount of money required for you to get my Program.

If times are tough for you right now, I understand.

That's why I wanted to write to you one last time and make you a very special offer, that'll take the "money stumbling block" away.

Before I reveal what it is, the following is a review and summary of the benefits you'll <u>absolutely</u> receive if you accept my very special new offer:

If you are a **Children's Performer**: How would you like to <u>get a steady stream of</u> <u>phone calls everyday</u> from parents interested in your service? How would you like to close over 70% of the people who call? Put an end to the "I'm just calling around for prices" objection? Have a list of names, phone numbers, addresses and birthdays of kids months before their party? <u>How</u> <u>about if this list cost you nothing</u>?

If you are a **School Show Performer**: How would you like to <u>dominate your</u> <u>market</u> even if someone else has been performing in the schools for years? Learn how to get booked over and over at schools, even when they tell you they don't have time for assemblies?

If you are a **Corporate or Trade Show Performer**: How would you like to attract prospects who are interested in using a magician for their event and are pre-disposed to hiring *you*? <u>Have</u> <u>qualified prospects calling *you* and asking for your help?</u>

If you are a **Performer of *any* kind**: How would you like to

1

FIGURE 5-1. (continued) The third letter in the sequence.

That's when Dave's mentor stepped in. Dave recalls, "Dan Kennedy said to me, 'You should package how you did your marketing to book so many shows and sell it to other magicians.'"

Dave took Dan's advice and placed a small ad in one of the four trade magazines for magicians. Before long, he was getting requests for information, and soon he had made his first sale. "At first I thought this information business would be a nice little residual income in addition to my shows," Dave says, "but sitting at home getting checks in the mail was a lot better deal than working."

It all started with a tiny $65 ad. "I didn't have a lot of money at the time. In fact, I was in debt, so I had to be very cautious," Dave explains. "I picked the number one trade magazine for magicians and placed my ad that said something like, 'If you wanna book more magic shows, call....' I had a toll-free recorded message that offered a free report, which was really a sales letter."

When that first ad worked, Dave expanded it to a half page ad and then a full page ad in the same magazine. Then he did the same thing in the other three trade journals.

Dave's marketing process was simple, but effective. He ran an ad offering a free report. People called the toll-free number to get the report. Dave mailed the report, which was actually his sales letter that told his story of becoming a professional magician who could book more shows than anyone else in the business. For nonresponders, he followed up with a second letter at day 14 and a third letter at day 28. Dave explains, "Some people just aren't going to reply to the first letter they get. They may not read it; they may misplace it; they may be thinking about it, so you gotta hit them multiple times."

The key to Dave's success was connecting with his customers. "The most important thing is to get your customers to identify with you—you need to let the reader know that you understand their ➡

pain. Because I was a magician, I knew what their pain was. For example, I knew their parents had told them it wasn't practical, that they wouldn't be able to do it, and that they wouldn't be able to live their dream. One of the most profound things someone said to me after reading my letter was, 'It was like you were under my kitchen table listening to me talk to my wife.'

"I spoke their language," Dave continues. "I talked about my pain, my struggle; about having a dream but not being able to fulfill it; about having a lousy job and knowing that magicians not as good as me were making more money. So I hit upon all those emotional hot buttons. This is the key. You've gotta hit upon the emotions. Selling is all based on emotion. So I talked about what their pains were, what their frustrations were, but I never gave them the solution. I told them I had the solution, but to get the solution they'd have to buy my product."

Dave's follow-up letter was similar to the first. "I took that first sales letter and put it on a different color paper," Dave explains. "I cut it down slightly, because the first letter was 16 pages long. Now someone might say, 'Who's gonna read a 16-page sales letter?' But if it hits their emotional hot buttons, they'll read it from cover to cover and then read it again. It can be 16 pages, 24 pages, whatever."

Dave's second letter was 10 pages, with "Second Notice" printed at the top of the page. He used basically the same elements, changing the headline, font, and paper color. "I also cut the third letter down a little, and I changed the offer up a little bit as well," Dave says. "The first offer had only one option, to pay in full. With the second letter, I gave them the option of making payments. The third offer was a scare: if you don't do this now, the price is going up. I stamped the deadline date to reply on each letter and said, 'You only have 21 days to buy. You have 14 days left. You have seven days left.' So each letter was counting down to the deadline." ➡

Dave had a great sequence of sales letters in place, so now he had to create the product. In a hurry. Fortunately he had learned a great tip from direct marketer Jeff Paul: "Good enough is good enough." Dave tells the following story:

> I had promised six audiocassettes with my course. When the first guy bought the course I had most of the written material, but I didn't have the audiocassettes done. So I quickly ran to Radio Shack and bought a little clip-on microphone. I didn't have any professional recording equipment—all I had was my stereo system, which was underneath my TV. The cord to the microphone was only about as long as my arm, so I had to lie on the floor next to my stereo to make my recordings. And then to duplicate my tapes, I had four boom boxes. This was true Kennedy-style renegade or guerilla marketing! If I had waited to make everything perfect—like trying to get into a recording studio—it would have never gotten done.

Dave also used an audiocassette (and later a CD) as an addition to his sales letter. "The free tape really helped, because then they could hear the passion in my voice," Dave explains. "They could hear me tell my story. We found out that some people weren't even reading the sales letter; they would just listen to the audio."

Good enough truly was good enough for Dave Dee. Eventually he built enough value into his business that he was able to sell it to someone else. What made it valuable enough to sell? "Customers," Dave says, "and a lot of product. I had customers that literally had come to each of my seminars for 10 years in a row and bought everything that I had. Plus, I'd built up a name in the magic business as the marketing guru guy. So this person wanted to buy it, and what was really neat is I actually sold it to one of my first customers."

While Dave no longer works in the magician marketing business he started, he is busy with several other information marketing businesses. Today he teaches others how to start their own businesses. ➡

"The one thing I want to get across is that everybody has some knowledge or can access knowledge that other people want. The key is to not limit your thinking. You can do it!" Dave exclaims.

Dave took his enthusiasm for information marketing and the great lifestyle it provides and created a new product called "Marketing Magic." He adapted his magician marketing system to service businesses such as doctors, lawyers, dentists, and chiropractors. "One of my favorite sayings is marketing is marketing is marketing," Dave says. "It doesn't matter whether the guy is a chiropractor or a magician. He's gotta generate leads."

Dave's program can be adapted to any profession, and he has even been asked to license "Marketing Magic" to someone else who wants to adapt it for an industry he is targeting. "Now think about this," Dave says. "This is a product that I created 10 years ago. I've learned a lot, and obviously I've added to it, but the core product is the same. So not only have I made a ton of money selling it to magicians, not only did I make money selling the magicians business to somebody else and then take that product, modify it, and sell to service professionals, now I've got people who want to pay me a large sum of money to license it to sell to their own niche!" Dave exclaims.

For more about Dave Dee's "Marketing Magic" visit **www.Dave Dee.com**, and for an expanded profile visit **www.InfoMarketing Book.com/Dee.**

Chapter 6

Step 5: Gaining Trust and Easing Fears So Customers Buy More

by Robert Skrob
President, Information Marketing Association

O NE MONDAY MORNING WHEN MY DAUGHTER WAS IN FOURTH grade, just before it was time to load up in the van to go to school, she dropped a bombshell. What made it worse was that I knew she must have been worried sick about revealing it to me all weekend, and she had waited until it was impossible to put it off any longer.

My daughter goes to a private Catholic school here in Tallahassee, so her revelation came as a huge surprise to us.

She confided, "The girls in my class are telling everyone that I want to take my clothes off for all of the boys." Yes, that'll wake you up when it comes from your 10-year-old. Since she is our oldest, this was the first time we'd had to deal with this sort of thing. Evidently one form of bullying popular among grade school girls is spreading false rumors. Somehow I think this is even worse than coming home with a black eye.

My daughter's frustration got so bad by Tuesday night that she told us she didn't have any friends "because I'm different."

We had a long discussion, and at one point I told her, "Of course you are different. And because you are different, you're going to be thought of as strange and unusual by your friends your entire life." I should tell you that I got a really mean look from my wife right about then.

I went on to explain, "You are smarter than the other kids in your class. Your grades show it, and you know it. Plus, you work harder than anyone else in your class. When you are struggling on times tables, you practice for 30 minutes a night until you don't have to struggle."

"You always tell me positive practice leads to positive results," she said.

"Yes, because you work when others play and because you are smarter than them to begin with, they will always think you are different. And, most importantly, you should take that as a compliment. Because you are different in their opinion, or more accurately, exceptional, you usually achieve exceptional results."

We live in a nation of cynics. Everyone is ready to believe the worst about you. They'll believe the worst about you even though they've grown up with you for the last five years. You can be assured that they will believe the worst about you if they've just heard about you *and* you are trying to sell them something.

Do you always believe what the United States president says? Do you believe that every time he speaks you are getting the entire story and all of the facts?

Of course you don't. Well, if you don't believe the president of the United States, the leader of the free world, how do you expect anyone will believe you?

Proof and risk reversal are two crucial tools in overcoming the fear, hesitation, and doubt in your prospects' minds.

When they are in a lawsuit, attorneys present every piece of evidence that proves their case. From the smallest drop of blood to the

A Step-by-Step System That Removes All the Guesswork, Waste, and Frustration From "Creating Copy That Sells" Once and for All—GUARANTEED!

Info-Marketer
Resource

As you can see from the last three chapters, the info-marketing business requires a lot of salesmanship. Quite frankly, no matter what business you pursue, there is no more important skill you can learn than effective sales copywriting. Today, it's never been easier to learn.

Bill Glazer created a groundbreaking web-assisted product that puts at your fingertips all the tools you need to become an expert copywriter. In addition, it walks you through the entire process step-by-step so by the time you finish the program, you have produced high quality sales letters, just like the marketing pros.

In part, this system includes:

- The *"11 Building Blocks"* that must be incorporated into just about every piece of copy you write.

- The *"20 Critical Copy Concepts"* that will take your work to the next level. Many of these are tools that only very successful pros think about. In fact, they are the tools (and tricks) that often separate the good copywriters from the professional copywriters.

- *"Kopy Kryptonite."* These are the *biggest mistakes* that people make when writing copy that will kill your results the same way that Kryptonite affects Superman. I've identified *seven of them,* and believe me, you need to know what they are and avoid them like the plague.

- The "Step-by-Step Questionnaire" I use to get me organized before I write copy and also *how to get the right "raw material" to mold into great copy.*

Visit **www.InfoMarketingCopyThatSells.com** for more information.

tiniest shred of fabric, all of it is presented in the most compelling light to the jury.

Your jury is your customers; you have to overcome their doubt to win your case. And you can't expect them to rule in your favor based only on your words. You have to provide proof.

> **KEY CONCEPT** You cannot assume people will believe you. If you are asserting it in your sales materials, back it up with *proof*.

Proof can come in three forms; social proof, documented proof, and guarantees. First, social proof.

How to Get Others to Sell for You

As info-marketers, we must prove our cases with facts and figures, physical demonstrations, pictures, and testimonials. And of those proofs, testimonials can be the most powerful.

Testimonials are what your current members have to say about you. Testimonials are very important because what *others* say about you is 10 times more believable than what *you* say about you.

Think about it. Are you more likely to try a new restaurant because your neighbor tells you how wonderful it is or because you saw an ad in the newspaper for it?

Of course you're more likely to try it if your neighbor can't stop raving about it. That's another marketing strategy—to make customers so thrilled with your products that they can't help telling others about you.

There are two basic types of testimonials; the first are so-called "good guy" testimonials, and the second are "outcome testimonials."

Outcome testimonials are where the customers explain in detail all of the great things that came to them as your customer. If they made more money, the dollar amounts and time frames are specified. This way the reader has outside validation that someone purchased the product, used it as directed, and had the outcome you are promising.

The good guy testimonials do not provide specific outcomes. They say things like your marketing system is really good, you are a great guy to work with, we've always been successful with his methods, or you are a great person. You should use all of the testimonials you have, but emphasize and work to get more outcome testimonials.

> What others say about you is more powerful than what you say about yourself.
>
> **KEY CONCEPT**

Testimonials can be audio, video, in person, or written. Many info-marketers deliver an audio CD along with their sales letters that features dozens of audio testimonials. Here are some testimonials excerpted from Ron LeGrand's sales letter from the "Ron LeGrand's Fast Cash Generator" product available at **www.IMAProductShowcase.com/FastCash**. To provide a lot of social proof for his sales message, Ron LeGrand uses a lot of testimonials.

Here are selected "good guy" testimonials included in the "Fast Cash" sales letter:

An Inspiration. I am pleased to say you have made more real estate entrepreneurs wealthy in this market than anyone else! You are an inspiration to everyone in real estate entrepreneurship!
—Dave Dweck, Boca Raton, Florida

Changed Our Lives. Just a note to let you know how much we appreciate the training you have given us. It has absolutely changed our lives permanently. Our minds can no longer return to normal.
—Dennis and Monica Quattlebaum, Norcross, Georgia

> **More Ron.** My life changed the day I stopped listening to the MORONS and started listening to MORE RON! Thanks again for the work you do in changing people's lives.
> —Bill Barnett, Fort Worth, Texas

Here is a selected "outcome" testimonial included in Ron LeGrand's sales letter:

> **The Right Direction.** I remember calling you and moaning and groaning, crying that I wanted all my money back. You gently pointed me in the right direction, and five weeks after that I made $26,000, and that is more than I made in the whole previous year. Thanks again for truly helping me.
> —Neil Blatt, Phoenix, Arizona

In addition, here is an outcome testimonial from Rory Fatt's Restaurant Marketing Systems sales letter from **www.IMAProduct Showcase.com/Restaurant.** Some individuals may be more comfortable giving you percentage increases instead of dollar amounts. Here is an example of a percentage increase outcome testimonial.

> *It has been absolutely amazing the results I am getting. I started in October, and sales were up 25 percent over the previous year. When everyone was complaining about the economy, I was growing. Then in November, we got the same kind of results. It has continued for nine months. We set new sales records every month. We are making money now! I'm looking at adding a new location—it's truly changed my life. I would try some other things, but I need to get on top of the growth; it's tough to keep up with a 20 percent increase monthly! Thanks, Rory!*
> —Steve Kraft, Habanero's Grill, San Antonio, Texas

Notice how every testimonial is documented with the individual's name and city. The more information you provide about the individuals giving the testimonials the better. You may even choose to include occupation and age information with your testimonials.

Let the Documents Speak for You

You should also include any documents, charts, or graphics you can to demonstrate that your systems achieve the promised results. Many info-marketers include copies of canceled checks, bank statements, or 1099s to prove their income claims are true.

Certainly any of these documents could have been fabricated along with the story; however, that doesn't discount their effectiveness. Find documents that prove your claims and include them in your sales messages to increase your believability and sincerity in the eyes of your prospective customers.

Remove the Risk of Loss

After proving your case, the info-marketer must remove all financial risk of loss for the customer. Very often the customer has to justify the sale to others. Even if he is a decision maker, he may have a bookkeeper or a spouse, and he doesn't want to be seen as someone easily fooled into making a bad purchase. No one wants to be "gotten." No one wants to have to explain why he purchased something he didn't need or that didn't work. You have to remove that risk of loss.

The way you remove that risk of loss is through guarantees. This way, your customers can make a purchase and if the product doesn't meet their needs, they can return it for a full refund. This way, your customers aren't worried about justifying a bad purchase. They can order your product and check it out for themselves.

There are two types of guarantees, conditional and unconditional. Conditional guarantees require the buyer to do certain things before he can qualify for the guarantee, for instance, try three tactics or implement certain steps to prove to you that he tried to implement your strategies before he gave up and requested a refund.

Unconditional guarantees allow the customer to ask for a refund for any reason or no reason within a certain time frame. These guarantees comfort customers because they know they won't have to deal with red tape or aggravation if they open the box and immediately figure out this product isn't for them.

Your merchant services providers will most likely require you to provide an unconditional 30- to 120-day guarantee to your customers. Refunds are a normal part of running an info-marketing business. If you don't have a few refunds you aren't selling hard enough.

> **KEY CONCEPT** You will have to give refunds even if you don't want to, so you might as well turn your guarantee into a positive sales message. Doing so won't increase refunds.

If refunds are normal and your merchant services provider is going to require you to give them to your customers anyway, you might as well use your refund policy as a tremendous bonus to your sales message.

Most info-marketers use a combination of conditional and unconditional guarantees. The following are a few examples from the **IMAProductShowcase.com** web site.

From Rory Fatt of Restaurant Marketing Systems (**www.RoryFatt. com**), an info-marketer serving the restaurant industry, here are his guarantees from his sales page to sell his marketing kit for restaurants, available at **www.IMAProductShowcase.com/Restaurant**:

This new system is so valuable, so certain to put thousands of dollars in your pocket that I can provide not one, but THREE very generous guarantees.

GUARANTEE #1: 100%, No Risk, No Hassle, No B.S., 12-Month Guarantee. If at any time within one year you aren't completely thrilled, head-over-heels happy with my Systems, you can send them back and get a full refund. This guarantee is very straightforward. You don't need a note from your mother. There isn't any teeny, tiny fine print. If you aren't happy, return it and get an immediate, full refund. Period.

Take 12 months to look it over. Read the manuals. Listen to the CDs. Use the System in your business. Discover how the System can generate good, loyal customers everyday. Use the whole System. Put it to work for you. Generate new customers. More referrals. Higher average checks. Benefit from it. Make money with it. And then, if you aren't totally elated with the System or the results for any reason, I insist you send it back for a prompt and cheerful refund. And keep the Free Gifts I will shower you with, plus any free issues of *The Restaurant Revolution Newsletter* you've received, just as a gift for trusting me and trying my Systems. Short. Sweet. Simple. Owning my system either makes you a ton of money—or you pay nothing. I'll buy it back from you, UNCONDITIONALLY!

GUARANTEE #2: $10,000 In-Your-Pocket, One-Year Guarantee! I'm so sure the System will work for you that I am willing to make you an unheard of guarantee: You will put AT LEAST $10,000 in additional income in the bank in the next 12 months. Every penny of this money will be directly attributable to the System.

This is money that you would NOT have otherwise had. It'll come directly from customers that came from the System. If you keep and use your system past the first 90 days, and you can show me proof that you have implemented at least one of my strategies, if at the end of A FULL YEAR (!!!) you write me a letter and can honestly say you didn't put <u>at least $10,000 in the bank that you wouldn't have otherwise, I will still refund every penny you paid</u>. You are the sole judge and jury. If you try my system and it doesn't make you money, send it back for a full refund.

This means that you can get, review, and use my System without risking a single penny of your money. ZERO RISK.

Ask yourself this question: Would I make a guarantee like that and sign my name to it if I didn't think the System will far exceed your expectations? I know this System will work for you—no matter what level your business is at right now. That's why I offer you such a rock-solid guarantee.

GUARANTEE #3: I also guarantee support. You aren't alone anymore. If you have any questions about how to use a marketing strategy or a new idea, you can call my team and get help. Our number is 604/940-6900. We are open from 8:30 a.m. to 4:30 p.m. Pacific Time, Monday through Friday.

You can also reach us 24 hours a day with our Fast FAX Hotline. The fax number is 604/940-6902. You can send in your questions, concerns, ideas, and successes 24 hours a day.

From Ron Ipach of CinRon Marketing Group (**www.CinRon.com**), an info-marketer serving the auto repair industry, here are his guarantees from his sales page to sell his marketing kit for auto repair shops, available at **www.IMAProductShowcase.com/AutoRepair**:

Q. Do you guarantee this will work?

A. Absolutely! It amazes me that anyone would buy or sell ANY-THING without a huge guarantee. Where I come from, if you're going to ask someone for their hard-earned money in exchange for providing a product or service, you'd better be prepared to back it all up with a great guarantee.

This SYSTEM has proven itself in thousands of shops already, and I'm so certain it'll put tens of thousands of dollars in your pocket, I won't just give you one guarantee, I'll give you <u>TWO</u> very generous guarantees:

Guarantee #1
Better-Than-Risk-Free, 180-Day Money-Back Guarantee!

If at any time within the first 6 MONTHS (!) you aren't completely head-over-heels, jumping up and down with joy, absolutely thrilled with my System, you can send it back and get a full refund of your purchase price.

This guarantee is very straightforward. No teeny, tiny print. No notes needed from your mother. Nothing. We're only interested in having extremely satisfied customers. So if you aren't happy, we're not happy either. Please return it and we'll send you your money back. Period.

Guarantee #2
TEN TIMES Guarantee!

Put my System to work for you for 180 days. If you find it hasn't made you an additional TEN TIMES what you paid for it, send it back for a refund of your purchase price.

You see I'VE DONE ALL THE HARD WORK FOR YOU! You won't have to "re-invent the wheel" like I had to. You can go ahead and spend a ton of money and years to put this information together on your own—but why?—When I'm prepared to hand it to you on a silver platter AND guarantee a massively profitable impact on your business!

From Chet Rowland of PCO Millionaire (**www.PCOMillionaire.com**), an info-marketer serving the pest control industry, here are his guarantees from his sales page to sell his marketing kit for independent pest control operator shops, available at **www.IMA ProductShowcase.com/PestControl**:

AND I GUARANTEE IT'LL BE WORTH A WHOLE LOT MORE TO YOU . . .

In Fact, I Absolutely, Positively Will Not Keep A Penny Of Your Money . . . Unless You Insist

I'll say it again—I do _not_ need your money. I'll be on my boat or out on my balcony overlooking the Gulf of Mexico. I'll still fly first-class … I'll do just fine whether you invest in my systems or not. So I have absolutely no desire to get money from you unless I earn it, deserve it, you make a lot more, and you are glad to pay me. In fact, I want you to be telling everybody you can about how many different ways you've benefited from knowing me, or I don't want a dollar.

So here's the deal I'll make with you …

Guarantee #1—Three-Month Test Drive, Zero Risk

I'll put everything into your hands … you'll be on my Tele-Seminar for new members (which I'll tell you about in a minute) … and I'll let you use _any_ or _all_ of it for three full months, on trial. That'll be plenty of time, even if you are slow, to prove to yourself that my SYSTEMS will make a huge difference in your business, bank account, and life. Anytime during those three months, if you decide I've let you down, in any way, and you do not want to keep and use my SYSTEMS and continue your membership, you just shove it all back at me, yell "cancel," and you instantly get every penny refunded. No questions. No hassle.

Guarantee #2—12-Month/One-Year $25,000 Profit Guarantee
If you stick past the third month, you've got a whole YEAR to let my SYSTEMS work for you. At the end of the year, if you can truthfully say you haven't gotten at least $25,000 in EXTRA PROFIT you know you wouldn't have gotten without me, you can still send me my stuff back, and I will still refund every penny you paid. <u>I'm promising you a $25,000 pay raise</u>. Go ask your wife if she'd have good use for an extra $25,000 this year. See what *she* says. Look, I'm deadly serious. As serious as a brown recluse spider bite. You WILL track and pocket <u>at least $25,000</u> (probably much more) directly from what I give you, or you get back what you paid me.

PLUS: Continuing Support: I Won't Hit and Run on You
No, I won't just ship you my box of stuff and then disappear. I'm totally committed and interested in what happens WITH YOU. I've decided it'll be a kick to make 100 pest control operators into cash millionaires in the next three years. So I'm signing on to assist and push you all the way. You'll be a Member of Chet's PCO Cash Millionaires Club.

Identifying, gathering, and using proof and risk reversal are critical to a successful information marketing business. Quite simply, you cannot skip this step and achieve much success within info-marketing.

As you are starting out, it probably will be impossible for you to have all of the proof that you want to have. Build the best proof that you have available to you. Use proof from your own story, and as you generate customers and they have success, integrate their stories and proof into your marketing.

Last point, honor your guarantees. If there is a shadow of doubt whether a customer qualifies for a guarantee, give it to him anyway. Honoring your guarantees is the best way for you to become known as an honest player within a market. If you are building a long-term business that you hope will sustain you for many years, honoring your guarantees provides you with a terrific foundation for success.

Chapter 7

Step 6: Make a Sale Once, Collect Money Every Month, for Life

by Robert Skrob
President, Information Marketing Association

W HILE I PRIDE MYSELF ON MAKING DELIBERATE AND RATIONAL decisions, not all of my decision making is as deliberate as it should be. My wife, Kory, and I met at an NC State vs. FSU football game. She had graduated from NC State the year before and happened to be sitting in front of me at the game.

We met again about three weeks later and about five weeks after that, we were engaged. Yes, that was quick. Another short four months later, on May 28, we had the wedding. This time the rash decision making worked out; we've been married ever since, but it was pretty quick.

A common tradition at weddings is that the groom has to remove the bride's garter and toss it to a group of less-than-excited single men to curse one of them to be designated as the next man to get married. But this time I had a surprise in mind for Kory.

Before the reception I sent two of my friends to JC Penney to buy the biggest pair of underwear they could find. Also, I specifically requested they buy the ugliest color or design. They had to be huge and hideous. My friends really came through for me. I had no idea women's underwear could be so disgusting to look at, but these things were bad. I promptly stuffed them in my sleeve so no one would see them.

We went through all of the normal rituals, and it was time for the garter ceremony. My wife sat on a chair and pulled up her dress partway to reveal her knee. She was very smug with herself as I got on my knee and started working with the garter.

Then I grabbed the hem of her dress and pulled it over my head. Kory started struggling with me and whispered, "Robert, *stop*, my father!" I pulled the garter off, put it in my teeth. As she shoved me away I slipped the underwear out of my sleeve. I stood up and held up the panties as if I'd just found the biggest prize under her dress. Kory couldn't believe it.

The whole room turned simultaneously to look at Kory's father, but he was laughing so hard he nearly fell out of his chair.

As newlyweds I thought it would be funny to continue this little prank by signing Kory up for the panties of the month club. While the courtship was short, our first year of marriage was very long. I had a lot of learning to do before I signed up my wife in any new continuity programs.

One of the most important factors of an info-marketer's business is the monthly continuity program. In a continuity program, the customer pays a monthly fee to receive continuing services and products such as CDs, newsletters, and tele-seminars.

A number of years ago info-marketers began creating membership programs based on what an association might do. They set an annual membership fee and offered memberships to their customers when they bought something. Many buyers opted into these membership programs, and that helped form long-term relationships between info-marketers and their customers.

More recently, info-marketers have built upon the membership program idea and have begun bundling continuity programs into their initial sales. For instance, a customer buys an information kit for $697. As part of that sale, the info-marketer bundles in two free months of his monthly membership program that includes a newsletter and a CD every month for $49. After 60 days the customer is billed $49 a month to continue receiving the benefits of the continuity program.

> Attaching a continuity program to a sale to a customer increases revenue from the customer and builds a long-term relationship without decreasing sales of the initial product.
>
> **KEY CONCEPT**

Not everybody chooses to continue the program. In fact, on average 10 to 25 percent of new customers opt out of the continuity program before they are charged for it. Still, the info-marketer gets a huge increase in long-term customers by offering a monthly continuity program. Through extensive testing we have found that many more people stay in the monthly continuity program than would have joined an optional membership program. This has tremendous implications for an info-marketer. In addition to the money made on the initial product, that first sale actually sells the continuity program! And the continuity program continues to make money for the info-marketer for many months or even years after the initial sale.

Benefits of Continuity Programs

There are three ways continuity programs outperform annual membership offers:

Continuity programs are easier to sell than annual memberships. One of the reasons buyers stay in continuity programs is the way the fees are charged. An annual membership fee might be $600, while the monthly continuity fee is $49. Most people prefer to pay $49 per month than a $600 annual fee. Most times when info-marketers test the two options against each other, the monthly continuity program generates more money for an info-marketer than the annual membership renewal.

There are no marketing or renewal costs for continuity programs. It used to be that an info-marketer would sell a product and then have to execute another entire marketing sequence to sell the customer into the annual membership program. Then, 12 months later, the info-marketer had to conduct another marketing campaign to renew the member. Continuity programs make it much easier to keep customers in the program, renewing their memberships automatically month after month.

Great customers surface through continuity programs. You will reach customers who never would have joined your membership program if they had to write a $600 check for annual dues. But because it was a free trial offer and it was only $49 per month, they thought, "If I don't like it I can drop it in 30 days." Twelve months later, most of these customers are still your customers!

Types of Continuity Programs

Monthly Newsletter. This is arguably the best continuity program. You can publish anywhere from 4 to 12 to 24 pages. The key is to provide compelling information your customers want to read about every month. You should have news or events, customer profiles, and any additional materials your customers are looking for. You want your customers to look forward to seeing your newsletter arrive every single month.

Monthly Mailing. Every month you send a special box filled with interesting items for your customers. Maybe it's a book. Maybe it's a gadget. Maybe it's a new thing. Maybe it's a magazine article. Maybe it's some contact or product or service you thought was interesting. Your customers will look forward to receiving their box of the month and the surprises they'll find inside.

Monthly CD. A lot of info-marketers are creating interviews with celebrities and experts both inside and outside their industries. They deliver those interviews on a monthly CD. They also create lectures or content CDs. The idea is to provide important information to customers every month.

Monthly Tele-Seminar. Many info-marketers offer monthly teleconference calls for their customers. Individuals have the privilege of calling in and speaking with you each month. You talk for a few minutes. They each ask their questions. They get to hear the questions other people ask. The best part is since your customers have already paid for that month's tele-seminar through the continuity program, you don't have to sell it! To make this better, put your tele-seminar on a CD and send it to customers after the call. That way they won't have the excuse that they're never able to make those calls. The CD delivers a tangible benefit right in their hands. If you try to "force" them to be on the call, after they miss one or two of them, they're going to be looking to drop out of the program.

In-Person Coaching. Some info-marketers offer in-person group coaching meetings, either monthly or quarterly, where the customers prepay a certain amount each month and receive a set number of in-person meetings with you so they can discuss their challenges and find ways to solve their problems.

Automatically Implemented Products and Services. Recently a number of info-marketers have come out with products and services with which they do everything the customer needs done to implement a particular strategy. For instance, a lot of info-marketers teach their business clients that they should be sending monthly newsletters to their customers. All the research shows that monthly newsletters get customers coming back more frequently, keep customers in the program, and make more money for the info-marketer. Even though that's well established and even though it's easy to get people to believe it's true, getting them to actually publish a newsletter every month is almost impossible. Business owners find every reason not to do it, especially if you try to convince them they have to do it every single month. So instead of trying to convince business owners to publish their own newsletters, info-marketers do it all for them for a monthly fee. Business owners don't have to write it. They don't have to print it. They don't have to mail it. So they're happy to pay the info-marketer each month to get it done!

Automatically implemented marketing is another example. Jerry Jones of Jerry Jones Direct (**www.JerryJonesDirect.com**) is marketing postcard lead generation mailings within the dentistry profession. So when a dentist decides he wants new patients, he doesn't have to learn how to create postcards that generate patients. He doesn't have to figure out where to buy mailing lists. He doesn't have to learn how to get the postcards graphically designed or how to get them printed. He doesn't have to label them. He doesn't have to deal with mailing them. Instead of doing all that, this dentist is very happy to pay Jerry Jones a monthly continuity fee to have his marketing automatically implemented for him.

You can create automatically implemented programs for just about any product or service you promote to your customers.

Make Your Own News

Sometimes the best marketing tools are the simplest, most obvious ones. If you're looking for a time-tested, proven way to attract new customers and promote new products to your existing customer base, Chris Mullins of Mullins Media Group™ LLC says to look no further than the good old-fashioned customer newsletter.

Chris has found that publishing a monthly newsletter is a great way to provide ongoing marketing of you and what you do in an educational, how-to, informational format for your clients. Your customers view the newsletter as a benefit—a seminar in print or training in print—delivered to them every single month. But the biggest benefit actually accrues to you: You're staying in front of your customers and prospects, reminding them that you're the go-to expert!

Some Basics

If you've never published a newsletter, you may be daunted by the task, wondering things like "What should I call it?" "How long does it need to be?" "Do I need color photos?" "Where will I find content?" Chris has learned a few lessons along the way.

Newsletter Name: Chris uses her own name to continually brand herself. Her company publishes *Chris Mullins' Nuggets® For Sales*. If you think about the products and services you provide, a logical title containing your name will probably come to mind quickly.

Newsletter Format: To begin, Chris recommends aiming for four pages, using black ink on white paper. It's basic, it's readable, and it works! Once you get the hang of publishing a monthly newsletter, you can expand to eight pages or more. Monthly inserts, which ➡

can be full-color brochures or promotions for a seminar or a product, give you additional opportunities to connect with your customers.

Newsletter Content: Chris says you can write as much or as little as you wish. She personally writes 75 percent of her newsletter's content, but not everyone will choose to go that route. Chris long ago established the habit of writing articles to be published in magazines, trade journals, and newspapers, so now she uses her writing habits for her own newsletter. In addition, she is always writing for her clients, coaching classes, training sessions, etc., so she can modify that material for her newsletter. "I schedule one hour of writing time every morning. It's amazing how much I get done since I have put it into my schedule," Chris says.

Don't have time to write? Well, IMA members have a great resource for newsletter content: the Copyright-Free Content CD. These CDs are loaded with articles, free reports, tip sheets, and other newsletter-ready content from famous authors, speakers, and experts. All you have to do is cut and paste! Once you get started, you'll probably find your own ideas for articles, and writing them will come more naturally to you.

Let Your Clients Inspire You

If you've decided to write your own content like Chris does, let your clients inspire you! For example, Chris is known as the Mystery Call Phone Sales Doctor™ for inbound and outbound sales. Her clients are learning about good phone skills, etiquette, and sales, so she writes about that. Chris explains, "My primary goal is to be sure I share ideas, how-to tips, and reminders to my paying clients, but my other goal is to announce to them all the other ways they can get more of Chris Mullins's advice in areas they don't realize I cover, like script writing, presentation skills, communication skills, telemarketing, how to ➡️ coach a sales team, customer service, and all kinds of other areas that cross over into my primary purpose. I can write about these areas because they are all part of every business, and again I position myself as the expert."

Chris also writes about herself—her own lessons in business and life. In Chris's Personal Diary, she focuses on exercise, running races, and what she has learned through that process. She also writes about her colleagues, her own inner circle, sharing lessons learned so readers will find and apply those lessons in their own professional and personal lives.

Another source of content is celebrating the success of others, in this case, your clients' successes. Chris recommends having a dedicated space in your newsletter so your clients can send announcements about their accomplishments, awards, or newsworthy events.

Chris Mullins' Nuggets® For Sales has an ongoing "Do It For You Recognition Club" and Sales Hot Shot™ program that spotlights a client's team member. The client nominates a staff member, Chris personally interviews him by telephone, and then the interview gets transcribed word for word and published in the newsletter. Chris's readers get to learn all about why this particular hot shot is so successful and how they can learn from this person's success. The hot shot gets a gift of hot sauce with a specially printed "Sales Hot Shot" label, plus books and a clock from Chris's office. Chris also mails five copies of the newsletter with a handwritten personal note to family members and other folks the hotshot wants to share his success with. In short, *Chris Mullins' Nuggets®* encourages her clients to *brag*! In addition, Chris coaches the business owner on how to make the most of this important moment for the sales hotshot back at the office, how to give a speech to the team, etc. "It's really a do-it-for-you recognition program for businesses," Chris says.

Another aspect of the recognition club is that Chris continues to turn her clients (team members) into celebrities by putting the name of that month's hotshot and other noteworthy team members on the front of the newsletter envelope on a fluorescent label. Chris has even done this for her clients' customers, turning them into celebrities on behalf of the client, and then sending copies of the newsletter to each of her client's customers on behalf of the client.

Chris says, "Providing 'bragging rights' to my clients (and even their clients) is a great way to market my business. It shows my clients and prospects about all the different businesses I work with; continually marketing yourself while educating others is the purpose of your newsletter, and each segment of your newsletter can do that for you!"

Chris also solicits newsletter content from her clients, staff members, and business associates via fax and e-mail. She and her staff even interview those who they believe have important information to share and include interviews or articles based on interviews in their newsletter.

Let Others Write It for You

Chris has found that it's easy to get others to write for you if you remind them why it's important *to them*. When they write for your newsletter, they receive important exposure to your other customers, and perhaps even more important than that, they can get copies of your newsletter containing their published articles and send them to their own prospects and clients as gifts. This positions them as the expert and boosts their credibility because now they can say they are a published author.

The majority of Chris's outside content comes from her clients: what she teaches them in coaching, exercises they do, etc. Chris also does weekly free tele-clinics for newsletter subscribers, and she uses a lot of those lessons; every time someone comments about the newsletter, their services, students—anything—Chris publishes it.

Chris says you can also seek out experts that are of interest to your clients and prospects and ask if they'd like to be a monthly contributor. "You may want to joint venture with someone who already has a monthly newsletter, but be sure you get to put some of your personality in it," Chris advises. "However you obtain your content, you need to become part of it. Your newsletter needs to showcase who you are, mostly that you're human with the same needs and desires as your clients."

Review all of Chris's newsletters and free monthly telephone training calls at **www.GreatBottomLine.com**. You can learn more about how Chris Mullins uses her newsletters at **www.Info MarketingBook.com/Mullins**.

Look for the Upcoming Guide
Information Marketing Association
Official Guide to Newsletter Profits

In this book, we'll dissect the simple and easy ways to make a great living or side income by publishing newsletters. This book will detail the easy ways to generate content and sign up subscribers. Coming soon from the Information Marketing Association and Entrepreneur Press.

Chapter 8

Step 7: The Source of Real Profits From Your Business

by Robert Skrob
President, Information Marketing Association

"While most information marketers think that the purpose of getting a customer is to make a sale, the successful information marketer thinks the reverse. The purpose of the sale is to get a customer!"

—Dan S. Kennedy

I
F YOU THOUGHT SELLING $1 CONSTRUCTION PAPER FANS WAS GOOD, LET me tell you how Robert William sold a single piece of folded copy paper for $5.

You remember back in Chapter 3 when I told you about my son, Robert William, selling folded construction paper fans. Well that's not the end of the story. No, it gets better.

Folding paper into little "fortune tellers" became the rage of second grade. So one day after school he folded paper into these fortune tellers.

When I got home, he had to read my fortune. Robert opened the fortune teller by sticking his fingers in the slots and saying, "Pick a color." He counted the letters in that color and then asked me to pick a number. After counting out that number he pulled up one of the numbered tabs and told me I'd suffer some terrible symptom like an upset stomach. Then we repeated the process.

On about the third week of this ritual of having my fortune read several times, and perhaps after having a couple of beers with dinner, I suggested that he start selling some of the fortune tellers. I figured we might as well spread this joy around to others.

So Robert and I worked together to build a new sales presentation. Now, immediately after he sells customers a fan, when they go to their wallets to grab the dollar, he offers them an up-sell to a $5 fortune teller. He talks about the item's construction and the good luck that comes from knowing your future.

In addition, when he sells fans by mail, he always includes a thank-you note with a pitch to buy a fortune teller. These fortune tellers have transformed the profitability of his business. Now, instead of a customer value of $1 or perhaps $2, if they buy two fans, a lot of his customers immediately upgrade to fortune tellers and are worth $6. In some cases, when they don't have change, they become worth $10.

The real power of the information marketing business is in what info-marketers call "the back end." The back end refers to generating income from existing customers. Everything up until now has focused on getting customers, or the "front end." Until you actually have customers, the front end *is* the most important thing. But info-marketers who have been in the business for just 6 to 12 to 18 months focus on creating and maximizing back-end opportunities.

When you start selling your first product, you will have a baseline cost of sale. This is the cost per sale calculated by taking all of your marketing costs and dividing it by the number of sales you had from that marketing funnel. For example, you place an ad that costs you $1,000, and you get 100 leads. Your cost per lead is $10. Of those 100 leads, 10 of them buy your product. That gives you a cost per sale of $100.

Early in your business, you are going to be able to improve your lead generation ads and your sales message to minimize your cost per sale. However, there are always a certain number of "early adopters" in every market. Early adopters are the ones who buy your product first. The folks already doing well in a business and who are looking for a competitive advantage are going to be very quick to buy your product. Others who are doing exceptionally poorly and are looking for a life raft will also be early buyers of your product.

These early adopters will give you a relatively low cost per sale at the beginning of your offer. Once those early buyers have snapped up your product, you are going to have to convince the folks in the middle that they need to buy your product, too. You will find over time that even though your ads are getting more effective, your cost per sale will increase because you are trying to sell to customers who aren't immediately responsive. So, as your cost of sale increases, the back-end part of your business will become even more important than the front end. Your business will transition from the front end being a revenue generator to where all of your profits and revenues are coming from your existing customers.

> **KEY CONCEPT** Most info-marketers generate the majority of their profits from sales to existing customers. What you do with a customer after the initial sale will determine your business's profitability.

The one thing that distinguishes the information marketing business from all other providers of information is the focus on developing and maximizing back-end revenue. This single focus is what generates the million-dollar business. While everything else is important, and you need to become an expert in generating new customers, you must focus on Step 7. This is the most important part of your business, because this is where all of the money is made.

Hard Work and Research Pay Off

E d O'Keefe with Dentist Profits has also built back-end continuity programs into his business. "We'll give our dentists the kit for free when they sign up for our $450-a-month coaching," Ed explains.

Another strategy Ed uses to build his business is developing strategic relationships with others who are working within his niche. "I've always believed that being in the same tent and working together is better than trying to compete with each other," Ed says.

Ed cautions info-marketers to know the difference between sales and cash flow. "$30,000 in sales does not mean $30,000 in cash flow," Ed warns. "Number one, you need to get your customers into a continuity program as quickly as possible to recoup some of your advertising and marketing costs. Number two, you should raise your membership fee to whatever it needs to be so you can afford spending more money on the front end."

Ed practices what he preaches. His Silver membership is $450 per month. Three and a half years ago, that membership was priced at $19.99. Ed finds that he has better customers who complain less at the higher price, and now he has customers automatically worth $5,200 per year.

For more information about Ed O'Keefe and his products visit **www.DentistProfits.com** or **www.InfoMarketingBook.com/OKeefe**.

One of the key profit centers of Ed O'Keefe's business, Dentist Profits, is his monthly continuity program. In 3½ years he has increased the price of his continuity program from $19.99 a month to $450 a month. Here is an insider's peek at the benefits of Ed's continuity program:

Ed O'Keefe's Inner Circle Member Benefits

FOR THOSE INTERESTED IN DOING WHAT
THEY DO <u>FASTER</u>, <u>EASIER</u>, AND <u>MORE PROFITABLY</u>!

'Silver' Inner Circle Membership at $450 per month. Participation in Silver includes:

- Ed O'Keefe's monthly Insider Marketing Newsletter
- Access to the "Members Wealth Portal" virtual masterminding on our exclusive web-based forum with access to audio/video training modules
- Access to downloadable, customizable, successful ads being run by other dentists all across the country. Get what's working and get it now!
- Monthly Exclusive "Ed O'Keefe Interviews ..." CDs
- Weekly Insider Marketing Tips via fax
- Three live coaching calls with Ed every month
- One special Closed Door Meeting with Ed and the other Silver Members per year
- Two H3 Marketing Critiques
- 'Gold' Inner Circle Membership at $850 per month.
- Participation in Gold includes every benefit offered in Silver, plus:
- Customized Consultations with Ed; Gold members get two customized consultations each year where Ed will record his answers at your fingertips
- Two private emergency access calls per year to get immediate answers from Ed
- Our monthly "Magical Smiles & Motivational Mentor" patient newsletter, free for one year
- Five pre-arranged private phone consultations per year
- Three Closed Door Meetings per year with Ed and the rest of the Gold Members

- Six H3 Marketing Critiques
- Free tuition to the 2006 Ultimate Dental Practice Profit Explosion Super Conference
- Exclusive access to all celebrities brought in to our live seminars

Look for the Upcoming Guide
Information Marketing Association Official Guide to Building Super-Profitable Info-Businesses

In this book, we'll detail the techniques and business models top info-marketers use to provide their existing customers with additional value for maximum profits. This book will detail the easy ways to generate additional revenue from your existing customers. Coming soon from the Information Marketing Association and Entrepreneur Press.

Back-End Products That Require Labor

These products can fall into any category. You can offer tele-seminars to provide specialized information and additional training on a particular product. You can provide coaching. A lot of info-marketers have a six-week jumpstart program. A jumpstart program delivers weekly information on how to get started in the business. This information can be a combination of printed materials, audio CDs, a tele-seminar, and over-the-phone coaching.

Another back-end product is specialty items that weren't in the initial kit. For example, an info-marketer can sell a no-money-down real estate buying kit and then offer a specialty program on becoming a landlord or buying homes that have gone through foreclosure or buying HUD foreclosures or buying tax liens. All of these were not part of the original sale, and they are going to interest customers who have bought the initial real estate kit.

You can also offer one-on-one consulting to help your customers implement what they have bought from you. Many customers will buy your marketing system and think it's great. But they don't have time or don't want to learn how to do it themselves. These customers will be willing to pay you to either walk them through it or to do it for them!

Info-Marketer Resource

Champions of the Info-Summit

Who Else Wants to 'Pick-the-Brains' of the Sharpest Information Marketers in the World?

Imagine ... Just ONE IDEA Can Make You Independent for the Rest of Your Life! One of the most important topics each year at the Glazer/Kennedy Information Marketing Summit is back-end opportunities to increase the profitability of an info-marketing business. Each year this seminar provides tremendous profit-enhancing opportunities for new info-marketers as well as the experienced pro. Bill Glazer has consolidated the best presentations:

- Big Breakthroughs in the Information Marketing Business
- How a Successful Info-Business Was Increased by 500% in 12 Months
- How Agora Did It
- Copywriting Secrets From the Pro
- How to Most Successfully Market Your Million-Dollar Seminar or Boot Camp
- How to Sell High-Priced Coaching
- Integrated Media Magic: How to Crossbreed Online and Offline Marketing for ANY Information Business
- How to Sell Information Online ... Even If You're a Total Computer Dunce!

- Secrets of Online Copywriting
- Tele-Seminar Selling Secrets
- How to Turn Unconverted Leads Into a Flood of Extra Profits by Adding Inbound and/or Outbound Telemarketing to Your Marketing Funnel
- The 5 Gold Rings of Wealth Production From Info-Entrepreneurship
- How to Turn Your Info-Products Into a Lot of Extra Cash, Automatically, on eBay

For more details visit **www.InfoMarketingChampions.com** for a special limited time offer just for buyers of this book.

Another back-end product that requires labor is providing specific services to your customers. Craig Proctor, an info-marketer who serves real estate agents, trains his customers that they need to use prerecorded messages to help get new listings and to sell homes more quickly. He could simply give them a list of vendors to choose from, but Craig has turned this into a back-end product. He has joint ventured with a provider of prerecorded messages, so he receives a commission on each customer who uses the service. Now, even if a real estate agent decides to drop Craig's continuity program, Craig continues to get revenue from that customer in the form of commissions.

Info-marketer Brian Sacks has a business called **www.Mortgage WebSuccess.com**. Brian serves the mortgage broker niche and helps mortgage brokers get more customers. He teaches mortgage brokers that they need to create a web site that offers several free reports. When potential mortgage borrowers opt in to receive the free reports from the mortgage broker, they receive a series of e-mails that promote the mortgage broker. Brian's marketing kit contained all of those free reports and e-mails, but some mortgage brokers weren't able to implement the program successfully. They couldn't seem to find a web developer that could create a site to collect the leads and send the free reports.

Brian packaged the web site as a turnkey system for mortgage brokers who didn't want to create the sites themselves. He created a template these brokers can follow, and not only that, they can pay a fee and have the entire web site customized for them and up within five minutes. By turning the system into an automatically implemented web site, Brian not only gets the sale of the kit and a new customer, but he also gets continuing revenue from the web sites and provides his customers with a lot more value.

Info-marketer Dr. Ben Altadonna serves the chiropractic niche. He has been teaching chiropractors that they need to publish a monthly newsletter. However, few are able to get it done consistently. So as a back-end product, Ben publishes the newsletters for them. His customers don't have to take time away from their practices to pull together information, put it in the form of a newsletter, and mail it out to their clients. Instead, Ben gets their customer lists, customizes the newsletter for each doctor, and gets them printed and mailed. Ben has several hundred chiropractors who pay him monthly for that service. It is a huge revenue generator for his business.

Another back-end idea is direct-mail marketing campaigns. Ed O'Keefe does direct-mail lead generation campaigns for dentists. Dentists can sign up for Ed's system, select the types of patients they want, and then Ed takes care of all of the marketing. The dentists are notified when the postcards go in the mail, and the next thing they know, they have new patients calling the office. Ed's customers don't have to learn anything. All they have to do is ask Ed to take care of the service, and he handles everything.

Now let's take a look at back-end products that do not require manual labor.

Back-End Products That Do Not Require Labor

Almost every back-end product that requires labor can also be done in a way that does not require labor from you. However, each product does require either technology or someone else to take care of it for you.

For example, tele-seminars can be done once and then be rebroadcast for new members as they join. Or you can outsource live tele-coaching to an outside vendor. You will need to create a coaching manual for the vendor to follow, so you will need to conduct the first few coaching programs so you will know what your members are asking.

Once you have gone through the series, you can write down the frequently asked questions, provide the answers, and give a curriculum to the team who will handle your coaching program for you. Web site services, prerecorded messages, direct-mail campaigns, and monthly newsletters are all being done by existing info-marketers. You can partner with them to sell these products to your customers. That way you don't have to do any of the work, but you still generate significant revenue from those products being marketed to your customers.

Helping Info-Marketing Clients Implement Turnkey Marketing Tools Automatically Without Having to Touch the Actual Key

There are hundreds of reasons why people won't get around to implementing a marketing campaign you give them, even if they *know* it will work and all they have to do is send it! The trouble is when information marketers can't get their clients to implement, it becomes harder to create loyal clients who come back and consume more.

Info-Marketer Profile

Nigel Botterill (the Glazer-Kennedy Insider's Circle "Information Marketer of the Year") recently partnered with Infusion Software to create a true turnkey marketing system for his clients.

Nigel Botterill and his wife, Sue, own My-Mag. They help individuals publish their own community publications. Their clients solicit advertisers and publish those ads together with community-related content into a monthly publication distributed within their neighborhoods. While many of Nigel's clients were doing well, others were not able to effectively implement their marketing sequences and were losing important advertising revenue.

Although all of the necessary follow-up campaigns were already provided in a kit that Nigel's clients purchased, many were not sending those letters to prospective advertisers. Frustrated with this lack of implementation, Nigel realized his clients needed an ultra-simple way to manage lead follow-up. They needed a system that would *do the marketing*.

Together with Infusion, Nigel created several lengthy follow-up sequences that included e-mails, postcards, letters, faxes, and voice broadcasts. All of the steps in these campaigns were preloaded into Infusion's marketing software.

Now all the clients have to do to become very effective marketers is to enter the contact information of their prospects and press a button. Immediately, Infusion CRM takes over and executes a lengthy multistep marketing campaign:

- The prospects receive an immediate e-mail with a custom message such as: "Hey, John, it was nice meeting you at the BNI Networking meeting last Thursday. Here is the first step in the free marketing course I promised to send you."

➡

- Also on the first day, Infusion CRM sends a notice to a local fulfillment vendor to have a postcard sent to the prospects. The postcard includes testimonials and information about a special offer (with a deadline of course). *Again, this is hands off—the franchisee does nothing.*
- For the next five days, the prospects receive the free marketing course, which helps establish trust and a "guru" status.
- On day six the prospects automatically receive a reminder (via e-mail) that they've got seven days left for the special offer.
- On day 11, a final notice for the first offer is sent.
- On days 12 and14, a voice broadcast is sent.
- On day 15, an invitation to a tele-seminar is sent.
- On day 17, a fax broadcast of a news article is sent.
- On day 26, a "Frankly, I'm perplexed" e-mail (with a second offer) is sent.
- And for 270 days the prospects continue to receive follow-up messages from the franchisee.

In addition to the follow-up sequences, the clients also have lead generation campaigns they can send to cold prospects, lead tracking tools for their manual follow-up, and a "happy client" campaign that automatically starts when a new client is acquired. This sequence "wows" the client and over time asks for referrals, testimonials, etc.

The best part for Nigel's clients is if they sell only one additional ad each month, they completely pay for the entire cost of the marketing system. It makes the sale of this system extremely easy to cost justify.

Many information marketers are already using Infusion's CRM Software to automate their *own* follow-up. But now that information marketers can provide the same type of automated marketing machine for their clients, many new opportunities are available.

This unique mix of marketing content from the marketing guru and marketing automation through Infusion provides several benefits:

1. Information marketers can now offer a completely scalable, automatically implemented solution without having to actually *do* much at all.

2. Information marketing clients can become very effective marketers literally overnight. All they have to do is put their prospects' names and info into the system and press a button.

3. Additional revenue streams are immediately available:

   a. Automatically implemented system can be easily integrated into a high-priced coaching program to add value and enable a higher price point; or

   b. Can act as a standalone offering that provides additional *continuity income* to the information marketer.

To learn more about using Infusion's software to manage your marketing, visit **www.InfoMarketingCRM.com**. For more information including an expanded profile visit **www.InfoMarketingBook.com/ Botterill.**

Instead of Selling How-To Manuals an Info-Marketer Sells Automated Lead Generation Systems

Who knew that when you put together a golf pro with a "web guy" you'd end up with a Mega Marketing Machine™?

This story belongs to Matt Gillogly (the golf pro). At age 27, Matt was one of the youngest golf pros in the country and working at a top golf resort for Marriott Corporation. Matt took what he learned as a golf pro to a start-up company that bought struggling resorts and transformed them into moneymakers. He became a "turnaround specialist," moving from resort to resort every 15 months or so. Then, after four years as a golf pro, Matt's career took a dramatic turn.

After attending a Robert Allen info event and subsequently connecting with Ted Thomas, Matt bought into a real estate program and began doing short sales. Soon he was coaching his mentors' students, and three years later Matt began his own coaching business for real estate investors. He provided back-end coaching for speakers who didn't want to do the coaching themselves.

Then Matt attended his first Dan Kennedy event where "there were so many light bulbs going off it was like the paparazzi at a Hollywood premiere." Reed Hoisington made a presentation on tear sheets, and right then and there Matt knew he had to buy the license to provide tear sheets for real estate investors. Nine months later, he was doing $500,000 in tear sheets. Then a light bulb really went off.

Matt says, "You know, they want the coaching, yes, but what the clients really want is marketing, and they want it all done for them. So I still provide coaching for about three speakers, but

➡

Tear Sheet

A *tear sheet* is a mail piece that looks as if it was torn out of a magazine or a newspaper. After the page is printed the left edge is ripped so it is torn and jagged.

A tear sheet usually includes a "sticky note" with an attention-getting message. The most common message is, "Try this, it works! J."

where I'm carving my niche is in marketing. But it's a different kind of marketing. Basically I've taken my kit, put it online, and put it on steroids."

A Different Kind of Marketing

About 18 months ago, a group of Matt's platinum members came to him and said, "We want you to teach us about marketing." So he did a tele-seminar and created a kit called "Ultimate Marketing Dominance." It sold well, but it didn't have a long lifespan. So, Matt recalls, he did exactly what Dan Kennedy and Bill Glazer told him to do. He sent a survey to his list of 20,000 real estate investors and asked them to list their biggest problem, challenge, or goal. Number one was finding leads, and number two was marketing those leads.

Matt had had good success with tear sheets, but the downside was buying big lists and only mailing to them once. In addition, it ➡

was labor intensive, and Matt didn't want to be the one doing the labor. He began to wonder if someone, somewhere could manage multiple mailings to a list for him—a turnkey approach to marketing. Matt asked around, and after he had about 10 guys tell him he was completely nuts, he figured he was onto something.

Five months and a couple of conference calls with the web guy later, Matt was ready to test his product with a few of his clients. Fifteen minutes into the presentation, every client was sold.

Matt's system takes a complicated problem—managing multi-step marketing campaigns—and makes it as easy as clicking through a few online forms. By using the Mega Marketing Machine™, real estate investors can pick a multistep campaign; charge it to a specific niche; buy a list that's targeted to that specific niche; and send the pieces, the multistep campaign, and the list to a printer that will then print them out and mail each batch spaced 30 days apart. These investors can literally set up the marketing program once and then forget it and never have to do it again. By using this system, Matt's members get a steady flow of motivated, high-level prospective clients contacting them.

The Mega Marketing Machine™ offers investors several different mailing sequences and access to different targeted lists (e.g., credit-challenged homeowners, homeowners that have an adjustable rate mortgage, homeowners that have self-primed credit loans, and bankruptcy). Matt explains that by offering different mailing sequences, his system solves problems for investors throughout the country. Different markets need different solutions. "I wanted different niches within my market to be attracted to this system and say 'This is for me,'" Matt says. "Plus, when they have more choices, members continue to subscribe because they haven't given the system a real chance until they have completed all of the mailings." ➡

Following some guidance from Dan Kennedy, Matt offered his Mega Marketing Machine™ system after a training seminar on "how to do your own marketing." After studying the complicated steps of conducting a marketing campaign, 37 of the 170 attendees were ready to have someone else do the marketing for them—especially after Matt conducted a live demonstration and actually produced a campaign for a coaching member in the audience—so they bought the system. Other speakers at the event asked Matt to pitch the system at their events and tele-seminars, so the initial launch was extremely successful. Matt continues to do two or three tele-seminars per month, plus live events.

For more about Matt Gillogly's automated system, visit **www.PlaidJacketMarketing.com** and to read the expanded profile go to **www.InfoMarketingBook.com/Gillogly**.

Big Payday Opportunities

You need to step up opportunities to receive large paydays from the group of your customers who are excited and glad to buy your products and services. Most info-marketers use events to create large paydays.

After you have sold your products and services to a significant number of people, a number of them are going to be interested in coming to an event to hear you talk about what you have taught them and to hear from other experts you bring in.

These events, if done properly, can be an excellent big payday for you. Some events cost as much as $2,500 to attend if they provide specialized content not revealed anywhere else. One hundred people at $2,500 adds up to a large amount of money, and the registration fees are not the whole opportunity.

Your event is a terrific forum for you to market your existing back-end products and to offer brand new back-end products for your info-business. In addition, you should look at your event as an opportunity for other individuals to make a sales presentation to sell their products and services to your customers. Many info-marketers make anywhere from $100,000 to $2 million at these events.

These info-marketers invest heavily in bringing customers into the event, and once they are there, they take advantage of the opportunity to generate maximum revenue by promoting other products and services to their customers.

Another way to generate a significant payday is by offering a coaching program. A number of individuals within your customer base will pay to come to a coaching meeting. These can be structured in a number of different ways.

Seminars/Boot Camps

The "fill the seats" business looks a whole lot easier and more profitable than it really is, but there is one best way to make very, very good money from promoting and hosting seminars. You can make $100,000 to $1 million or even more, net profit, from a single two- or three-day event.

A lot of people attending seminars count heads, multiply by the registration fee, erroneously conclude the seminar promoter is making a killing, and think, "I can certainly do what I see him doing!" Ah, but it's what you *don't* see that matters most. In most seminar situations, it actually costs more to fill the seats plus put on the seminar than is paid in registration fees, so the promoter is "negative," i.e., in the hole when the doors open, making up that loss/investment and seeking his profit from on-site sales of books, tapes, coaching programs, and other goods and services.

Filling seats via media advertising, for example, is very, very costly and risky. Some info-marketers use newspaper, radio, TV, and direct-mail to fill seats at "free introductory seminars," where they sell an actual seminar, routinely spending $200 to $300 per person to get them into the room.

The Easy Way to Minimize Liability, Reduce Stress, and Increase the Profitability of Your Events

Info-Marketer Resource There are thousands of dollars of potential liability when you sign a hotel contract for your boot camp or event. In addition, the document is so long, it's difficult to figure out what it even says.

Bari Baumgardner has been negotiating hotel contracts and managing events for her clients for over 15 years. Her clients benefit from her experience and the volume pricing she is able to negotiate with hotels. Because Bari works with several info-marketers, hotels make concessions to her so they will be considered for other future business.

Hotels have experts who negotiate with event planners every day. You need an expert on your side. Outsourcing the complicated and time-consuming event management work to Bari so you can focus on marketing and on-site sales can add tens of thousands of dollars in new revenue to your event.

For a complimentary meeting evaluation, phone Bari at **704/334-0909** or e-mail **BBaumgardner@SageEventManagement.com** today.

Profits from these events come when speakers offer additional products and services to attendees after their presentations. Typically an info-marketer offers several of his own products where there is no revenue split, and the sales of invited speakers are most often split 50/50.

Mastermind Meetings

Small group mastermind meetings typically have somewhere between 10 and 25 customers sitting around the table with the info-marketer. The info-marketer provides a little bit of teaching, but primarily each coaching customer comes prepared to give a 15- or 20-minute presentation about his business. Then you discuss some

---

Look for the Upcoming Guide
Information Marketing Association Official Guide to Building Seminars and Speaking

In this book, we'll detail the methods that the most successful seminar promoters use to fill seminar rooms and make maximum profits from their events. This book will explain the marketing, arrangements, and on-site logistics to make it easy to create events that attendees love to attend and that are profitable for you. Coming soon from the Information Marketing Association and Entrepreneur Press.

---

issues each presenter is facing, and the coaching members and the info-marketer help solve each problem.

When run correctly, the info-marketer does not have to do a whole lot in these forums. When you put together 15 or 20 people, whether they are in the same line of business or in a diverse industry, one of them will present a problem and almost assuredly two or three people in the room will have already faced that problem and come up with a solution to it. By hosting these coaching groups, not only can you make a lot of money for yourself, but you can help your customers find shortcuts to improving their businesses.

Group Coaching Meeting

Another model for coaching is the large group model. In this model, 25 to 150 (or conceivably even an unlimited number of people) work together with a facilitator. The facilitator makes presentations about specific areas of expertise and then the groups sitting at each table are given individual exercises and group exercises to work on together. Using this process they can work through specific problems and help solve them. The benefit of this program is that you can sell it to a lot more people.

Now, you might assume you could charge a lot more for the small format model, but most info-marketers have found there is not a lot of price resistance to coaching in either model. Whichever model you choose, most info-marketers offer their first-time coaching programs at $10,000 to $12,000. Info-marketers who have mature businesses have been able to increase their prices and still meet their goals for participation in both the small and large formats. A lot of info-marketers prefer the strategic coach (large) model because they can sign up 50, 100, or 150 customers to meet three or four times a year; charge them $10,000 to $12,000; and have significant paydays for their businesses. Then they can hold monthly tele-seminars with these same members. The info-marketers who use the mastermind (small) model have 12 to 20 participants. The price is still in the neighborhood of $10,000 to $12,000. They have the same three or four meetings a year. They offer the same tele-seminars. But they make a lot less money from their coaching programs than the info-marketers who use the strategic coach model.

You need to create a program that makes the most sense for both you and your customers. Some businesses lend themselves well to the strategic coach model. Other types of businesses are served better in small groups. You need to research your market, examine the type of coaching model you are interested in, and make a choice that considers what will be best received and provide the most value for your customers and generate the most revenue for your business.

Ultra High-End Products

You should also consider coming up with an ultra high-end product for a small percentage of your customers. Some info-marketers have developed an area-specific product they will sell to only one customer within a specified geographic area. It could be a unique marketing campaign, a particular service, or special coaching. You should study the models that info-marketers are using to create very high-priced products within their businesses. If you offer your initial product at $500 or $1,000, a monthly continuity program for $49, and a coaching program at $10,000 to $12,000, you should have another product that sells for $30,000, $40,000, or $50,000. This product should be a way for an elite customer to get "more of you." You can outline what the product is and then wait to create it until someone buys it. At the end of the year, this high-ticket item can be a significant source of net income for your info-marketing business.

Automatically Implemented Systems

Another way to set up big paydays is to market automatically implemented systems. We talked a little bit about the automatically implemented systems in the programs that require labor, but they are also a source of large payday revenue for you. For example, if you have 150 or 200 or 500 or 5,000 people paying you to publish a newsletter for their customers, it is a very powerful way to set up a big payday for your business.

Tollbooth Position Revenue Opportunities

When you have customers who have bought your product and are participating in your monthly continuity program, they are going to listen to your recommendations and implement them for themselves. This puts you in what info-marketers refer to as a "tollbooth" position. It simply means you are in a position to charge money (a toll) to allow others access to your market of customers.

Joint Ventures. One way to leverage your tollbooth position is through joint ventures. Joint ventures are arrangements where two individuals agree to work together to create and market a product. In many cases, one info-marketer has the potential customers and another info-marketer has the product. They create a relationship in which the one who has the product has an opportunity to sell it to the other info-marketer's customers.

This helps the info-marketer who has the customers because he doesn't have to create a product, sell it, or fulfill it. The info-marketer who has the product doesn't have to go through all of the expensive work of finding customers.

Joint ventures drastically reduce the cost per sale for both info-marketers. Joint ventures are a terrific way for an info-marketer just starting out to generate sales for his product and get new customers. They are also a great way for an established info-marketer to get paydays from his business simply because he has a tollbooth position to provide access to his customers.

Endorsements. Another way to generate revenue through your tollbooth position is through endorsements. You can endorse a particular product or service that you believe is valuable for your customers by creating an endorsement or affiliate relationship with the service provider. You endorse the service provider to your customers, and when your customers use that provider's products or services, you get paid. You can negotiate being paid some money up front in addition to receiving monthly fees. Many marketers have on the bottom of their web sites a link for their affiliate programs so you can sign up automatically to promote their products and services and make an affiliate commission based on your sales.

List Sales and Exchanges. Another tollbooth opportunity is to sell or exchange your list of customers. If you have a significant number of customers or a significant number of leads, list brokers or other info-marketers will want access to those names. You may also want to exchange lists with another info-marketer who works with the same type of customers. This is a great way of finding new customers without having to go through the expensive lead generation process.

Inserts. You can also agree to put inserts promoting another info-marketer's product into your monthly newsletter or your product kits. This can be under a joint venture or an affiliate relationship. You simply take a sales message provided by somebody else and insert it into your newsletter or kit. In exchange you get a commission from the provider based on the sales you generate.

Events. Another way to leverage your tollbooth position is at your events. Whenever you have a room full of potential buyers, chances are there are other vendors who would be more than happy to pay you for the privilege of being in that room to promote their products and services.

Multiple sales to your current customers are where the profits in information marketing come from. This is the most important opportunity you have within your business. It is never too early to consider the types of back-end products and services you will offer to your customers. In fact, you should set up the sale of those back-end products in the initial product or service you are promoting to your niche. The place to begin is with your back-end business. You should create your entire marketing sequence of lead generation and sales conversion based on the types of customers who will be more likely to buy your back-end revenue opportunities. Always ask yourself: How can I build my entire business to maximize my back-end sales?

Life at the Beach With Reed Hoisington

What were you doing yesterday at 3:00 in the afternoon? It's a good bet you weren't working on your tan like Reed Hoisington often does.

Reed completely changed his mortgage business marketing systems by creating advertising that offered free reports to potential borrowers. It was a big change for Reed's staff. "My sales reps were saying, 'What's a lead? Wait, this guy doesn't want a loan, he wants a free report,'" Reed laughs. "They thought I was crazy at first."

Crazy like a fox, maybe. Reed built a huge business by offering free reports that built trust with his prospects, educated them about what to look for, and asked them to contact Reed's company for additional information.

By 1997, Reed was an enormously successful mortgage company owner. Operating in 23 states via a centralized direct mail and outbound telephone center, his 185-staff member operation took in 600 loan applications a day.

Then he flew out to see Dan Kennedy and hired him to write new lead generation ads and a sales letter with free report offers.

Reed ended up becoming an information marketer and a member of Dan's Platinum Coaching program before the day was out.

After taking Dan Kennedy's advice to "take what he already knew and stick it in a box," Reed was selling 100-plus kits per month after only 90 days in the business! Ultimately he sold over 3,000 of the kits that showed his customers how to build an operations manual, structure commissions, and write noncompete contracts—virtually everything needed to run a mortgage company.

Reed built his first kit by delegating the work to two of the top staff members in his mortgage company. He gave them the basic content and an outline to follow. "I gave the project to two of my top folks who are extremely bright and who can write," Reed says. "A month later, the kit was done."

Most people have the luxury of following in someone else's foot-steps. Not so for Reed. "We were the first broker in North Carolina, and everybody else just copied us," Reed says. It sounds familiar now after hearing commercial after commercial on TV, but Reed was the first to show customers how to "get another loan, pay less, get more money, and pay off those credit cards." Other loan officers were interested in learning how they could repeat Reed's success.

Reed knew his kit was working. The next step was to build a back end, so he started a monthly newsletter. Back in the early 1990s, forced continuity was a new idea, and not everyone thought it would work. Reed did. "I gave them two months free and then auto-matically started charging for subscriptions," Reed says. "There was some concern that including the forced continuity in the sales materials would suppress the sale of the front-end kit. Or maybe after the fact people would be saying, 'Hey, I didn't want that thing,' but that didn't happen."

Reed built his business using fax broadcasts and newspaper tear sheets. "We were the fax kings," Reed says. "We sold lots of kits through faxing." They created a lead generation marketing piece, then fax broadcasted it to fax number lists they purchased from brokers.

The main thing Reed's mortgage broker customers want is to have leads generated for them. "The idea is to dummy proof it," Reed says. "Why teach them to fish? Just give them the fish!" Reed pro-vides the entire mailings ready to go: "We ship it to them, addressed, stamps on them, everything ready—or else it won't get done."

Today, Reed's continuity package (**www.ReedH.com/mail**) is comprehensive, providing the following benefits to his members:

- A newspaper tear sheet to generate leads
- A newsletter for each member to send to his own clients
- A hotline for each member's prospects to call to request free reports
- Lead lists to generate new clients
- MortgagePro CRM, an automated system that tracks and follows up with new leads, pending loan applications, prospects, and clients
- A web site for each member's business (**www.ReedH.com/mbw**)

With all of these components, the pain of disconnect is increased for Reed's members. Even if one of the benefits is not valuable for a particular member, the strength of the other benefits in the package keeps that member in the program.

Reed's goal long term is to grow the client newsletter benefit, mailing newsletters to his members' clients because, as Reed puts it, "Publishing newsletters doesn't require me personally day in and day out doing boot camps."

So what does Reed like to do day in and day out? "I am a happy guy," Reed says. "I have a terrific gal. I live at Wrightsville Beach. When Robert called me at 3:00 in the afternoon, I had just gotten back from a walk on the beach with my dogs splashing in the tide."

Not bad for a mortgage company owner. Forget that fat little guy in a rumpled suit chasing after his next loan. Reed is living the good life in coastal North Carolina where you're more likely to find him working in his swim trunks at home.

For more information about Reed, including an expanded profile, visit **www.InfoMarketingBook.com/Hoisington**.

Foreclosure Can Be a *Good* Thing— Just Ask Ted Thomas

Ted's first career was as an airline pilot. He worked for Aloha Airlines, and from there he went into the real estate business in California. He used to buy apartment houses and office buildings all over the West. During the 1970s, Ted built a company that owned over $200 million worth of real estate. That all changed abruptly in 1986.

"In '86 they changed all the rules," Ted remembers. "You couldn't write off real estate anymore, and so all the commercial real estate we had bought—and I owned 1,800 apartment houses in Phoenix alone—dropped anywhere from 25 to 35 percent in value."

In less than a year, Ted had lost everything. "With the stroke of Congress's pen, it all just went away," Ted muses. "I went from the clubhouse to the outhouse in six months. In 1986, I was living in the country club, right close to the clubhouse. Just like that, it was all over. I lost my house to foreclosure."

But Ted didn't let that foreclosure stop him. "I redirected myself. Believe it or not, losing my house to foreclosure is what got me into the foreclosure business!" Ted exclaims. "I started looking at my situation, and I said, 'Gee, I wonder if anybody else is as stupid as me.' So I went down to county records to find out. It turns out I lived in a very wealthy county, Contra Costa County, right across from San Francisco. And 75 people a week were going into foreclosure!"

Ted pulled himself out of bankruptcy by purchasing foreclosure houses and reselling them. Putting his marketing savvy to work, he even used direct mail to buy and sell houses. "This was back in the 1980s," Ted says. "The *San Francisco Examiner Chronicle* called me for an interview, because they couldn't believe I was buying houses

➡

using direct mail. At first I turned the interview down. The guy called me back in a couple of days and said, 'Look, we're going to do the article, so if we can interview you we can make sure it's accurate.' So I did the interview. That's when people started calling and saying, 'Can you teach me how to do it?' Bingo. I was in information marketing."

Not one to start small, Ted began charging $1,000 day, and his typical consulting took five days. From there he branched out into writing reports that outlined his steps to follow, and that led to a book. "In 1988 I did a big, thick book," Ted says. "It was 450 pages, and I self-published it. It sold for $100. Back then, no one could sell a book for $100."

Then Ted heard about the American Booksellers Association. Thinking it might be fun, Ted and a friend went to a convention in Las Vegas. "I didn't know there would be 25,000 people there!" Ted laughs. "There were all these booths with big New York publishers like John Wiley and Simon and Schuster. I ended up selling my book to John Wiley right there at the book fair!"

From books, Ted moved into audiotapes, something relatively new in 1988. Ted recalls: "A guy called me up and said, 'Why don't you have audiotapes?' I said, 'What are audiotapes?' He said, 'I'll read the book onto the tapes, and I'll give it to you if you'll order the audios from me.' And that got me into doing audiotapes."

The next big thing for Ted was newsletters. He started sending his book and tapes to newsletters to see if they would be a good way to market his materials. "I didn't know any better, so I sent it to them," Ted says. One of Ted's packages landed on Howard Ruff's desk.

Howard Ruff was a gold investor who wrote a newsletter that went to a list of 300,000 people. "Howard Ruff called me up and said, 'Ted, I read your book, and it's really good. Could you make ➡

this into a seminar for my clients?' I said, 'Yeah, it'll probably take me two or three weeks,' and he said, 'Oh, it'll take three weeks just to write the mail piece.' Stupid me, I said, 'What's a mail piece?' I didn't know!"

Ted had something else to learn, too. When he asked Howard how they would split the money from a seminar, he was shocked when Howard said 70/30—with only 30 percent going to Ted! As the author, Ted thought 70 percent might go to him. "I didn't know that it cost money to market a seminar," Ted remembers. "But the payoff was huge. Howard charged $5,000 for a three-day seminar. Nobody did that in 1988!"

Nobody but Howard and Ted. For the next 10 months they had 50 people at each seminar, each one paying $5,000 for the privilege. They took in $2.5 million with $800,000 going to Ted. "Did that get me out of bankruptcy or what?" Ted laughs.

Howard had a few more lessons for Ted. Like sequential mailings: "Howard said, 'Look, you mail once, they like it, you mail it again. They like it, you mail it again. You just keep doing it.'"

Another tip from Howard was to record the seminars and sell tapes. "We mailed our seminar offer to 50,000 people," Ted says. "Only 500 people bought at $5,000, so Howard had the idea to record the seminar and send a notice that people could buy the tapes. We made another $150 million that way."

Today, Ted is still in the real estate business, using the same techniques he sells in his information marketing business. His success has inspired many others to copy his formula. "I have kept doing real estate, buying houses and wholesaling them, and I still use direct mail and the system I created. Everybody's copied it now. If you go to a Bill Glazer or a Dan Kennedy seminar, you'll see all these real estate guys doing real estate foreclosures. They've all just ➡

taken it to another niche. One guy copied it and made it so you could do it with a computer program. Another guy copied it and made it so you can do the letters automatically. I still do the same old system. I still sell it, and I've been selling it since 1988."

Visit **www.TedThomasWorkshops.com** or **InfoMarketingBook. com/Thomas** for more information about Ted and his products.

The "E-Zine Queen" Rules

Info-Marketer Profile

Just a few years ago, Alexandria Brown was an account manager and copywriter for a small advertising agency in New York City. Today she is the "E-Zine Queen," runs a million-dollar-plus info-marketing business, and she likes—no, loves—being in charge of her own destiny.

Alexandria thinks back to her New York days: "I knew I wanted to work for myself because I had moved from job to job looking for *the* job that would make me happy. I finally realized I just wanted to be on my own."

Hers is a familiar story. Old-fashioned bosses. Bureaucracy. Management by committee. "I had better ideas than my bosses did, and they wouldn't let me make any changes. I like to make changes fast," Alexandria laughs. "It took them five months to decide what new fax machine to buy. It was just driving me crazy, and I started thinking I could go to Staples today, buy everything I need, and have clients by next week. So I left—but I was in for a rude awakening. I didn't realize how important marketing is. For a while there, I starved!"

Alexandria did everything you're supposed to do. She studied marketing. She went to networking meetings. "But it just wasn't clicking for me," Alexandria says. "Finally I tried an e-mail newsletter to promote my services to people I'd already met. I started with 10 people, which included my parents and my cat," she laughs. I didn't have a web site, products to sell, or anything."

She started out by sharing a marketing tip of the week. Soon people started forwarding Alexandria's e-mails, and her list began to grow. Within a few months Alexandria had gotten some referrals to big clients like Dunn and Bradstreet, New York Times Digital, and Scholastic Books. "I wasn't selling my information yet, but the information was definitely marketing for me," she says.

At the beginning of her information marketing career, Alexandria took a fairly straightforward, no-nonsense approach to her e-mail newsletter. "Up until three or four years ago I didn't feel like I should share anything personal in the newsletter," Alexandria says. "I had moved to California, and all this stuff was going on in my life, relationships and things, but I didn't share anything. I just talked about marketing."

All that changed the day Alexandria got a new kitten.

"I already had another cat—actually two other cats—and I was delighted, but at the same time I had forgotten how crazy kittens are," Alexandria laughs. "This kitten was bipolar, sweet and sleeping one minute and the next running around like *Tom and Jerry*. The cats were all chasing each other around the house, knocking things over, going up the drapes, across my desk, jumping on my head, and there I was trying to write the newsletter! I was getting aggravated, so I started writing just a little bit about the kitten, saying, 'Oh, you know, it's funny. I'm trying to get this newsletter out today, but this kitten is driving us all crazy. She's so cute but what a handful.' That was it. Really just a sentence or two. I had this great article underneath it on how to write headlines, and I'm thinking, 'They're going to love this article. This is going to rock their world.'"

Alexandria pressed "send," and the response rocked *her* world.

"I went out for the day," Alexandria recalls. "I came back and had dozens and dozens of e-mails about the cats. The cats! They cared about the cats. People were writing me back saying, 'What are your cats' names? How many cats do you have? How long have you had the cat? What kind of kitten is it? Can you show us pictures?' People were sending me pictures of their cats. Some of them were dressed up. It's kind of freaky. This one woman wrote and said, 'Now that I know you love cats, I'm going to buy everything you have.' And I still see her name on my customer list," Alexandria marvels.

With those few lines about her cats, Alexandria discovered that great marketing—whether in person, in print, or online—is all about making a connection. "When it comes to online marketing, we think it's different, but actually it's even more important that you build a relationship with your online readers," she says.

Now Alexandria makes it a habit to share information with her customers about what's going on in her life. She includes a few personal notes in her e-zine, and she uses her blog (**www.Alexandria Brown.blogspot.com**) to post photos and write more about herself. This creates a strong connection with her list. "Some people tell me outright, 'I didn't even read your article, but I wanted to hear about your vacation and your first time waterskiing,'" Alexandria says. "I like having the blog because if anyone wants to see photos or read more about my life, they can go there. It's amazing that when you're a little bit vulnerable with customers and you share what's going on in your life, they will respond to that. People buy from people they know, like, and trust."

Alexandria built on the success of her e-zines by publishing an e-book on how to use e-zines to market products and services. "Within a year or two I had people saying, 'Hey, Ali, you're not at these networking meetings anymore, and we see you wearing nicer suits, ➡

and you're obviously getting better clients, and everything's going great for you. What is the secret?' I said, 'Well, you gotta start one of these e-zines,' and they said, 'How do we do it?'" Alexandria recalls.

So she looked in the bookstores, and she looked online. "I was not really happy with any of the books or courses I found on e-zines, so I decided to write one. At first I was going to write a 'real' book until I realized that it's time consuming and you don't make much money on printed books," Alexandria says.

Alexandria put together her first e-book and sent a quick e-mail to her list. "That was the moment my life changed!" she exclaims. "By that time I had amassed a few thousand people on my list—my 'herd' as Dan Kennedy refers to an info-marketer's customer base—but I didn't know the power of what I was doing. I started my e-zine to get more clients, and when I came out with this e-book, I thought maybe my clients would be interested in it. So I put up a crappy web site and wrote a note to my e-mail list saying, 'Hey, you may be interested in this. It's a course on how to publish an e-zine that makes you sales and clients and makes you more money.' I remember pressing 'send,' and then the sales just came in.

"That was the day my life just completely changed, because I had shifted from selling my *time* to selling my *knowledge*. I suddenly had leverage. I suddenly realized the amount of money I could make was no longer linked to the amount of hours I worked. I was done with that book, and the sales kept coming in and coming in and coming in. And to this day it still makes me money. I have a much more advanced version of it now, but it's essentially based on the same information. And now I sell five different information products, run three virtual coaching programs via Internet and phone, and host my live 'Online Success Blueprint Workshops,' which teach solo-entrepreneurs how to do exactly what I did—take their current business and knowledge and ➡

transform it into more time, money, and freedom using e-mail and the Internet."

Today Alexandria runs her booming business from a beautiful new beach house in Los Angeles, working only four days a week. "I'm happy to keep a business with smaller numbers but with a higher value. I'm always looking for ways to work less to make the same money or even more," she says. "The big selling point for the information marketing industry is the lifestyle. I'm a big vacation person. I love going away—a lot. It also makes me feel really good that I can get on a plane anytime and go visit my elderly parents. I don't have to ask anyone for permission, and I can work from wherever I am if I want to."

Part of Alexandria's freedom stems from the way she has chosen to run her business. She uses a virtual team of five stay-at-home moms who play different roles in Alexandria's operation. "I have no one working with me in my home. I don't necessarily want to get dressed every morning. I don't want to see anybody in the mornings. I don't want to talk to anybody in the morning," Alexandria chuckles. "It's very valuable for people to get clear on what they want their lives to look like. I almost did the office thing, and I'm so glad I didn't!"

For the complete profile on Alexandria Brown visit **www.Info MarketingBook.com/Brown** or visit **www.AlexandriaBrown.com.**

Chapter 9

Step 8: Crucial Keys to Build a Strong Business So You Don't Blow It

by Robert Skrob
President, Information Marketing Association

A LTHOUGH I'M A LICENSED CERTIFIED PUBLIC ACCOUNTANT, MY career before info-marketing was association management. I work with an association management company. We provide staffing, support, and infrastructure for several associations at one time, providing economies of scale and a one-stop, low-cost solution for our clients.

Since associations are nothing more than nonprofit information marketing companies with products, newsletters, and seminars, I've created and operated more than 30 info-businesses over the last few years. Until I started creating how-to info-marketing information, I had never operated a business within any of the industries I marketed to.

I remember my first meeting with three clients as the new executive director of their association. It was many years ago. My wife and I took Jeff, Rick, and Christina to the University Center Club here in Tallahassee. These three were the top decision makers within the industry, and this was my night to impress them. Boy was I excited about making a great impression.

Christina is a tough-minded attorney; she wants work done precisely and on time. She is always dressed in a well-pressed designer business suit. You always know where you stand with Christina, which is good. But you better get it right, or she'll let you know about it. At this dinner, I decided to sit next to her to get in her good graces.

After a dinner of several courses it came time for dessert. Our server recommended the house specialty, baked Alaska. I didn't know much about baked Alaska, but since everyone around the table ordered it, there was no reason for me to choose otherwise.

The server brought out the baked Alaska for Jeff and lit it on fire! (Evidently there is a flaming aspect to this dessert.) Jeff gave a half-hearted puff at the flames, but they didn't go out. Then another light puff. Still flaming. After about four light puffs he was finally able to extinguish his flaming dessert.

The same story was repeated around the table. Everyone had trouble. One by one, each person had to puff away at the baked Alaska until finally, after several attempts, the flames went out.

Well, I took this as a personal challenge. There wasn't any way I was going to allow this to beat me. I knew I had to get my flames out in a single puff. As the dinner's host, I was the last one to receive my dessert. Everyone else had their flames out, and they were waiting for me before starting to eat their desserts.

Have you ever seen a 4-year-old at his birthday party, blowing his head off at the candles on the cake? Well, that was me. I geared up and gave the hardest blow I could.

That's when it happened. Evidently, hiding under the flames of every baked Alaska, is a really light meringue topping. When I blew at my dessert, flaming meringue went flying all over the table. And, worse, all over Christina (and her designer business suit) sitting next to me. That's when I learned about baked Alaska—bits of frothy egg whites were everywhere!

Christina actually took it quite well. After we got the flames out and provided her with some soda water, she was as good as new. In the end, I think she even enjoyed her dessert. Now, whenever Christina sees me, she has to laugh!

I learned a powerful lesson at that dinner. Now, whenever I tread on unfamiliar territory, I'm careful not to allow my ambition and determination to succeed make me blow it. (Sorry for the pun.)

Step 8 is about making sure you don't rush into the info-marketing business without some crucial business fundamentals necessary to ensure your success.

In the first seven steps, I taught you the marketing sequences, the product development, and the market research issues you need to consider when building an information marketing business. Those really are the most important factors, and Step 8 actually belongs last, but it is something you need to think about as you grow your business. You cannot go through Step 7, do everything from getting customers to creating a back end, stop there, and expect to have a successful business. You also need to build an infrastructure. I am not talking about staff or buildings. I am talking about systems to run the business and to monitor what is going on so you can keep track of how well your business is running at all times.

It's All About Math

One of the most important things to learn about the information marketing business is that it's all about the math. It does not matter if customers are returning product, if they are not buying at huge percentages, or if they are complaining.

What really matters is this: Are the numbers acceptable for your business?

Let's say you sell your product to 100 customers. Twenty of them complain, and 10 return the product. After you factor in the cost of generating the lead and making the sale, and subtract the refund rate, are you still making a profit? If you are, you can do some things to minimize the refund rate, but you should still go out and get more customers, get more complaints, and have to make more refunds. That may sound crazy, but if you're making a profit with 100 customers, 20 complaints, and 10 refunds, there is no reason not to expand your business to 1,000 customers that include 200 complaints and 100 refunds. Of course, you should try new things to minimize refunds and reduce complaints. But don't allow complaints and refunds to reduce the actions you take to promote your business. You must focus on the math.

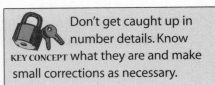

KEY CONCEPT Don't get caught up in number details. Know what they are and make small corrections as necessary.

Protect Your Niche With a Strong Back-End Business

The next thing you need to consider is the fact that eventually the front end will no longer be profitable. As explained in Step 7, the back end is much more important to your business. As time goes on, your cost per sale is going to increase.

How soon that will happen depends on your niche market and your marketing strategy. Sometimes it pays to start out with an extremely high cost per sale, because it can build your back-end business and protect your niche. Many info-marketers are able to create very profitable businesses, even though it might cost them $1,500 to sell an initial product of $997. They are willing to go negative to create a customer. In fact, that's what Dan Kennedy calls "buying a customer."

If your back-end products are true moneymakers, and you understand how much revenue you will get from a customer over time, then it may be wise to buy your customers, to go negative on the front end, so you are able to get more sales, generate greater revenue, and build your business. This is a good thing for two reasons: (1) your back end will become your business; and (2) you are going to be less susceptible to people who want to knock off your product and sell it themselves. You know you are spending $1,500 to generate a $1,000 sale, but others jumping into the business will not know that. They will see your ads and sales letters and think you are making money. When they try to duplicate your ads and sales letters and it costs them $1,500 to generate a $1,000 sale, they are going to jump out in a hot second.

If you focus on building a terrific back-end business, you will be able to get customers no one else can get. In addition, you will have a tremendous advantage over anyone else who might try to get into your niche market.

Expand the Definition of Your Niche

Next, you need to consider expanding the definition of your market and your niche. A perfect example of this is when Bill Glazer created BGS Marketing. Bill took over his family-owned menswear store business. He created a marketing program for his two stores and generated a lot of customers for them.

Then he decided to get into the information marketing business. His first information marketing product was directed toward menswear stores. He focused his niche on identifying the media within menswear stores. He identified what they wanted, created a terrific product, and made a lot of money selling his product to menswear stores.

Bill soon found, however, that his niche was very small. He reached the point where the cost of acquiring a new customer was growing quickly. The back-end business was good, but it was not enough to meet his income goals. So Bill took the same products and services he was offering to menswear stores and made it appropriate for several other niches, including jewelry stores, furniture stores, and others he identified as terrific sources of customers. Now he is operating in several different niches, all within retail, at the same time. This is a great way to expand a business when it becomes unprofitable at the front end.

> **KEY CONCEPT** An info-marketer can expand his business by offering more products to one niche or by expanding the definition of the niche he serves so he can market to more people.

Essential Metrics for Info-Marketers

To make good business judgments you need a firm grasp of your numbers. You must know which ads are performing so you know how to adjust your future spending to maximize your marketing investment. Fortunately, info-marketers have always been measurement oriented.

A marketing campaign might involve five e-mails, three mailings, a tele-seminar, newsletter inserts, and telemarketing. How can you determine which pieces were essential to the sale, or which had the most impact? It's rare that an info-marketer has the patience and discipline to set up controlled experiments to test all of the variables involved.

Despite these difficulties, info-marketers must learn to always focus on a few key metrics that are easy to gather and analyze. Well, they may not be "easy" to gather, but at least they are straightforward and provide essential business statistics.

Essential Metric #1: Cost per Lead

The cost of a lead is determined by each individual medium. If you place an ad in a magazine, and the ad costs you $1,000, and you generate 100 leads from that ad, then the cost of the lead is $10. (Computation: $1,000 ad cost ÷ 100 leads = $10 per lead)

Let's make this a little bit more complicated.

If you place one ad for $1,000 in Journal A and another ad in Journal B for $500, and Journal A continues to get 100 leads while Journal B generates 25 leads, your cost per lead for Journal A is still $10, but your cost per lead for Journal B is $20. You will want to create tracking mechanisms so you know which leads come from which publications so you can calculate your lead cost for each ad.

Publication A		Publication B		Publication C	
Ad Cost	$1,000	Ad Cost	$500	Ad Cost	$1,500
Leads Generated	÷ 100	Leads Generated	÷ 25	Leads Generated	÷ 125
Cost per Lead	$10	Cost per Lead	$20	Cost per Lead	$12

You should not automatically abandon the more expensive lead generation systems for the less expensive. Even though you may not be making a profit with a particular medium, if you are able to generate new customers and offer them additional products and services later, it is still wise to continue to use the more expensive lead generator.

Essential Metric # 2: Product Cost/Gross Margin

One of the benefits of selling information products is that their manufacturing costs are quite low. Usually you are able to sell a product for 10 times or more what it costs to create. The cost of creating the product has nothing to do with the value of the product to your customer. In the info-marketing business, your product costs should be no more than 10 percent of your sales price. The marketing costs are going to be a large enough factor that most info-marketers try to avoid products with a sales price anything less than 10 times the cost of creating it.

Example: If you are selling a product priced at $500, then the cost to print materials, purchase binders, produce and print covers, reproduce audio, create audio jackets, generate reports, and pay for handling and storage should cost you $50 or less.

Please note: The 10 times markup is presented as a general industry average for a new product. Many info-marketers choose their prices for different reasons, including market conditions and volume considerations. This example is not to be considered price setting or creating minimum markups for the info-marketing industry. You are encouraged to set your own prices at whatever you wish to meet your individual business goals.

If your product sales price is $500 and your fulfillment cost is $50, then $450 is your gross margin.

Sales Price	$500
Fulfillment Costs	– $50
Gross Margin	$450

Essential Metric #3: Marketing Cost per Sale

Let's return to the example we created to illustrate cost per lead. Our cost of advertising in Journals A and B combined was $1,500 per month; those ads generated 125 leads.

Now you have to spend money to convert those 125 leads into sales. In your marketing sequence you have four or five letters, some faxes, and maybe some audio CDs to help sell your product, and these items cost you $20 per lead.

The good news is that 20 people purchased your product. Most people would be quick to focus on the response percentage (20 ÷ 125 = 16%), but that is meaningless. Instead, you should compute and track the cost per sale.

Cost of your sales process to convert a lead into a customer	$20
Number of leads put through that sales process	x 25
Total cost of sales conversion process	$2,500

Now your total market costs are $4,000. You spent $1,500 in lead generation materials to produce 125 leads. Then you sent a marketing campaign to those leads costing a total of $2,500. Therefore you have:

Lead generation advertising	$1,500
Marketing campaign to leads	+ $2,500
Total marketing costs	$4,000

Now we can calculate your marketing cost per sale.

Total marketing costs	$4,000
Divided by number of sales	÷ 20
Total marketing costs	$200
Plus product fulfillment costs	+$50
Total cost per sale	$250

So after considering all of the lead generation costs, marketing costs, and product fulfillment costs, you spent $250 to sell the $500 product. Many info-marketers would consider this a nice profit on a sale to obtain a new customer. Now you have a customer to sell the monthly subscriptions described in Chapter 7 and additional products described in Chapter 8.

Essential Metric #4: Return on Investment (ROI)

Return on investment is one of the key statistics info-marketers use to evaluate a medium. It is calculated by comparing total revenue to the lead generation media cost.

Let's return to our example from above. Our lead generation ads cost $1,500. From those leads we made 20 sales at $500 for total revenue of $10,000.

We calculate return on investment from those lead generation ads as follows:

Sales revenue	$10,000
Less total marketing costs	– $4,000
Return	$6,000
Divided by marketing costs	÷ $4,000
Equals ROI	150%

There are a lot of variations on the ROI calculation. Some info-marketers use net revenue to factor in sales and fulfillment costs. However, this is the calculation you hear quoted most often.

Essential Metric #5: Lifetime Customer Value

As your info-business transitions from a one-product business into an integrated info-marketing company, one of the key metrics will become lifetime customer value.

Lifetime customer value is calculated by tracking the purchases each customer makes over a period of time. Then you divide that figure by the number of customers that have purchased from you during the same period.

It is common to have a few customers that have purchased every-thing they possibly could from a business. Then there are a lot more customers that have made one purchase and never bought another item. This calculation tracks your ability to encourage your customers to buy additional products and services from you.

It is important to track this calculation based on segments of your customers. Here are several ways to compare the lifetime value of your customers:

- The lifetime value of customers who participate in your continuity program versus those who are not subscribers
- The lifetime value of customers who attend your boot camps versus those who do not
- The lifetime value of customers generated from one lead generation campaign versus the others
- The lifetime value of customers by region of the country, sex, and/or ethnicity

These details help info-marketers maximize their business opportunities. These metrics will show the info-marketer where to invest advertising dollars in order to find the customers that are most likely to have the highest lifetime value.

Business Issues

There are a number of business issues you need to consider as you develop your information business. Number one is merchant accounts.

Merchant Services Providers

Merchant services providers, as a rule, do not understand the information marketing business. At the Information Marketing Association we are working to educate them. All of our businesses have an FIC code that we assign to ourselves from the table of codes provided by the Internal Revenue Service.

Most info-marketers choose the code for a publisher. Publishers typically sell products and have relatively consistent revenues.

Certainly there are spikes when they come out with a new product, but the revenue generally falls within a range. An info-marketer's revenue can be very different. For a while you sell kits for $500 or $1,000 and continuity programs for $50 or $100 per month, and your revenue falls within a normal range.

But then you decide to hold a boot camp. Your registration fee is $2,500, and you have 200 people sign up. Suddenly you have half a million in sales! You have marketing expenses to pay, so you look in your checking account, but you don't see a deposit for all of this money. Not only do you not see the deposits for the boot camp, you don't see *any* deposits. Because your deposit pattern has changed with your merchant services provider, it has put a hold on all of your transactions.

Since merchant services is the primary way info-marketers get paid, you should be prepared to deal with people who do not understand your business and are, in general, suspicious of you. Your $30,000-a-year merchant services rep works all day in a cubicle, and it's his job to protect the credit card company from thieves who rack up a bunch of charges on customers' cards, don't deliver anything, and then take all of the money out of the checking account and skip town.

As an info-marketer you need to understand that people don't understand how your business works. That's why you must develop a strong relationship with your merchant services providers. You need them to trust you. You need them to be willing to work with you when you have revenue spikes in your business.

Finally, a Merchant Services Provider That Appreciates Info-Marketers, Understands the Business, and Wants to Help You Make More Money

Info-Marketer Resource

Info-marketers everywhere are shocked to learn that their merchant services providers consider them to be a liability. Even after these providers unconditionally accept your business, they can impose six-month holds on your money without notice, refund your customer charges, or cancel your account altogether.

Now there is an alternative. One merchant services provider likes info-marketers and wants your business, too. For a free, no obligation evaluation of your current merchant services needs and your future opportunities, visit **www.InfoMarketingMerchantServices.com**. Complete the quick form and someone will contact you right away.

Merchant Services With Info-Marketers in Mind

Info-Marketer Resource

Info-marketers, let Charge Today provide you with full-service merchant accounts and credit card processing solutions for today's demanding marketplace.

From merchant accounts, ACH/check services, secure gateways, and virtual and physical terminals to shopping carts, **ChargeToday. com** is the info-marketer's premier partner for credit card payment and processing solutions. For more information visit **www.Charge TodayInfo.com**. Complete the brief form and Charge Today will be in touch with you within 24 hours.

Look at your business from the merchant services providers' perspective. They feel like they are giving you a loan. Your boot camp customers have a right to charge back their $2,500 registration fee on their credit card for up to six months after the transaction. At five months and 28 days, your customer can call the credit card company and say "This is not right. I do not want to pay it." The credit card company has to give the customer credit, and then it has to look to you to collect the $2,500. If the credit card company doesn't believe you are going to be around in five and a half months, then it is not going to allow a charge to go through. If you are doing $50,000 per month in charges, in six months the merchant services provider will have $300,000 on the line. You know you are trustworthy, but your provider has to consider the worst-case scenario. It is your merchant services provider's job to protect the bank, not grow your business.

The Information Marketing Association has created a special relationship with merchant service providers to provide hassle-free credit card processing to help info-marketers get paid quickly for all of their transactions. For more information about making more money by more efficiently processing credit card transactions visit **www.Info MarketingMerchantServices.com**.

Regulatory Requirements

Info-marketers need to consider the regulations that might govern what they are doing. If you are providing weight loss information, then you need to understand the U.S. Food and Drug Administration's rules on weight loss offers. If you are selling to the dentistry or the chiropractic niche or to CPAs or attorneys, then you need to be aware of the types of regulatory issues that arise within those environments. While you do not have to warrant that the marketing programs you are doing are 100% legal for every person in every city in America, you need to be aware of regulatory issues so you are not systematically encouraging your customers to break the law. This needs to be part of your research within your niche. Make sure the products and services you offer comply with regulatory requirements.

You also need to be aware of the regulatory requirements within the info-marketing business. Whenever you make a claim or provide a testimonial, you need to be prepared to provide documentation for that claim or testimonial. Imagine that an investigator from the Federal Trade Commission shows up tomorrow with your sales letter and says, "Your letter tells the story of an individual who bought your product and made $100,000. Who is this person? Where is he, and how can we verify this?" You need a piece of paper with that story on it and the individual's signature that certifies the story is true. Does every info-marketer have every claim within every sales letter documented? I doubt it. However, you need to be prepared in case you are asked to document any of the claims you have made within your marketing materials.

If you have testimonials within your materials that claim a certain benefit, you need to know that those testimonials are viewed by the Federal Trade Commission as if you wrote them. They actually become your claims. So if a certain claim is illegal or not allowed, even though it was written by another person and then just dropped into your sales letter, you will be prosecuted as if that claim had been written by you. You are responsible for all of the claims within your marketing materials, whether they were written by someone else or by you. The FTC does not make any distinction between the two.

The Information Marketing Association provides ongoing information for all info-marketers to help them comply with the Federal Trade Commission's rules related to claims made and other marketing issues within sales letters.

Software

Some of the first things you will need within your information marketing business are software and technology tools to help automate your business. Whenever you create a multistep marketing sequence, you need a way to:

- Capture a prospect's name, address, fax number, and e-mail address
- Identify what lead generation marketing sequence created the lead

- Keep track of what you are sending to the lead
- Know when that individual chooses to buy so you can take him out of the marketing sequence and put him into the next sequence you do for your customers, such as a welcome sequence or a back-end sales sequence
- Keep in mind that you have different customers in all different stages of your marketing sequence. Some convert to customers right away, while others need to go through more steps of your marketing sequence before they buy. It can get unwieldy very quickly. Luckily, there are software solutions that can help you address this situation quickly and help you manage your processes.

Info-Marketing Lead, Order, and Fulfillment Processing Systems—A Comparison

With so many systems on the market for providing data management services, deciding which would be best for your business can be confusing to say the least. Some programs only perform one function, while other systems offer "all in one" programs that can do it all. An "all in one" may be the right choice, but as your business grows, it may be more beneficial to segment and use different systems for different functions. Why would anyone use several different systems? There are many reasons why, but the most important one is that each of the systems discussed below is the BEST on the market for at least one function of information and direct-response marketing. I will outline the strengths and weaknesses of each of these systems and show how, together, they can provide superior service for your direct-response marketing business. I will also discuss some of the "workarounds" necessary when using combinations of these systems.

InfusionSoft. By far, this is the best software for tracking client data and processing one-time online sales as well as offline sales. Information is easy to upload, store, search, download, and modify.

Clients can be entered with multiple addresses, telephone numbers, e-mail addresses, etc. On and offline campaigns, by way of action sequences, which can include e-mails, fulfillment, and timed step-mailings, are excellent and can be used to provide the regular contact with clients that direct-response marketers strive to achieve.

The search feature in InfusionSoft is superior. Clients can be found with minimal data, which is helpful when removing bad addresses from a mail campaign. We were recently able to find a client with only the first letter of the first name, first two numbers of the address, and three digits of the ZIP code visible on the returned envelope.

The contact merge feature is simple and useful when contacts appear multiple times, which happens when lists are uploaded from different sources. "De-duping" can be done on the entire list, new imports, or contacts that haven't been checked recently and can be checked by a single criterion, like e-mail address, or by multiple criteria, such as name, address, and/or e-mail address. Once the duplicate contacts have been identified, merging is easy and quick. Contacts can also be merged manually when a specific contact is found in the system more than once. During manual merges, you can choose specific information from each record that will be merged into the client's final record.

InfusionSoft's use of web forms for user-initiated online purchases is outstanding. While it is necessary to create a different form for each variant of a product you carry, this process is simple. Each form generates its own unique link that can then be integrated into your e-mails and/or web sites. Once a transaction is completed, an action sequence is initiated that can send customers an e-mail, take them to a success or thank-you page (or a failed transaction page for declined orders), put them into a group, remove them from other groups, and do a variety of other useful functions.

InfusionSoft is a high-quality program that has lots to offer direct-response marketers. While initially the sheer enormity of its potential can be quite overwhelming, there is customer support available, both online and offline.

For a free product tour, auto responder test drive, and online demonstration visit **www.InfoMarketingCRM.com**.

1ShoppingCart. 1ShoppingCart (**www.InfoMarketingShoppingCart. com**) surpasses all others in the area of online shopping carts. Its ability to allow multiple purchases per transaction is excellent. 1Shop also allows use of e-checks and PayPal as payment methods, allowing a wider audience to take advantage of your offers. 1Shop also offers an excellent affiliate program, allowing you to track sales by affiliate and to pay out commissions accordingly.

Regular use of 1Shop for daily e-mail contact is available, but 1Shop doesn't offer the ease of use or features found in AWeber. Clients can be contacted by use of auto-responders or put into groups to receive daily e-mail messages. These e-mails can be queued in advance and sent to multiple groups or to your entire database.

1Shop also allows easy use of the "bounce-back" offer for upgrades and add-ons to specific purchases. These can be cumbersome in InfusionSoft.

AWeber. This is the easiest system available for sending e-mails to multiple users. Lists are easy to create and can be used to assess marketing effectiveness. E-mails can be sent to one or multiple lists and uploaded and queued in advance for delivery on specific days and times. They can also be tracked for deliverability, "opened," and "click-through" rates. Each e-mail is also assigned a spam rating based on content, prior to sending. Content can then be modified to provide higher deliverability rates. With the increased use of BrightMail by ISPs to filter incoming mail, this feature is especially important in getting your message to your users.

AWeber (**www.AWeberEmail.com**) has strict rules regarding spam, including a 100% double opt-in by use of carefully tailored forms and an auto-responder e-mail from the list owners to verify their requests to receive your e-mails. These features have helped to increase AWeber's e-mail deliverability to ensure that your messages are treated as white mail, rather than gray mail.

Integration. One way to use multiple systems to maximize your marketing efforts is the following: XYZ Corp uses AWeber to send out a daily newsletter to its entire list pitching Package #134. A link in the newsletter sends clients to a web form created in InfusionSoft. Once the client purchases, he is sent to a " thank-you" page, which offers an opportunity to buy an upgrade product or products at a discount.

For another way to use multiple systems, consider the following example: Your clients opt into your AWeber newsletter by way of an online form on your web site that also requests a free report. Those clients are then downloaded from AWeber and uploaded into Infusion. An action sequence is applied that will download those names at specific intervals for the purpose of direct-response mailing pieces. Subsequent action sequences resulting from purchases will remove them from this group and will automatically put them into another group to receive different marketing pieces.

Info-Marketer Resource

Turnkey Customer Service for Info-Marketers

As you are beginning, especially if you are working out of your home without an office and without experience in these software products, it's a good idea to hire an expert to handle the setup and integration of your software. Best yet, the same company can also handle your customer service calls, sales, and product fulfillment. When you have a product and a marketing campaign and you are ready to get into business but need someone to help you get everything implemented, call Randy Sheiff of Sheif Services at 512/757-3603. He has a complete call center and a fulfillment and marketing systems staff to help you get your business implemented and run with the least amount of work necessary from you.

Info-Marketer Resource

Info-Marketer Information Systems

www.InfoMarketingCRM.com: A comprehensive customer relationship management system that provides marketing campaign execution, order processing, and member management. The largest information marketers use Infusion to run their businesses.

www.1ShoppingCart.com: This is the tool of choice for many online info-marketers. It is simple to implement and use. It has terrific affiliate campaign management and training systems. However, it is not convenient if you take a lot of orders offline since it only manages e-mail campaigns.

www.AWeber.com: The e-mail auto-responder system that currently provides the best e-mail deliverability in today's difficult e-mail delivery environment. This system easily integrates with Infusion's Manage Pro or 1ShoppingCart.

> **www.ConstantContact.com:** This is an e-mail auto-responder system that is similar to AWeber.com.
>
> **www.DydaComp.com:** Mail Order Manager—M.O.M. provides order processing along with inventory management and good reporting features. It does not have the marketing support features that are built into Infusion's ManagePro.

Knockoffs

One of the things you need to deal with as an info-marketer is other people who want to copy what you're doing and capture some of your success for themselves. They may be your own customers. They may be people who see your advertising and think you must be making a ton of money. They want to take advantage of the opportunity you have discovered by copying your product.

A lot of info-marketers spend a lot of time worrying about knock-offs. They order the knocked-off products, examine them, and get angry that the knock-off artist has stolen their stuff. And it *is* stealing. You do need to protect your intellectual property. You do need a good attorney to help you go after thieves and kick them out of your business. *But* you need to keep these knockoffs in perspective.

Instead of focusing your creative energy on getting rid of these pests, you should work at making your products so unique and your marketing methods so effective that it is totally impossible for anybody to compete with you. That is your best long-term strategy.

eBay

It's almost a compliment in the info-marketing business when someone starts selling your products on eBay, the world's flea market. Some people buy your product, keep it, and like it. Then after a few years go by, they decide to sell it on eBay. That doesn't hurt your business much. It's just one kit. Sometimes, however, people sell the original kit and then think, "It's just paper and CDs. I'll make copies and put those on eBay, too." This creates a black market for your product.

There are a number of ways to follow up on these eBay sales. You can contact the dispute resolution program and tell eBay you are the copyright holder. You can track the eBay user IDs that repeatedly sell your products and report them to eBay. You can even put a disclaimer in your product that your buyer does not have the right to resell it on eBay. That will eliminate any question that these are not legitimate sales.

One of the most successful ways to eliminate pirates who are selling your products on eBay is to sell on eBay yourself. You can create a very low-cost product that acts as a lead generating technique. Your eBay kit will include your name and some of the information in your full product. This strategy will actually help you find and sell to more

The Most Hated Martial Artist on the Planet

Info-Marketer Profile

Lieutenant X is the most hated martial artist on the planet. Chris Pizzo is a cancer survivor. So what do they have in common? They are one and the same man.

Cancer is a challenge no one wants to face, but overcoming that obstacle in his life is one of the things that led Chris into his successful career as an info-marketer. Likewise, no one (usually) sets out to become the most hated anything on the planet, but Chris's alter ego, Lieutenant X, is another key to his success.

Chris began his working life in the military, where he served for six years. After receiving a medical discharge so he could fight his cancer, Chris used the GI Bill to go to college. He is a classically trained graphic designer so he tried his hand on Madison Avenue—he left after five days because he didn't like the big city. He ended up ➡

designing toys for a while, which "was fun," Chris says, and eventually ended up teaching high school commercial art and business.

Not surprisingly, Chris's first product was education-based: **HomeWorkMotivator.com** helped students do better in school. He has since licensed that product to others.

After successfully fighting off cancer, Chris was ready to get back in shape. He turned to the sport that had always been a part of his life: close combat martial arts. That's where Lieutenant X enters the story.

Chris created his Lieutenant X identity after one of those accidents that turn out to be a good thing. "At first I was making more money with my educational products, and by accident I sent out an e-mail for the martial arts information to the educational parents. And that didn't go over too well. So I realized I had to have two separate identities," Chris explains.

Chris muses, "I'm a nice guy, but (as Lieutenant X) I am the most hated martial artist on the planet. Lieutenant X and **TopSecretTraining.com** became the scourge of the Internet discussion boards. Because nobody knew who Lieutenant X was, everybody was being accused of being Lieutenant X."

Chris kept his identity a secret for a long time. As long as he was selling his video on the Internet, it was easy. When it came time to do seminars and boot camps, his secret came out—but people weren't all that interested in letting Lieutenant X retire. "What's funny is right before the Glazer-Kennedy Info Summit last year, I actually tried to get rid of the Lieutenant X personality, but nobody even cares about Chris Pizzo; they want Lieutenant X. I couldn't get rid of it. So now I'm branded Chris 'Lieutenant X' Pizzo," Chris laughs.

Chris sought out partners to help him develop his info-business in the martial arts industry. "I brought people in because it's a very strange market. There's a lot of competition with very big players ➡

in it," Chris says. "My big pet peeve is why reinvent the wheel? I needed a lot of content very fast, so we structured a deal where everybody wins. My partners are now making more money than they ever dreamed of, and so am I."

Product Packaging to Increase Customer Value and Earn More Money

Chris believes there are only three or four ways to make money in martial arts. "You can open a school and bang your head against the wall. You can become a fighter and get your head knocked in. Or you can sell videos. And so I analyzed what everybody else was doing and figured out a way to improve it," Chris says.

For $87 per month he provides a 20-minute video, a curriculum lesson, and on-demand streaming video on the Internet. "I just hooked up a high definition camera in the training school, and we record lessons we are teaching anyway and then broadcast them on the membership site," Chris explains.

For more information about Chris Pizzo visit his web site at **www.NobleTraining.com** or see the expanded profile at **www.Info MarketingBook.com/Pizzo**.

customers. So, yes, fight the pirates who are stealing your product.

From Computer Manuals to "Info Millions"

Bob Serling is a software engineer with a flair for writing. He got his start in information marketing as a direct-response copywriter, but his first writing job was rewriting computer manuals to make them understandable for his colleagues at the bank where he worked.

"Those manuals were written so poorly that even the IBM engineers who worked on mainframe computers in the 1970s couldn't understand them," Bob says. "So, I reworked the technical writing and threw in a little humor to make them easier to get through." A PR agency saw Bob's work and asked him to do some copywriting. "I still remember my first assignment. It was for a Valentine's Day brunch for a restaurant chain," Bob laughs. "But it was fun, and I didn't have to work on boring computers, so I started my new career in copywriting."

Bob started studying his new craft. He happened to know Gary Halbert, so he started with Halbert's materials, publications by Melvin Powers, and a book by Victor Schwab called *How to Write a Great Advertisement*, a classic direct-marketing book. "I realized I had a bit of an edge with my background in computers and in banking and finance, so I started running ads in the trade magazines for people who needed copywriters who understood technical and financial information," Bob says, "and I quickly built a pretty good client list."

He used his technical copywriting skills as a bridge to get into direct-sales copywriting. "I'd write their brochures and some of their collateral pieces, and then eventually I'd ask my clients if I could write direct-mail pieces for them. It just grew from there," Bob explains.

Bob's transition into information marketing came when he realized he was "giving out a lot of free advice." So he redefined himself as a consultant and started charging for his information. "I was making more money than I was writing copy, which is very labor intensive," Bob says. "I enjoyed consulting more, and then it was just natural to create information products—both as a passive stream of income and also as lead generators."

His first information product taught people how to create their own info-products quickly and easily by using a tape recorder. "I showed them how to use a tape recorder and their own voice—either interviewing themselves or interviewing others," Bob explains. Paul Hartunian and a couple of other people picked up ➡

on that book and really spread it around, so I had a lot of joint ventures helping to sell my first product."

To market his information products, Bob mails to his own list and to others' lists through joint ventures. To build his own list, Bob uses an e-zine and regularly sends press releases that offer a bait piece—10-minute interviews with 21 different marketing experts asking them for their absolute best, most reliable marketing technique or strategy.

Bob's list got a tremendous boost when Yahoo Business picked up one of his press releases. "It just flattened my web site twice," Bob laughs. "We added more servers and more bandwidth and brought it back up, and within six hours it was flattened again. The traffic that came from Yahoo Business was immense!"

This software engineer turned copywriter turned information marketer has only good things to say about information marketing. "It's given me two things. First, it's given me a lot more freedom to pursue the things I love, like sailing. It's really fun to go on vacation or even go out to dinner and then come home and check your sales log," Bob says. "I mean, you can go on vacation, spend $10,000 or $15,000, come home after 10 days, and you've generated $30,000 or $40,000 in sales that more than paid for that vacation and everything else while you were gone."

Because of his background of being a software engineer, Bob describes himself as being "process oriented." He stresses the importance of coming up with a process so you don't have to repeat yourself over and over again: "It's important in creating your products to have a system, and that's what I developed into my first info-product course called 'Info Millions,'" Bob says. "It's a recipe. I do step one, two, three, four, five, six, and then, boom, I've got my product. You don't have to reinvent that process over and over again. That way you can spend your own personal time doing the things that are the most important—like the strategy to grow your business or the mar- ➡

keting you're going to use to implement that strategy."

Bob believes another benefit of having a process is the ability to turn day-to-day activities over to an assistant or even have them automated. "You can have a follow-up sequence of e-mails, or you can intersperse e-mails and letters, but a lot of that's automated and the part of it that isn't automated can be run by someone other than you because it's a repeatable, reproducible system that's run the same way over and over again," Bob explains.

Bob has two products that can be offered to others' lists as a joint venture. His "Information Products Master Course" is a complete course on creating and marketing information products. It expands on his original "Info Millions," adding comprehensive information on using the Internet to market products and to research what is selling well in the business arena.

Bob's second product, "Killer Copywriting Simplified," shows people how they can use seven simple blocks to create e-mail copy, web-page copy, sales letters, and space advertisements.

When seeking others' products to offer to his list as a joint venture opportunity, Bob looks for three main topics that are important to his customer base: (1) product development; (2) traffic generation; and (3) conversion.

Bob's web site is at **www.DirectMarketingInsider.com**. For an expanded profile of Bob Serling and his info-business visit **www.InfoMarketingBook.com/Serling**.

From Making Corporate Sales Calls to Making Money in His Sleep

Troy White used to sell computers for big companies like Hewlett Packard. "I just got sick of it," Troy says, "and decided to follow that entrepreneurial dream and go out on my own."

Troy started "playing around with words" and discovered how important they are to marketing. "I didn't really understand what a copywriter was, so I took an Internet Marketing Center course with Cory Rudl (**www.Info-Marketing.org/Internet**) and worked with Ted Nicholas for a year. So it was a pretty good start to my copywriting career."

Troy's wife had planned a lot of weddings, so a natural first product for them was a themed wedding planning how-to. He also does a lot of freelance copywriting for other people. "That's about 75 percent of what I do, but I want to change that," Troy says. "I've been teaching seminars locally for the average small business owner who's never written a promotion in their life. I just try to make it simple for them."

Troy is quick to point out that most of his clients already know the value of good copywriting. "People who don't understand the importance of words won't understand why somebody would pay thousands of dollars to have a promotional piece written," Troy says, "but people who are already doing decent marketing and who have experimented with this—they get it."

Troy has a number of home study courses that consist of mainly printed materials in binders with accompanying CDs or DVDs. He also sells books as well as recordings and transcripts from live seminars. His "Classical Sales Letter Success" course is for the average business owner who wants to learn how to write better promotions.

➡

Originally a one-day event, Troy no longer presents the materials on stage; he just sells the course.

Other products include a yearly calendar of templated letters themed around unusual holidays, a how-to on using newsletters, and a prewritten marketing letter that can be personalized. "These products are mainly for people who are doing O.K. in business but know they could be doing better. They just need someone to show them how," Troy explains.

Troy markets his products via a number of web sites that collect leads. "I do different types of campaigns for those leads, including a print newsletter—a four-page freebie that I send out to both clients and prospects—and I'm bringing out a paid newsletter about small business strategies as well," he says.

Since Troy has done a lot of work with authors writing Amazon campaigns, he is targeting that niche. "I've partnered with a lady who has used PR to sell millions of books and other products over the years. We're starting to help a lot more authors, and I'm thinking about how I can niche one of my sales letter products into the author market. Most authors don't understand that the book is definitely not a business," Troy explains. "They think they'll get rich off a single book, and it's just never going to happen. That or they're so caught up in the information they don't care whether it'll make money!"

For more information about Troy White visit **www.WildWest Wealth.com**, call 403/259-4566, or fax 403/259-2092. For the expanded Troy White profile visit **www.InfoMarketingBook.com/ White**.

Chapter 10

Step 9: Avoiding the Common Info-Marketing Mistakes Before They Find You

by Robert Skrob
President, Information Marketing Association

I'M OFTEN ASKED, "ROBERT, HOW DO YOU GET IT ALL DONE?" I PER- sonally publish three monthly newsletters and two bimonthly newsletters. My office publishes several other newsletters in which I have less involvement. This is in addition to all of the member sales letters, tele-seminar notices, e-mail sequences, etc., that have to be written, plus several consulting engagements a month, monthly coaching calls, and best practices calls.

I distinctly remember a few years ago listening to Dan Kennedy say that success is messy. He said you have to create a mess, with more customers than you can accommodate, and sometimes you'll fall behind on deadlines—that is what success is all about. While he hated falling behind on deadlines and did what he had to do to get caught up, sometimes customers would become aggravated.

I thought to myself, "I can be better than that. I'll be successful, but I won't make mistakes. I'll make deadlines; I'll get everything perfectly formatted and never send out anything with errors."

I cannot possibly explain to you how much money that attitude cost me. Lots of people talk about missed opportunities, and they throw out all these big numbers. So please don't allow my big number to put you off—being overly particular has cost me over $1 million. At least! While I'm formatting a letter so the margins are the same at the top and the bottom, I'm losing the opportunity to send out another sales letter to other prospects.

If you are trying to be perfect, to eliminate all errors, learn from my mistake. Let go of your fear of getting embarrassed. Sure, it is humiliating to be caught in a mistake. When it happens to me I feel like an idiot, and I'm afraid of a negative backlash of members' comments.

The only reason I accomplish as much as I do is because I decided to let go of the illusion of perfection. Instead I'm grasping for production and what I call "finish."

Yes, I drive everyone in the office crazy with "finish." They may spend hours creating a sequence of e-mails or working on a product. However, I have to tell them: If it isn't finished, it's as if you never did anything at all. It's enough to make someone cry (as I've come to learn).

But it's true. Even if you spend 100 hours creating an information product, if you don't have a sales letter out there generating customers, if you aren't making sales and shipping product, then you have completely wasted your time. Your goal is creating sales, not creating products. Skip straight to the sales part; the products will come along.

The last bit of work to make a job complete often drags out. Vendors get slow, outside contributors go missing, or interruptions prevent you from getting a task completed. It often seems like a conspiracy. As if the whole world were ganging up against you.

My work production has increased so much I've had to go from one graphic designer to seven. I've hired designers from in town, around the country, and as far away as India. At the same time I've had to identify seven different printers. Since all of my newsletters have to get designed, printed, and mailed at the end of the month, no one team can get all that done in time. I need several teams moving on a parallel track.

Before I became an info-marketer I would have had all of this laid out in advance. There would have been a production meeting, and everyone would have talked. We would have coordinated everything so there were no problems in production. That's when I was totally broke. Of course I had time to carefully plan each step of every project—I didn't have enough customers to keep me busy!

The real truth is I would *never* get anything done with those habits. The only reason I get so many new products created is because I've already sold them and have customers expecting delivery. By focusing on the selling, I create a situation where I can't help but deliver what was promised. It's a lot more painful, but I'm convinced this discomfort is a good thing. Having a lot of products moving forward, all with dozens of unanswered questions, is a necessary part of success. Otherwise, you have nothing.

My humble advice: I've done it the wrong way for years. I was too fussy. I told myself I could be better than Dan Kennedy. I told myself I could match his production *and* get it done without errors, on time. Wrong.

By letting go of my compulsion to make everything perfect, by focusing on my goal of making sales and only then creating the products to fulfill those sales, I've been able to make huge leaps in productivity *and* in financial reward.

I am going to talk through some of the common mistakes info-marketers make so you can prevent problems within your business before they start. This will get you started quickly and save you a ton of money and aggravation.

Putting the Product First

Info-marketers can get too wrapped up in the product they have created. It's almost like birthing a child. They've been on this yearlong odyssey to create something people will want to buy. Now they are so proud of it that they cannot see beyond it. They can't be objective about who would want it and why it was created in the first place.

Successful info-marketers always keep the market first. They always focus on evaluating their customers and what they want. Successful info-marketers pay attention to their customers' responses to marketing. They ask customers questions. They respond to questions they receive by making improvements in their business. With each comment they receive, they are always evaluating the market and what their potential customers want from them. They put the market first.

And if they have to throw away their product and create a new one, well, they are not all that happy about it. But because they are keeping their market first, they are not so worried about their unwanted product. They focus on the need to replace it with a new one that people do want. The minute a product is proving unsuccessful within a market, you have to get rid of it and create a new product. You cannot fix a bad product with good marketing. Sometimes you just need to start over.

Becoming Obsessed With the Product

There is no perfect product for any particular niche, so there is no reason for you to be obsessed or worried or hopeful that you are going to create the perfect product. What you need to do is create *something*. Get something done and move forward with it as fast as you can. Then you can move on to the next product and the next. If you become obsessed with a two-year quest to put together the perfect product, you are not going to make money at it.

A lot of authors let book selling become their obsession. They have devoted their entire lives to some particular study, and they decide to impart their wisdom to everybody in the world. So they create this very detailed treatise on a particular issue, and it turns out nobody wants to buy it. The book is so thoroughly researched and so well done that they lose sight of the fact that nobody wants it. They continue marketing it in spite of all good common sense.

As info-marketers we are not concerned about a particular product or a particular delivery mechanism. We just want to give customers what they want in a way that meets our needs and solves their problems. Beyond that we are not going to lose sleep over the two weeks spent creating a product. Sure, we hate to throw it away and have to create a new one. But we just move on, create the next product, and generate the next customer.

Insufficient Research

It is startling to me how quickly I can stump a new info-marketer about the research he has done about his marketplace. I ask about the number of customers, the number of customers by region, the types of things individuals buy, the types of individuals within the market area, the terms used in the market. It turns out that very few individuals know all that much about their marketplace.

You must become the foremost expert in the market you are selling to. Quite honestly, there cannot be anybody who knows more about this particular market than you. And if you are marketing in a niche, if you are marketing to a subculture, you need to live and breathe this group, understand what these people feel, see life from their perspective, and do every bit of research possible to make sure you know what is going through their minds. That's the only way to be prepared to sell to them.

Copying Something That Is Not Working or Not Profitable

It is easy to look in a magazine and think you know what is happening in a business you see advertised. Maybe you are looking through a business opportunity magazine, and you see somebody selling a particular business opportunity, so you write to him. He writes back and says it is $10. You pay your $10. You get the sales letter, and the kit costs $495. You could buy that kit and make money. But you look at it and think, "Maybe instead of just buying this, I ought to knock off what he is doing. I have the ad, and I have the sales letter. Now for 500 bucks I can have the product and get into my own business of selling it."

Or let's say you go to a boot camp and hear a speaker who offers a product for sale. Maybe it is a $1,000 product. Maybe 80 people get up, go to the back of the room, and buy the product. You look at that and go, "Man, $80,000 just got made there. That is fantastic."

What you must remember is that in all of these businesses there are costs involved in making those sales that you can't see from the outside. You should not be too eager to jump in without doing adequate research into a business that you may not completely understand.

As we discussed in Step 7, many businesses are operated on the front end at break even or even at a loss. By the time you factor in the ad costs and the leads that did not convert, it might have cost $1,000 to get a $500 sale. If you are too eager to jump into a business without completely understanding it, you could end up losing a lot of money. To make money you have to have the back-end revenue opportunities in place. You must completely evaluate a business and determine what is going on before you try to jump in. Better yet, rather than trying to copy something you do not know is working (or how it is working), do your own research, find your own market, and sell your own product.

Bad Economics

We discussed before that an information product is usually sold for at least 10 times its cost to produce. I see too many info-marketers selling a new book or other product for $19.95. That just doesn't provide enough money to do sales properly.

You can generate a whole lot of web traffic, capture a bunch of interested individuals, and have a decent conversion on a web site. But if you are only selling a $19.95 book, you are doing a lot of work for very little money.

It is better to create a $500 product and then figure out what you need to do to justify a $500 price tag to your customers. Then when you get one sale you will generate $500 in revenue. It would take 25 sales of your $19.95 book to come up with that same $500. Just because a product costs 25 times as much does not mean it is 25 times harder to sell it.

Do not be afraid to try to sell something at a higher price. It gives you a huge advantage within the marketplace because you can afford to do more marketing. That is a very strong position to be in. If the economics of your business allow you to spend more than anyone else to acquire a customer, then you are going to have a huge advantage over everybody else doing business within that niche.

Bad Projections

A lot of info-marketers have an entirely wrong idea of how many people are going to respond to their particular ad or sales campaign. In general, accurate projections are only going to come through experience.

You cannot take someone else's projections, the numbers you hear thrown out in an article or a seminar, and try to estimate what you are going to get. Unfortunately, the numbers never work the same twice, so you shouldn't base your projections on them.

Instead, you should base your projections on your revenue generated per ad minus your cost per sale, and your production costs and refunds. Do not create unrealistic projections and set yourself up to be disappointed.

Being a Pioneer

You do not want to try to pioneer a new method, a new market, a new anything. Instead, you should apply time-tested techniques and messages to slightly different situations. So if you find a market with no info-marketer in it, do not try to reinvent info-marketing for that market. Use one of the tried and true methods and adapt it.

You do not want to be the pioneer blazing new territory. That is the most expensive position to be in. It is actually a lot easier to go into a niche or a market where someone is already selling, create a product that is unique from anything else being offered, and then offer your product to that market. That way someone else has already done all the hard work, and you are able to walk in and make a lot of money.

Not Realizing Good Enough Is Good Enough

As I explained at the beginning of this chapter, one of the most difficult things for me in the information marketing business was getting over my compulsion to make everything perfect. Quite frankly, the customer does not care if all your grammar is correct. They do not care if all your spelling is correct. They are buying what you know because of the promised benefits they are going to receive.

The way the product looks and comes across, whether the CDs have labels or not, and whether the book is spiral bound or in a three-ring notebook, have nothing to do with whether or not the customer will like it. The color of the cover does not matter.

Here is what *does* matter: Does the content deliver the promised benefit? As long as your customers get the promised benefit, then your product is good enough. If you start having to make refunds, that is the time to address how to improve the product. But do not try to anticipate every possible outcome before you try to sell the product.

Good enough is good enough. Get it done, get it sold, and then worry about making small changes in your product and marketing later. You are never going to have everything 100% perfect. Anything you publish today you are going to hate three months from now. So you might as well just get it published, get it done, and learn from doing.

Don't get paralyzed by continually adding to the idea, tweaking the idea, thinking about it, and worrying over it until you never get anything done (other than think about it for a long time). Good enough is good enough. Get it done, get it out, and move on to the next project.

Chapter 11

The Big Picture: Advanced Info-Marketing Business Models

by Robert Skrob
President, Information Marketing Association

N
OW THAT YOU'VE SEEN THE DETAILS OF BUILDING THESE BUSI-
nesses, it's important to take a step back to look at the big
picture of how these businesses are built.

An analysis of all of the business models could easily
fill a book in itself. However, I will show you the things that make
each model unique as well as the things that are pretty consistent in
all of them.

I've listed these business models in chronological order, that is,
roughly when they were developed and publicized within the info-
marketing industry. There was a lot of crossover, and there were early
adopters doing certain things before others were, so this won't be a
completely accurate historical account. But you will see that it makes
sense to use a chronological format, because one idea builds upon the
other.

Product Sales

A product sales info-business is the oldest business model. For hundreds of years individuals have been selling information. There are plenty of historical accounts of nomads who sold maps and directions to businesspeople so they could find new markets in which to sell their goods.

Product sales businesses sell individuals products. Generally you can recognize this model in a mature business because it will have dozens of products. To get the most value out of its past customers, a business has to create and offer new products to get repeat sales from its customers.

A lot of info-marketers have catalogs of products, either printed or online. Each product has different elements or addresses different topics within its market.

One of the advantages of this model is the info-marketer has numerous products to attract different types of new customers. Info-marketers using this model can offer their products in several markets at the same time or rotate several product offerings within the same market. This allows them to attract customers in many different ways.

A lot of info-marketers use the multiproduct model today, but most use it in conjunction with one of the other models. The downside is you must create a new product and get a customer to make an individual buying decision each time you make a sale.

Running an Info-Business in Only 27 Minutes Each Day

Info-Marketer Profile

Robert W. Bly is a newcomer to the information marketing industry, but chances are you have seen his work in print—and you may even know his name.

Before putting his own information product online, Bob spent 25 years as a freelance direct response copywriter. His clients include Agora Publishing, Rodale, AARP, American Writer's and Artists Institute, and dozens of newsletter publishers, technologies companies, financial services, and health-care companies.

He is also the author of more than 70 traditionally published books. His best-known book is *The Copywriters Handbook*, published in 1985 by Henry Holt, and he has written on a wide variety of other topics.

"A lot of them have been on business and marketing topics," Bob says, "and communications and writing. For example, I wrote a best-selling business-writing book called *The Elements of Business Writing*. But I've done other things. I've written a book on sex. I've written a book on Star Trek. I've written books on careers and computers. I wrote a book on Stephen King. I wrote a humor book called the *I Hate Kathy Lee Gifford Book*. So I've done a lot of different stuff."

While the books about Star Trek, Kathy Lee, and Stephen King were more fun to write, Bob's books on copywriting and business writing are what launched his career. "My first book, *The Elements of Technical Writing*, accelerated my career and was my means of establishing myself in advertising," Bob says. "Other people could run ads, give speeches, or network at direct marketing association functions, but I wrote books."

Traditional wisdom might argue against the value of writing books. Some beginning info-marketers believe if you put everything you ➡

know in a book and teach readers what to do, they won't need to hire you. Bob disagrees. "No, it's the complete opposite. What happens is when you write a book or an article or an information product, people listen to it and say, 'Boy, this guy knows what he's doing,' and 'Boy, that's a lot work; I don't want to do that. I'll hire him to do it.'"

So why would a successful published author "jump ship" into information marketing? Bob explains: "The book publishing industry is an industry with problems. A lot of people seek to have a 'book-book' published, because there's a status to it. But I've had it over 70 times. It doesn't do anything for me anymore."

Encouraged by friends and colleagues in the publishing business—including university publishers Johns Hopkins University and Harvard—Bob decided to try selling his books on the Internet.

At first Bob was hesitant. "I remember telling people, 'I'm really happy doing what I'm doing, and I'm so busy. Between copywriting and writing books, I work 12 hours a day,'" Bob recalls. "I also stayed away from Internet marketing because I viewed it as too detailed oriented. I'm not a detail person. It seemed like the technical parts were beyond me. Plus, I envisioned myself having to wrap up books in my bedroom and then mailing them out myself. I didn't want to do that, so I stayed away from the Internet."

Midlife finally nudged Bob forward. "About a year ago, I woke up one day and thought, 'I'm almost 50, and I've kind of lost interest in writing books,'" Bob explains. "I still love writing copy, but if I don't write books I want something else to do. My friend had been bugging me to do it, so without much thought I put together my first product."

Bob was able to assemble his product in just a day or two. He owned the rights to a series of columns he had written for *Writers Digest Magazine* on how to make six figures as a freelance writer. He added several more articles and other content he had written, ➡

gave it all to a graphic designer, and ended up with an e-book called *Write and Grow Rich*.

It wasn't long before Bob was sold on Internet marketing. "There's something about when you get the first check!" Bob exclaims. "That first sale on Click Bank or PayPal when you see, ding, $29 or $200 or whatever it is, it changes your life."

Bob has translated his experience into another product, "The Internet Marketing Retirement Program," to help others succeed. His program describes four stages of Internet information marketing.

At his web site, **www.Bly.com**, he has landing pages or domain names reserved for about 50 products. After only a year in the business, Bob already has 25 products and within a few months expects to have 50 or 60.

Bob is able to take his print books (to which he owns the copyrights), make simple updates, and convert them into e-books. For example, a 200-page book turned into three e-books, and the increase in income from the electronic version was dramatic. "When I sold it originally, it was a $10 book. I would get 8 percent (80 cents). My agent would get his cut, so I'd end up with only 72 cents for that content. Now it's three e-books priced at $29 or $39 each, so when I sell that same content, I get $90. Plus, I keep it all!" Bob says.

Bob works in his online business for just 27 minutes each day, and he's already making $200,000 a year, mostly by sending a weekly e-mail to his customer list. "I have a couple of assistants for my copywriting business, and I've given one of them some of the tasks of managing the online business. I outsource everything, so all I do is write my weekly e-mail," Bob explains.

Bob Bly's web site, along with links to his products and their sales pages, are available at **www.Bly.com**. For the expanded profile visit **www.InfoMarketingBook.com/Bly**.

Newsletter Publishing

One of the oldest and most traditional info-marketing business models is the publisher offering a monthly newsletter. Some common examples are Bottom Line Reports or Agora Publishing. Both are very large companies that publish a dozen or more newsletters that are marketed both to businesses and consumers. Publishers most often charge an annual membership fee, and the newsletters are delivered weekly, every two weeks, or monthly depending on the type of publication. Some publishers also offer daily e-mail bulletins.

These businesses rely on the front-end subscription price for the majority of their revenue. Many publishers offer add-on tele-seminars. They also offer meetings and events; however, meetings do not make up as large a percentage of their income as they do for traditional info-marketers.

It is difficult to sell a newsletter subscription as a front-end offer. In your offer you try to tell prospects how important this information is and how much they need it, and then you turn around and say "and that is why we are going to give it to you in equal installments over the next 12 months." If you get somebody excited about something and really wanting something, then they want a lot of it. And after they are excited about it, then you can dribble it out to them on an ongoing basis. That is what led to the development of our next business model.

JPDK

"How to Make $4,000 a Day Sitting at Your Kitchen Table in Your Underwear" by Jeff Paul was published by JPDK Publishing. JPDK stands for Jeff Paul and Dan Kennedy. They worked together to publish this product nationwide and have had an amazing amount of success. They have marketed through magazines, infomercials, and a variety of other media and have promoted this model of information marketing for many years.

What sets this model apart from its newsletter ancestors is an initial sale of a "kit." The kit is a group of products—CDs and binders with a couple of different manuals and a variety of sales and marketing techniques. All of the front-end marketing is devoted to selling this kit, this box of information. The power of this model is that the price of the kit is easily 10 times the cost of production. That pays for a lot of marketing to acquire a new customer. Once you sell the kit to a new customer, then you create a marketing sequence to get the member to subscribe to your monthly newsletter. Newsletter subscribers are then sold boot camps, coaching, and other programs and services.

The JPDK model was completely revolutionary because it drastically increased the marketing you could afford to generate new customers. Before JPDK, if your newsletter subscription was $200 a year, then $200 a year was all you had available to market and acquire another customer. However, if you have a kit sale of $1,000 where $900 of the price is profit, then you have $900 to go find a new customer. Plus, it is also much easier to convert your kit-buying customers into newsletter subscribers.

This model took a huge step forward when info-marketers discovered monthly continuity. It used to be you would sell a certain percentage of your kit-buyers on your monthly newsletter. This was far more subscriptions than you were able to sell without the kit sale. But it was only half of what you could generate if you sold your newsletter subscriptions by using forced monthly continuity.

Using forced continuity, you sell your kit bundled with two or three months' worth of free membership in your continuity program. Then after the free trial offer expires, your customers are automatically billed for the monthly continuity. Now, it is important to do two things. One, you tell your customers they will be billed, and two, you make sure they are comfortable with it, maybe even bribe them with a special offer if they don't cancel during the free trial period. You will get many more people into your program that stay in when it is forced on them through continuity. It is much more successful than getting people to opt in and send a check for your annual membership.

The JPDK model is a front-end kit sale where all front-end customers buy the kit as their first point of entry in the business. Afterward they are put into a forced continuity program and kept on a monthly subscription. That way the info-marketer can sell other back-end products and services to those customers.

A Different Sort of ELF™

Info-Marketer Profile

Joe Polish is a former carpet cleaner who began teaching ELF™ marketing to other carpet cleaners and has now expanded his business to target a growing group of marketing professionals in a myriad of industries.

Any visions of Santa and the North Pole aside, ELF™ stands for "easy, lucrative, and fun." Joe says you can have an ELF™ business, or you can have a HALF™ business, which stands for "hard, annoying, lame, and frustrating."

Joe explains, "I only want to teach and deliver processes and strategies that really are ELF™—easy, lucrative, and fun. My philosophy is you have to be willing to destroy anything in your life or in your business that is not excellent."

Life wasn't always ELF™ for Joe; he was living a HALF™ business nightmare, running a carpet cleaning company. "I ran my carpet cleaning company for a couple of years, living off credit cards, basically being broke. I learned marketing because I needed to eat, not because I ever thought I would be writing courses on it, teaching seminars, publishing newsletters, or creating audio and video information products," Joe says. ➡

Sometimes you just need a little help from a friend, and lucky for Joe, that's what he got. "A friend of mine gave me a Gary Halbert newsletter," Joe recalls. "I was fascinated with that newsletter, especially the Halbert Index, which is a unique way of classifying people. It was the perfect newsletter for me to read because I'd never been exposed to anything like it. Gary's writing is very 'in your face,' compelling copy. It was engaging, as any good marketing should be."

But Joe balked a bit at the newsletter's price. "When my friend told me he paid $197 a year to subscribe, the first words out of my mouth were, 'That's a lot of money. You can get a book for less than that.' It's a good thing my friend pushed back," Joe laughs. "He told me to keep reading, and a few pages later Gary had written, 'A smart person is someone that would rather pay $1,000 for 10 pages of useful information than $10 for 300 pages of fluff.' It was the perfect message for me at the time, and I've never forgotten it: smart people measure the benefit of information not by the pound but by the *value* of the information."

Joe was hooked. He immediately purchased a set of Halbert's videos for $2,000. (He had to put it on his credit card; at that point he was still a starving carpet cleaner.)

Joe wasn't starving for long. He put what he learned from Halbert's videos to very good use. "I started putting headlines in my ads," Joe says. "I started using education-based marketing and hired a local copywriter to write a consumer's guide to carpet cleaning, which was all of the same information I gave people over the phone. I had never documented that information in a form I could replicate, so my sales pitch was always live. To use a Gary Halbert term, I started 'canning and cloning myself' by taking my sales message and putting it into print. So my first sales letter was a consumer's guide to choosing a carpet cleaner."

FIGURE 11-1. To promote this new info-business and his elite networking group, Joe Polish buys display advertising in *Entrepreneur* magazine and several other business publications.

Choosing a carpet cleaner might not sound very exciting, but Joe learned to use compelling copy to draw his customers in. "One of my favorite pieces of copy was 'Crawling Critters and Crud: A Guide to the Slime, Grime and Livestock That's Seeping, Creeping and Galloping Through Your Carpet,'" Joe laughs. He reinforced those hair-raising words with photos of a dust mite magnified hundreds of times and a cute little baby. As you can imagine, the headline "Who's Crawling on Who?" really grabbed the attention of every mom who saw it!

Next, Joe began using a free recorded message to market his carpet cleaning services. "After I started doing that, people no longer called me saying 'How much do you charge?' because my free recorded message did what all good marketing should do—it sifted, sorted, and screened people, attracting the ones I wanted to attract and repelling the ones that were just price shoppers and didn't fit what I was looking for," Joe explains.

The results of Joe's new marketing strategies were nothing short of amazing. "I ended up taking this small carpet cleaning company that was doing $2,000 a month, and within a six-month period I took it to over $12,000 a month without buying a single piece of different equipment and without learning anything more about carpet cleaning. I simply changed the message on my communications, on my flyers, on my business cards, and on the side of my van. I put my free recorded message offer on everything," Joe says.

Joe "dipped his toe in the water" of information marketing by selling one of his ads to a couple of other carpet cleaning companies. The results were amazing. Within a few months, one of Joe's clients had made $62,000 from the $250 yellow page ad Joe had sold him. "After seeing these results I knew I needed to package this up and sell it to other carpet cleaners!" Joe exclaims. ➤

Joe ran a small lead generation ad driving people to a free recorded message to request a free report. "From that ad that cost me $138, I ended up selling $7,000 worth of marketing courses on my very first campaign," he says, "and within one year of launching my new information marketing business—doing nothing but selling a kit for between $497 to $697—I sold $250,000 worth of courses. The next year I sold a half-million dollars. The year after that I sold $1 million. The rest, as they say, is history," Joe chuckles.

Joe believes a big part of information marketing is getting people to trust you. One of the ways Joes earns this trust is through his "Genius Network Interview Series." As part of his information marketing business for carpet cleaners, Joe conducts a monthly interview. Each month Joe records a conversation with an author, a celebrity, or a successful businessperson to discover the keys to what has made that person successful.

Joe's "Genius Network Interviews" have become a product in and of themselves, allowing Joe to expand beyond his original niche into markets he never would have had access to otherwise. His 140-plus interviews include info-marketing gurus Dan Kennedy, Jeff Paul, and Gary Halbert; financial experts Robert Kiyosaki and David Bach; and many athletes, entertainers, and other celebrities. These interviews have given Joe access to a lot of bright people, and he is building a great list of contacts. This has opened the door to a new information marketing business based on these interviews, so Joe can expand his business beyond carpet cleaners to all businesspeople.

Go to **www.JoePolish.com** or **www.GeniusNetwork.com** for more information or e-mail **Support@JoePolish.com**.

For the complete info-marketer profile visit **www.InfoMarketing Book.com/Polish**.

Digital Delivery

As the Internet became more popular and marketing through the Internet became more common, a lot of info-marketers took the JPDK model and put it online. That is the majority of the businesses we see. Most info-marketers' web sites have a page you visit that promises to solve a problem and asks the web visitor to provide his name and e-mail address. This is called a squeeze page. When the visitor puts his name and e-mail address into the squeeze page, he sees the marketing message.

This is very similar to what you would do with lead generation ads. You qualify the customer: because he wants your information, he has to provide his name and e-mail address. Once you have that information, you can offer products and services until the customer unsubscribes from your marketing list. You send sales letters promoting a kit or a product or an e-book, something that promises a benefit. Then when the customer buys, you force him into a continuity program or present a back-end offer. This is very similar to the JPDK model. It has simply been automated by using technology.

Technology has completely automated the business for many info-marketers. They have automated traffic generators through Google ad words or some other search engine optimization. The page that collects the name and e-mail address, the squeeze page, is automated. When a buyer clicks "submit," the e-mail follow-up sequence can be completely automated. You can send a daily e-mail for 12 days and then an e-mail every other day for the next 12 days. That's 18 messages. Then you can send messages three times a week for the rest of the year until you have sent about 120 e-mails.

Once you have created your program, you just leave it and people come to the web site. They look at your sales message. They buy.

They receive the e-mails. Maybe even the back end can be completely automated. This model is nice from the standpoint that it does not require a lot of work. That was its real innovation, but it did not break new ground on how the information marketing business is done.

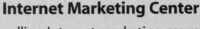

Info-Marketer Resource

Internet Marketing Center

The #1 best-selling Internet marketing course online for more than eight years running, "Insider Secrets to Marketing Your Business on the Internet," is the product that our affiliates consistently report **earns the highest commissions** for their promotions. The recently revised and updated version of this course boasts **1,300-plus pages** of the most up-to-date Internet marketing strategies and tactics. It contains two **8 x 11 full-color three-ring binders containing nine steps, broken down into 70 lessons** with step-by-step instructions included for every promotion and strategy. For more information visit **www.Info MarketingInternetCenter.com.**

Look for the Upcoming Guide

Information Marketing Association
Official Guide to Internet Marketing

In this book, we'll outline the ways to make big money selling information products over the Internet. This book will detail the easy ways to generate products, the marketing techniques, and the specifications for your web developers to implement. Coming soon from the Information Marketing Association and Entrepreneur Press.

Man Sheds His "Monkey Suit" and Kisses the Corporate World Goodbye

Daniel Levis's information marketing business is all about the entrepreneurial possibilities of copywriting on the Internet. His weekly column, "The Web Marketing Advisor," addresses Internet marketing issues with a strong emphasis on copywriting. Another column, "Selling to Human Nature," is more general in nature and helps salespeople learn how to sell more. At the same time, Daniel uses his column to encourage readers to "shed the monkey suit, say goodbye to the corporate world, and get into information marketing."

Daniel has a good reason to target salespeople, actually the best reason: he is a former commissioned salesman himself. He used to sell high-tech products to Fortune 500 companies. And that's what led him to shed his own "monkey suit" and join the world of information marketing.

"My first exposure to information marketing was using what I call lead generation magnets, which were essentially white papers that helped CIOs and IT professionals make more informed decisions," Daniel says. I would write the free reports to generate leads for my sales as an alternative to cold calling. This was about the time voice mail became popular, and I shifted from cold calling to the 'get them to come to you' Dan Kennedy style of marketing."

Daniel didn't yet have an actual information product since there was no price associated with his white papers, but essentially the marketing process was the same, so his transition into information marketing was a natural one. His first marketing efforts were conducted through the mail, but then in 2003, Daniel started using the Internet and discovered e-books.

➡

"I bought several e-books and found them very useful for figuring out the whole Internet thing," Daniel says. "It didn't take me long to put two and two together and realize that selling information, particularly online, was a pretty compelling business. I had already effectively slashed my marketing costs to the bone by shifting over to the Internet from direct mail, and here were these guys basically selling electrons for $30, $50, even a hundred bucks a pop and more, with essentially no fulfillment costs whatsoever!"

Daniel soon figured out that information marketing via the Internet was the business he had been looking for. "I started experimenting with it, moonlighting," Daniel relates. "Here was a business I could start up for next to nothing and that would allow me to immediately begin generating revenues. Aside from marketing costs, which I already understood and knew how to control, that revenue was nearly pure profit. It still blows my mind to this day because for years I'd been wracking my brain looking for a business opportunity that made sense, but I never found anything I thought was serious that didn't involve forking over a huge wad of cash."

Daniel decided to base his business on something he knew how to do and was passionate about: entrepreneurship. Specifically, he narrowed his topic to copywriting for the Internet entrepreneur. "I knew there was a starving crowd of other people out there who were equally passionate about this idea. I had direct experience with it because I was watching the world change literally before my eyes. The large corporations I was selling to back in the early 2000s were one by one downsizing their workforces, increasing their outsourcing to smaller firms and offshore, and in many cases to independent consultants and contractors," Daniel explains.

Daniel has successfully used a process, which he reluctantly calls "parasitic marketing," to create joint venture projects with ➡

successful people. One of his most successful is "Masters of Copywriting."

"Masters of Copywriting" is essentially a compilation of interviews with 44 different master copywriters. It includes well-known experts in the field such as Dan Kennedy, Joe Sugarman, Clayton Makepeace, Bob Bly, Michel Fortin, John Carlton, and 38 others. Daniel also included public domain works of deceased authors like Claude C. Hopkins and Bruce Barton that, Daniel points out, "all of us revere." By associating himself with these copywriting greats, Daniel positioned himself as an expert. In addition, because each of these writers appeals to a unique client base, Daniel was able to reach a larger universe of potential buyers who already knew one or more of the experts featured in the book.

Another benefit of including multiple experts was being able to get those copywriters to agree to drive traffic to Daniel's web site about the e-book. "This created a storm all over the subculture of the Internet," Daniel grins. "Right about that time Clayton Makepeace had hired someone to go out and find partners to help him start 'The Total Package,' his own information product business. I guess this guy happened to get an e-mail from one of the people endorsing 'Masters of Copywriting.' So he contacted me and asked me to endorse his e-zine to my list, and I said, 'Well, what's in it for me?' He didn't have an answer, so I gave him one: 'Why doesn't Clayton give me an interview that I'll put in my e-book?' That's how I got Clayton in my book," Daniel explains.

Most of Daniel's interviews were conducted via fax and were text based. "A few people got smart, and they started requesting audio because they knew how much work it is to write," Daniel says with a chuckle, "and I turned the recorded interviews into bonuses to go with my book."

➤

And the benefits of Daniel's "Masters of Copywriting" just keep coming. "Something else really interesting happened once the list started. People actually started approaching me from within that list and started literally begging me to write sales copy for them," Daniel marvels. "Today I command a fee of $17,500 plus royalties to write a promotion. And I do a lot of marketing consulting at $300 an hour. My latest venture is I'm adding a forced continuity program at the back end of 'Masters of Copywriting' to see how that works."

Daniel also lists public speaking, personal development, and motivational topics as possible topics to market to his list. Visit Daniel on the web at **www.SellingtoHumanNature.com.**

For the complete profile visit **www.InfoMarketingBook.com/Levis.**

Coaching/Products

Many info-marketers are now bundling their information products with their back-end coaching all in the front-end sale. It used to be that an info-marketer would offer a kit for, let's say, $1,000. A certain percentage of customers would buy with the first sales letter, but others were more reluctant. So the info-marketer would offer the kit on a three-month $333-a-month payment program along with a three-month free trial of the continuity program. After three months these customers would go right onto the continuity program, because the end of their trial offer coincided with their final $333 payment. Once a customer was in the continuity program, the info-marketer would start trying to sell coaching programs and other services as part of the back end.

Instead of waiting for the back end to try to sell their coaching and other products, many info-marketers have begun bundling them in as part of the actual front-end sale. So when you buy the kit you get the kit, but you are also signing up for a $333-a-month-until-you-cancel continuity program where you get tele-seminars, monthly newsletters, and maybe some automatically implemented templates and other things built into it. This has really changed the economics of these businesses. Instead of getting a front-end customer who buys a kit for $1,000, now you have a customer paying $333 a month, which is an annual value of $3,700. These customers are actually easier to get at a monthly rate. Plus these customers are more satisfied because they are not stuck with a box they have to sort through themselves. They have someone they can call for help. They have resources to rely on. They have coaching calls they can follow up on. Customers are much happier with this coaching/product business model.

Look for the Upcoming Guide

Information Marketing Association Official Guide to Building Profitable Coaching Businesses

In this book, we'll detail the profitable models to use to build coaching programs, including the benefits and drawbacks of individual coaching and small-group and large-group coaching models. This book will detail the easy ways info-marketers sell and deliver coaching services for maximum returns. Coming soon from the Information Marketing Association and Entrepreneur Press.

From Zero to $1.4 Million in Two Years: The Story of a Telemarketing "Baby Sitter" Who Cut Her Sales Teeth by Selling Frozen Meat

Info-Marketer Profile

"It's a sad story, Robin begins. "I don't even have an official high school diploma. When my parents divorced I had to drop out of school to work, so I got a GED (general educational development) certificate instead."

Robin spent her days, Monday through Saturday, cleaning houses and working in a flower shop. "The only day I wouldn't work was Sunday, because that was church day," Robin says. Her mother was part of a church that does not believe in accumulating wealth. "As a matter of fact, they won't save money in any savings account. They believe it's wrong. They won't own property because they believe that's accumulating wealth," Robin explains.

Robin had a lot to overcome before she could begin her journey to owning a successful information-marketing business. "I used to ride my bike to jobs because I wanted to save bus fare—up until I was almost 20. I mean, literally, I was poor."

Robin didn't share her mother's beliefs about wealth, but it took some time to develop her own opinions about how to approach earning money. She also viewed her lack of formal education as an obstacle. "I always had this hang-up because I felt as though I didn't have the education to really make it in the world, so I took a lowly sales job. Actually, the first 'official' job I had was with a telemarketing company that sold frozen meat," Robin remembers with a half smile. "Basically I was the administrative assistant to the telemarketing manager."

That first official job proved serendipitous. In a strangely wonderful turn of events, Robin was suddenly thrust into her boss's shoes. It turns out the telemarketing manager was arrested for tax evasion, so the owner asked Robin to "baby-sit" the telemarketing department ➡

until he could find a new manager. "He asked me to 'just sit there and make sure people don't dial 900 numbers and make sure they log in on time until we can find somebody,'" Robin laughs, "but I was curious, so I picked up the phone and tried my hand at setting sales appointments. The way I learned to sell was by calling people at their homes at night, trying to set appointments to have a guy come in and sell them frozen meat. Now if I could learn to sell *that* way, I began thinking that maybe I could be successful at selling other things, too!"

Robin made good use of her time in between telemarketing sessions. "I'd work the morning shift and then have a couple of hours off before the evening shift, so I'd watch Zig Ziglar tapes and learn the best I could. That way, I was ready for my next job selling computer training for a technology company. I was actually doing over a quarter-million dollars a month in sales!" Robin exclaims. "The average person was doing about $50,000, but I was so used to hitting the phone that I excelled. That was a turning point for me. I used to think sales was this horrible, lowly job that you did when you didn't know what else to do. But now, here I was in my early 20s, making about $70,000 a year! I was making more money than people who had college degrees. I was making more money than some of the senior engineers, the computer geniuses at the company! That was my ticket to freedom. Once I figured out I could make as much money as I wanted if I knew how to sell, that's when I got serious about it."

Armed with newfound confidence in her sales abilities, Robin continued learning everything she could. "I worked for Tony Robbins for a while, and I learned more during that tenure with him than I learned in anything else I've ever done. I got paid nothing, but the education I got was worth it, not only about selling and marketing in general, but also about how an organization should be run. Tony is a master ➡

What You Will Receive As A Gold or Platinum Master Mind Member

RR
RobinRobins

Open "Peer Advisory" Group Conference Calls And Member Forum
If you ever wanted to know what's working for your peers but couldn't because of competitive issues, this may be the most valuable aspect of your membership. **Because I will only allow one company to join per market at the Gold or Platinum Level,** you can join in on open group conference calls to connect with the other members of the group and find out what's working, get answers to operational questions, and even form alliances. This means you have a non-competitive peer advisory group facing the same challenges that you face every day and who are willing to help you find the fastest path to solving those problems.

You'll also have access to an online forum that allows you to post questions about technical issues, handling clients, quoting projects, marketing, vendors, hiring and compensating employees, and many other operational issues. The other members and I will provide you with insights and experienced-based advice about how to overcome these issues in your business.

A Complete, Done-For-You Website Template
After talking with many of my clients, I discovered that they DESPERATELY needed a better website. However, most of them don't have the time or the ability to write and design a great website that actually produces new customers. That's why I've created this done-for-you website template. If you hired a copy writer and web designer to produce a website of similar quality, you would have to spend $10,000 or more. But as a Gold or Platinum Member, you will be given this web template as part of your membership at no extra charge.

Monthly Done-For-You TechTip Postcard
If you struggle to get quality marketing campaigns out on a consistent basis due to lack of money, time, and staff, this service alone will be worth the membership investment! Every month you'll receive a fully designed mini newsletter template called the "TechTip Postcard." This simple, but highly effective campaign will help you generate leads, cross promote various services you offer, fuel referrals, position you as the obvious expert, and keep your name in front of prospective customers so they buy from you instead of your competition. **Best of all, you don't have to write it or design it; I'll do all the work for you!**

Automatic Updates To The Technology Marketing Tool Kit
As a member, you will receive FREE updates to the Technology Marketing Tool Kit. I am constantly learning and developing new strategies, tools, and campaigns to sell technology products and services. As a member, you'll get instant, up-to-the-minute access to every new strategy I discover.

Monthly Live Sales & Marketing Tele-Clinics
Every month you will be invited to attend a private, closed door tele-clinic. These calls will be 45-60 minutes of my best material on either one specific marketing strategy for generating more revenue in your business or I'll interview an industry expert on various business-building strategies such as selling managed services, public relations, management strategies, and more.

Access To An Ever Growing Library of INSTANT Marketing Campaigns
My library of instant marketing templates takes the guesswork and time out of marketing technology services. Instead of spending hours creating your own marketing campaigns, simply log on, download a template, and you're done. Here are just *a few* of the items you'll have access to:

- Lead generation campaigns and sales letters to attract new clients
- Campaigns to sell managed services to existing clients and new prospects.

FIGURE 11-2. Robin Robins is proof positive that anyone can succeed in the information marketing industry—provided she has the right tools, the best role models, and the will to work hard to achieve her dreams.

persuader, and I learned a lot about coaching from him," Robin says.

Now, as an info-marketer, instead of meeting quotas for someone else, Robin is free to pursue the things in life that matter to her. For one, she is a fitness buff, hitting the gym five or six times a week to teach aerobics classes and to work out with weights. Recently married, Robin and her husband have two Jack Russell "terrorists," and Robin walks them two miles every day. "The one thing I won't trade off is my health," Robin declares. "Another thing I won't compromise is walking my dogs. I love my dogs, I train them and do all kinds of crazy stuff like play Frisbee with them."

One of the ways Robin has streamlined her efforts is by focusing on a niche market. "It took me a little over a year to find my niche," Robin says, "but once I finally did, it went gangbusters from there."

Because of her work in an ad agency business, Robin was familiar with many industries, everything from MRI imaging to personal development to insurance. "I was all over the map," Robin laughs. "The first thing I decided to try being known for was lead generation, because I have a strong sales background. It wasn't a good fit for me, because I ended up getting a lot of different people from a lot of different industries. They all had the attitude that 'my business is different,' so I think it's harder to become a specialist in a general niche," Robin says.

Through a second serendipity, Robin ended up promoting her products to technology providers. Her clients offer computer consulting to small businesses and individuals, and Robin's products help her customers obtain more clients and maximize their revenues.

In her first year, Robin offered coaching as an option after clients purchased the kit, and about 23% accepted the offer. Now she uses a forced continuity program with much better conversion rates. "My clients get four free months of coaching and then get charged ➡

through auto-billing. When I switched to forced continuity, my conversion rate went up to 81%!" Robin exclaims.

Robin has several coaching levels: anyone can join her Silver group, while her Gold and Platinum levels are area exclusive. For a monthly fee, her Gold and Platinum members get an area exclusive, a newsletter produced for them, and tele-coaching for area-exclusive members. Her high-end coaching program is her "Genius League," and she conducts monthly calls with those members and meets in person with them twice a year.

For more information about Robin visit **www.Technology MarketingToolkit.com** or read the expanded profile at **www.Info MarketingBook.com/Robins**.

High-End Coaching/ Area-Specific Licensing

Building on the coaching/product model, many info-marketers are getting rid of the kit entirely. Instead they are front-ending their coaching program at a much higher price than ever before. Instead of promoting a kit, these info-marketers offer a coaching program: "We are going to show you how to solve this problem in your life. Not only that, we are going to help you do it. We are going to have monthly tele-seminars. We are going to have three in-person meetings a year." They go through the entire pitch for the coaching program and front-end it to the cold list. The nice thing about these businesses is they generate a lot more cash than other businesses because they are selling such a high-priced product on the front end. They are also easier to operate because info-marketers do not have a lot of product sales and a large number of customers. Instead, relatively fewer customers receive more personal service.

Some info-marketers are increasing the price even further by agreeing to sell their coaching to only one person within a particular geographic area. This works especially well with professional and trade niches. For example, if you are marketing how to get more customers for a veterinarian practice, you can sell your program to a particular veterinarian by saying, "You are the only one I am going to sell this coaching program to in southern Chicago. So when you buy it, no one else in southern Chicago is allowed to have it. You will be the only one who has this information and this program of sales techniques." That's a powerful offer!

Many information marketers are actually offering similar content to what would have been in a kit. But instead of delivering it all in one box, they are delivering it as part of their coaching program on a monthly basis. Members participate in the coaching program, receive the information, and then go out and implement what they have learned before the next coaching call. This generates a lot of cash without as much front-end work to create kits, sell kits, and then try to convert customers into coaching clients. Instead you go straight to selling the coaching.

None of these business models is better than all others. Each info-marketer must weigh the positives and negatives of each business type and create a business that meets his needs.

Info-Marketer Profile

Creating a $3-Million-a-Year Income in 18 Months

Scott Tucker discovered Dan Kennedy-style marketing and applied it to his mortgage business. Scott became the savior of individuals whom no one else would help, and he learned how to speak their language so they would respond to his marketing in droves. With his marketing he earned $719,000 as a mortgage broker, a sum in the top 1% of the profession.

That's when Dan Kennedy suggested he offer his marketing system to other mortgage brokers, but because his materials were extremely specialized, Dan suggested that he offer them with area exclusivity.

Scott branded himself as a rebel within the mortgage industry and created the **www.MortgageMarketingGenius.com** web site. Scott offers biannual seminars where mortgage brokers from around the country come to hear about his marketing methods. For those who live in an area where Scott doesn't already have a coaching member, Scott offers them the opportunity to become a member for the 30-minute drive time area around their office.

Scott's coaching members receive a license to use his proprietary direct-marketing materials, his proprietary web-site design, a monthly group coaching call, and three two-day in-person meetings a year. The response to Scott's program has been enormous, allowing him to sign up 163 coaching members in his first 18 months. At $1,497 a month Scott has been able to multiply his mortgage origination income several times.

This model allows Scott to work with small numbers of customers and still make a significant income from his information marketing business. For more information on Scott Tucker and his program visit **www.MortgageMarketingGenius.com**, and for an expanded profile visit **www.InfoMarketingBook.com/Tucker**.

Chapter 12

The Story of the Cat That Licked Stamps—How Anyone Can Get a Fast Start in Info-Marketing

by Dan Kennedy
President, Information Marketing Association

I
N THIS CHAPTER, I'VE BEEN CHALLENGED BY THE INFORMATION Marketing Association to tie together all of the pieces presented in this book, in the simplest possible way, so even a complete novice can get a fast start and learn as he earns. This is a daunting challenge. After considerable thought, I decided to go back in time and tell you two stories of information businesses I personally started, then extract the "steps" from the stories.

If you happen to already be active in information marketing and doing well, you could skip this chapter without harm. On the other hand, everybody can benefit from a back-to-basics review from time to time.

In both these cases, the opportunities to use web sites, e-mail, and broadcast fax did not yet exist. The use of tele-conferences, promoted as tele-seminars, to sell was barely in infancy, little understood, technically difficult, and expensive. Had I those tools and the know-how I have now, the information and examples that you've read about in this book, and the resources offered by the IMA, each of these businesses could easily have generated millions of dollars more than they did—although both were very successful. As a matter of fact, the chief asset I had with one of my very first forays into information marketing was a cat that licked stamps. Not a computer, not a web site, not a big budget. At the time, I was quite poor. I was starting from zero. My cat happened to like the taste of the glue on postage stamps and was happy to sit facing me on my coffee table while I watched TV in the evening and labeled and stuffed envelopes. I held out a strip of stamps. The cat licked the entire strip from left to right. I stuck the stamps on the stuffed envelopes, plop, plop, plop, plop. In retrospect, consuming postage stamp glue was probably not all that healthy for the cat—but, heck, they have nine lives, right?

Anyway, in example #1, somewhat by accident, I identified a very small niche market: about 3,000 people, all in the same business, with profound interest in and limited knowledge about a subject that I happened to be very knowledgeable about. I did my research at a convention attended by about one-quarter of this group. I came home and did just about the simplest thing anyone could do in info-marketing. I created a very simple catalog offering about 30 different "special reports," each on a very specific topic, each of different length and price—as I recall from as low as $5 to as much as $50. I used a list of these people compiled from the membership directory of the association they belonged to, manually culling a small number I judged unlikely prospects. I mailed about 2,000 of the catalogs at a pace of about 100 a day. As orders came in, I wrote, copied, and sent out the reports. (Today we have a fancy word for that. It's called Publish on Demand.)

Three things occurred. One, I made some money. About $15,000. Two, I saw which topics were of the greatest interest. Three, I created a "hot list" of about 250 buyers.

Next, I created a newsletter for this niche. More accurately, I created a sales letter for a newsletter, focused on the topics these people had demonstrated the greatest interest in. I chose the newsletter because I didn't have to create, publish, and inventory product. I first mailed my sales letter to the 250 buyers, several times in sequence with additional cover letters. Within a month, I had nearly 80 subscribers at $149 a year. Gradually I mailed to the entire universe of 2,000. I kept at it. Within the year I had nearly 1,000 subscribers.

I could go on, but this is sufficient demonstration. Know, though, that with all the ideas in this book about developing a multi-product, multifaceted complete information business, even as few as 1,000 subscribers can easily provide an income of $250,000 to $1 million a year.

In example #2, similarly, I identified a niche market for which both ad media and mailing lists were readily available and in which there was profound interest and limited knowledge about a subject I was very knowledgeable about. This list was considerably larger, about 35,000. In this case, I used advertising and direct mail to direct these people into small, free seminars in their own cities. Initially, I tested different seminar titles and promised content in different cities and, fortunately, quickly hit on the best offer. I kept one speaker busy 20 days a month, myself five days a month. Over a period of three years, I put nearly 10,000 of those people through those introductory seminars, sold them info-product packages, and also built a newsletter business. I used the seminars as my sales method for a number of reasons, but one was that these particular customers were accustomed to going to such seminars, welcomed the opportunity to do so, were responsive to free seminars, and I had a speaker eager and happy to travel. Nearly $10 million in business was done in three years, in the early 1980s. As I said, had I the resources and knowledge you have at your disposal, it would have been $30 million or more. Still, some of those customers have followed me through the years all the way to Glazer-Kennedy Insider's Circle Membership, my three newsletters, tele-coaching, coaching, and seminars today.

The first business was launched with a budget of about $300, for printing, postage stamps, and cat food. Then it was bootstrapped with its own money. The second business was launched years later, when I was already doing well, with about $10,000, and then it, too, funded its own growth. In the first business I had affinity with the market; I was one of them. In the second I had no affinity.

Now let's extract some "steps" from these two stories. In both cases, the first thing I did was identify a particular, specific, relatively small, manageable, affordably and directly reachable target market. Your choice of market is critically important. There are many different criteria to consider, including but not limited to those I listed here. You should also know that few info-marketers can profitably go after an entire market. Instead, you are looking for a hungry, responsive market within a market. As an example, I work with an info-marketer in the dental profession who does very well with dentists age 50 and above, in practice no less than 20 years, nearing retirement. To be successful, he must focus on that segment of the market, not all dentists.

Second, I determined what I knew they would be happy to pay to read about and hear about, through research and testing. The less you do based on your own assumptions, opinions, and ideas, the better. The more you can "listen to the market," the better.

Third, I devised info-products promising the benefits they told me they wanted. This is a very important point made throughout this book. It addresses a critical, costly mistake most insist on making: building product, content, or a business and then going in search of buyers, as opposed to finding buyers and then building to suit them. Too many people become so emotionally committed to an idea and invest so much time and money in birthing a product that they are blind to economic and market realities, deaf to what the market tells them.

Fourth, in these cases, I started with very simple publish-on-demand info-products. Today the opportunities are even better and more varied to do this. Information sold can be delivered electronically online, via tele-seminars or webinars, or if offline, in print-on-demand formats. Vendors that serve info-marketers are accustomed to producing info-products in small quantities or per order and handling the entire fulfillment process for you. One of the many virtues of this type of business is keeping your money out of dormant product inventory and turning over again and again in advertising and marketing.

Fifth, I used different sales methods for the different markets, but with all of them I communicated directly.

Sixth, I turned a one-time buyer into a customer of continuing value. In the two examples I used here, our approach was primitive and simplistic by today's standards. Today's info-marketers thoroughly understand that the asset is the customer and that a customer's value increases through membership, continuity, and ascension to different levels of services and pricing, in long-term and ongoing relationships. In one of my most popular info-products, "The Renegade Millionaire System" (**www.RenegadeMillionaire.com**), I teach a business principle particularly appropriate to info-marketing: Most business owners get customers to make sales, but we make sales to get customers.

And there you have it. To review:

1. Identify a viable market.
2. Determine what the market will buy.
3. Develop info-products to match what they want.

4. Start with simple products.

5. Select direct marketing methods appropriate for the market.

As you've seen in this book and will appreciate more by rereading the book several times and accessing the other IMA resources, today's info-marketing businesses are much more complex creatures than the two I've described here. Today they also tend to start in more sophisticated ways. With what we know now, it's quite common for someone to go from "start" to a million dollars or more in revenue in 12 months or less and to have continuity, multiple levels of continuity, and multiple products and services in place or at least planned from the beginning. Still, the first three fundamentals I've listed above govern even the most sophisticated of these businesses. And even today, you could start with nothing more than those three steps and a cat to lick the stamps.

Want to see the current, evolved version of Dan's info-marketing businesses?

Info-Marketer Resource

Visit **www.IMAKennedy.com** and, for a complete inside look, accept his invitation for The Greatest Free Gift offer, including a free three-month subscription to his most popular newsletter. Also read free chapters from Dan's most popular books and see video interviews with Dan and Kristi Frank from Donald Trump's *The Apprentice* at **www.NoBSBooks.com**.

Appendix A

Glossary of Info-Marketing Terms

Here are common terms you will hear within the information marketing business.

Affiliate: An affiliate relationship is one in which there is an agreement between two people to sell a particular product. One individual has customers he wants to market the product to, and another one has the product or service he wants to offer to customers. Typically, the individual who has the product will create an affiliate program. Many of these are executed online, and most of the popular shopping cart software programs today have this feature built in. The affiliate completes an application. Upon approval of the affiliate relationship, the affiliate is assigned a unique web-site address and given access to the affiliate toolbox that has e-mails, web sites, ads, and other things the affiliate can use to help sell the program. Then the affiliate uses the link, uses those sales techniques to help sell the product, and an affiliate commission is paid on those products. Commissions vary substantially by the different products and services sold. Very often the terms are negotiable for individuals who are able to sell a lot of affiliate programs, but for most folks, you normally have to earn a higher commission rate by performing well for a particular affiliate.

Affinity: This is a measure of your relationship to a market. If you have been a member of a market for a number of years, perhaps having established a career there, then you would have a high affinity with that particular market. If you are new to a market (for example, if you are going to sell to Harley Davidson owners and you have never owned a Harley Davidson and you do not know anyone who owns a Harley Davidson), then you would have very little affinity with that market.

Alexa.com: This is a web site that allows you to gather information about competitors and about web sites within a particular market. It provides a lot of information about the site, including how much traffic it is receiving from the Internet.

Back end: This is the most profitable part of an information marketing business and what distinguishes info-marketers from all other types of information publishers. Info-marketers are able to sell coaching, consulting, seminars, automatic implementation products, and newsletters, and offer other people's products to their customers as additional revenue opportunities.

Churn: This term refers to the number of new members joining a market at a given time. For instance, the real estate agent industry is a market where there is a lot of churn. Many individuals are joining that market with the hopes of making lots of money as a real estate agent. In contrast, the funeral director industry has very little churn. Most of the entrants in that market have been family-owned businesses for many years, or they are large corporations buying the family-owned businesses. There are not a lot of new companies jumping into the funeral director business that were not in it 12 months ago. The real estate agent industry has lots of churn, and there are lots of new customers to sell to. The funeral director industry has little churn. The customers in it today are pretty much the same ones who will be in it 12 months from now.

Claims: These are the benefits you are telling potential customers they will receive from using your product. Income claims refer to the amount of income you state others have received from using your product.

Coaching: This is an arrangement where you provide advice and counsel to customers to help them implement their own problem solutions. You may have already provided them the information they need, but through a coaching program you are able to give them specific information for their particular problems as well as specific case examples to help them solve the problems. This is generally distinguished from consulting. Consulting is actually doing it for them, whereas coaching is helping them to get it done for themselves.

Continuity: This is a program where on an established interval, usually monthly, customers are charged a set fee for a given level of product and service. Most programs are on a monthly continuity. This entire concept was pioneered and made popular by the Book-of-the-Month program, where customers trusted a publisher to send them a book every month related to their interests. This created an ongoing continuity relationship between these customers and the publisher. Info-marketers have used continuity to completely revolutionize their businesses and add many more subscribers versus using the annual subscription model. (See *Forced Continuity*.)

E-book: This is a book in a digital file that communicates information to your prospects and can be delivered electronically over the Internet. Rather than printing a product, weighing it, putting postage on it, and mailing it, you are able to instantly deliver an e-book and put your product in the customer's hand immediately.

Endorsed mailing: This is a mailing where an individual is given a letter of endorsement, usually a brief letter that is added to the front of his sales message, that gives credibility and recognition to the offer and sales message that it would not have gotten if it had to stand on its own.

Forced continuity: This is an arrangement where the customers are provided a free trial period of a program and then at the end of the free trial, they are automatically added to the continuity program. It does not require customers to act in order to opt into the monthly continuity. Customers can always opt out if they choose to; however, they do not have to act to opt in. (See "Continuity.")

Front end: This is marketing your products and services to new customers. This is the first step of your info-business. After you are able to obtain customers through your front end, you can develop the back end of your business by selling additional products and services to the customers who have already made a purchase from you.

Group coaching: This is a model where, instead of the coach interacting with one student at a time, the coach interacts with many students at one time. In general, a coach is providing advice and counsel, examples, and encouragement to students and is not performing actual services for the students. In the group coaching environment, there are many students interacting at the same time with one or more coaches.

Guarantee: This is your assurance to your customers that your product is everything you say it is. You promise to stand behind your product and offer their money back if your customers are not satisfied with it.

Guarantee, conditional: This is a guarantee where you force the customers to go through certain hoops in order to receive their money back. They may have to implement certain features within your product to demonstrate they have tried some things before you will give them a refund.

Guarantee, unconditional: This is a guarantee where the customers can simply ask for the refund, and they are given the refund without any conditions whatsoever.

Herd: A term Dan Kennedy coined to refer to an info-marketer's customer base. Expanding on the herd analysis, Dan teaches info-marketers to build a fence around their herd to protect them against poachers and to prevent customers from escaping.

Joint venture: This is where two or more individuals get together to create and market a product to a particular industry. In many cases, one of the joint venture partners has a list of customers, and the other joint venture partner has a product or will develop a product or service for those customers. The partners work together to sell the product and then split the proceeds.

Kit: This is a collection of materials you are delivering all at one time to your customers.

Lead generation: This is the process of identifying individuals within a market who are interested in more information about the product or service you are offering.

Market: This is a collection of customers who have something in common and, most importantly, have a common problem you can solve as an info-marketer.

Mastermind meeting: The idea of the "mastermind alliance" and "masterminding" grew from Andrew Carnegie, Henry Ford, Harvey Firestone, and Thomas Edison as reported in books like the popular bestseller *Think and Grow Rich* by Napoleon Hill. One of the factors successful people share is a group of people they can work with to help solve problems. By working together to solve each other's problems, each of them benefits. Many information marketers have been able to duplicate the benefit of mastermind meetings through their coaching programs.

Monthly CD: This is an audio program or other program offered through podcast and other means that individuals subscribe to. They can be provided by one person as a monologue, or they can be in a conversation or interview format between an expert and a host.

Multipay: This is an arrangement where the info-marketer helps customers afford the product by putting it on a payment program. It can be two-pay, three-pay, five-pay, etc., but this helps lower the initial price of the product and decreases the risk that customers may perceive from the sale. For example, if a customer looks at an offer that is $250 a month for four months, it may be more acceptable to him than paying $1,000 all at once, even though he could probably self-finance that $1,000 through a credit card. It feels like $250 is all he is risking, so he is more apt to participate in a multipay program than in an all-upfront sale.

Newsletter: This is a publication that is published, usually monthly, by an information marketer to communicate with customers and provide ongoing help and information and to reinforce what the info-marketer has taught them in the past.

Niche: This is a group of individuals with a like interest or a similar demographic. Normally these niches are defined as business oriented—the customers could be plumbers, restaurant owners, chiropractors, doctors, or accountants, for example.

Offers: This is what you are agreeing to provide your customers for a fee. Most teachers within the info-marketing world will tell you your offer is the most important part of your marketing campaign. You should create your offer before you create a product or anything else. You should create a compelling offer, a collection of resources, tools, techniques, manuals, CDs, videos, coaching: whatever you want to package in your offer. You should decide what your offer is going to be first, and then you can go about the job of creating the product and offering it to the marketplace.

One-step sale: This is a process where you go straight from introducing yourself to the customer to asking for the sale within one marketing piece. This is contrasted to lead generation marketing, where you first generate a lead through a lead generation ad and then create a sales sequence to sell to that lead. Through one-step sales, you are trying to sell at the point of first contact.

Online marketing: This is a method where you use the Internet to communicate with a large population of people using automated software to handle the lead capture, marketing, and sales process as well as, many times, the product delivery.

Order form: This is also called a response device or an application. This is a piece of paper, the document, or the web form the customer uses to make a transaction. This is where the customer fills in his name, address, and credit card information. The order form is mailed, faxed, or completed online or on the telephone. If completing a telephone order, the person taking the order usually has an order form to fill out for the customer.

Prerecorded message: This is a message, usually through a toll-free number, that you offer within your lead generation ad to encourage your customer to leave his name and contact information so you can deliver the rest of your sales message to him.

Reachability: This is a term referring to a niche that describes the amount of ease with which you can put your marketing message in front of your prospective customers. If a niche already has several magazines, others already marketing there, or its own cable television channel, then that market is highly reachable. If there are no magazines specific to that niche, then its reachability is low.

Response device: See *Order Form*.

Risk reversal: This is a marketing term for a guarantee with which you ease a customer's fear of making a purchase by taking on all of the risk of the sale. As the customer evaluates whether or not he wants to buy your product, he is deciding whether or not he can trust you. By offering a refund of the purchase price and to pay for return shipping if the customer returns the product, you are taking on all of the risk of the sale. This will help your customer buy from you with confidence.

S&D: This is a term coined by Bill Glazer that means "steal and distribute." Rather than reinventing new ways of doing business or new marketing programs for a particular niche, you should be adapting programs that have proven themselves successful in other areas and implementing them within your own market.

Self-liquidating leads: This is where your lead generation ad charges the potential customer a fee to receive the rest of the marketing sequence. For example, the ad will have an offer, invite people to respond, and charge them $9.95 to get the rest of the marketing sequence. This type of lead has two benefits: (1) it provides income from the lead generation process that helps pay for more lead generation ads; and (2) it increases the quality of the lead because even though it is a nominal fee, only the most motivated individuals will be willing to go through the work necessary to respond. When you use a free lead generation system and all people have to do is pick up the phone, you are going to dramatically increase the number of leads you get and the number of opportunities you have to sell to individuals, but you are also going to increase the marketing cost.

Squeeze page: This is a web form that captures a name and address from a prospect before you allow the prospect to see the rest of the sales message.

SRDS: This is the acronym for the Standard Rate and Data Service. This is a manual that has details about every list commercially available for sale. From the SRDS manual, you will be able to learn about markets based on the types of lists available for them and evaluate how easy it will be for you to reach this market through direct mail.

Subculture: This is a way of evaluating a potential market. Whereas niches are based on professional designations such as doctors and plumbers, subcultures are based on hobbies and interests of particular individuals. Golfers, fishermen, hobbyists, Star Trekkies, bird lovers, fish lovers—all of these are subcultures you can market to.

Subniche: These are specialties within a particular niche. For example, a plumber could be a commercial plumber who only works in 30-story buildings, or he could be a residential plumber. There are many subniches for doctors: dermatologist, surgeon, gynecologist, anesthesiologist—all of these are subspecialties or subniches within the niche of medicine.

Tele-coaching: This is a process of delivering coaching services over the telephone rather than in person or by mail.

Telemarketing: This is a process of delivering a sales message over the telephone.

Tele-seminar: This is a seminar delivered over the telephone. Most tele-seminars offered by information marketers are free and designed to provide a sales presentation. The sales presentation can be for a tele-coaching program as a back-end product, and many info-marketers also use tele-seminars to convert sales on the front end. So not only will they offer printed sales letters and CDs, but they will also invite their leads to call into a tele-seminar to hear a sales presentation.

Tollbooth position: Once you have developed a list of customers, there will be other individuals who want to sell products and services to your list. Because you have a relationship with your list, you are in a position to charge others for access to your customer list, either through an affiliate program, JV opportunity, endorsed mailing, or some other agreement.

Try-before-you-buy: This is often called a "puppy dog close" because it was borrowed from the pet stores that allow you to take a cute and cuddly puppy home for the evening. Once you have taken a puppy home, gotten used to him, shown the puppy to your neighbors and friends, and taken him for a walk, the likelihood of you bringing that dog back to the store is extremely low. An info-marketer very often may offer a try-before-you-buy where the customer is able to complete an order form, fax it in, receive the product, examine it for 30, 60, or 90 days, and then the charge goes through automatically if the customer has not returned the product.

Wordtracker.com: This is a web site that allows you to find out exactly how many people are searching for particular key words and phrases. When you are trying to determine how to position your product within a market, you can examine the types of key words and phrases individuals are searching for on the Internet. That will give you a hint of what you should be offering them.

Appendix B

Info-Marketing Resources and Vendors

One of the toughest parts of the information marketing business is finding vendors who understand what you are trying to accomplish and are able to get you there. Too many fail to deliver. An info-marketer must be able to act quickly. Once you get new customers, incompetent vendors can kill a business.

Here are vendors who understand info-marketers and are ready to help you become successful.

Customer Service

Turnkey Customer Service, Marketing Implementation, and Product Fulfillment

To streamline their businesses, smart info-marketers have outsourced all of this time-consuming work to Sheiff Services. Randy and Camille Sheiff are in the office each day supervising a call center, managing an InfusionSoft ManagePro CRM system for their clients, and making sure orders are fulfilled and customer service questions are handled promptly.

In fact, because they are doing all of this, their info-marketer clients are able to start up their businesses more quickly, get more marketing steps implemented, and generate a lot more money without any additional effort. In addition, they don't have to deal with the dozens of customer questions that come in each day.

For more information about how Randy and Camille Sheiff can take over the administrative hassles of your info-business, call Randy at 512/353-5037 today.

Event Management

The Easy Way to Minimize Liability, Reduce Stress, and Increase the Profitability of Your Events

There are thousands of dollars of potential liability when you sign a hotel contract for your boot camp or event. Plus, the document is so long, it's difficult to figure out what it even says.

Bari Baumgardner has been negotiating hotel contracts and managing events for her clients for over 15 years. Her clients benefit from her experience and the volume pricing she is able to negotiate with hotels. Because Bari works with several info-marketers, hotels make concessions to her so they will be considered for other future business.

Hotels have experts who negotiate with event planners every day. You need an expert on your side. Outsourcing the complicated and time consuming event management work to Bari so you can focus on marketing and on-site sales can add tens of thousands of dollars in new revenue to your event.

For a complimentary meeting evaluation, phone Bari at 704/334-0909 or e-mail **BBaumgardner@SageEventManagement.com** today.

Media Duplication

Deadline Driven, Complete Business Solution

Allow McMannis Duplication to handle your follow-up mailings, product fulfillment, or call us for a duplication job.

Media Duplicated for You
- CD Duplication
- DVD Duplication
- Cassette Duplication
- Complete Line of Packaging

Call Tony Wedel at 620/628-4411 and ask for the special pricing for readers of the info-marketing book. Free for IMA members, call Tony and ask for the audio program "T. J. Reveals How McManus Duplication Makes It Easy for Me to Use the Greatest Marketing Secret We Ever Learned From Dan Kennedy." It's yours, just for calling and saying hello.

Merchant Services

Finally, a merchant services provider that appreciates info-marketers, understands the business, and wants to help you make more money.

Info-marketers everywhere are shocked to learn that their merchant services providers consider them to be a liability. Even after these providers unconditionally accept your business, they can impose six-month holds on your money without notice, refund your customer charges, or cancel your account altogether.

Now there is an alternative. One merchant services provider likes info-marketers and wants your business, too. For a free, no obligation evaluation of your current merchant services needs and your future opportunities visit **www.InfoMarketingMerchantServices.com**. Complete the quick form and someone will contact you right away.

Merchant Services With Info-Marketers in Mind

Info-marketers, let Charge Today provide you with full-service merchant accounts and credit card processing solutions for today's demanding marketplace.

From merchant accounts, ACH/check services, secure gateways, and virtual and physical terminals to shopping carts, **ChargeToday.com** is the info-marketer's premier partner for credit card payment and processing solutions. For more information visit **www.ChargeTodayInfo.com.** Complete the brief form and Charge Today will be in touch with you within 24 hours.

Software

A Software System That Puts Your Small Business on Autopilot by Automating Your Marketing, Sales, and More

Web-Based CRM Software for Info-Marketers

Are you tired of never being in control of your prospect and customer information? Does your business suffer because you use three, four, or five software programs to manage your business? We understand your pain, and we have a web-based CRM Software program built specifically for your info-marketing business.

Contact Management

ManagePro CRM is your customer relationship management system. Finally you will be able to put your customers at the center of your business where they should be. All your customer interaction via e-mail, phone, fax, or in person is tracked and managed in one place so you can close more sales and maintain better relationships with your existing customers.

No more trying to track which leads are in which step of multiple marketing sequences. ManagePro CRM lets you SUPERCHARGE your follow-up sequences. In addition to sending follow-up e-mails, ManagePro CRM will send direct mail pieces, faxes, voice broadcasts, and more—automatically.

For a free product tour, auto responder test drive, and online demonstration visit **www.InfoMarketingCRM.com**.

The Shopping Cart Used by the Most Info-Marketers for Online Orders, Follow-Up With Prospects, Run Affiliate Campaigns

All of the shopping cart and marketing tools that info-marketers need to automate a successful online info-marketing business. With 1ShoppingCart, info-marketers have the ability to take orders online, accept credit cards, e-mail customers, use automatic e-book delivery, use ad tracking tools, have unlimited auto responders, discount/ update modules, and have access to a built-in affiliate program. **www.InfoMarketingShoppingCart.com**

Create Products Fast

We help info-marketers uncover quick-profit niches and help discover what their prospects and customers want to buy "most." With the Ask Database you can create new products from scratch, effortlessly grab more testimonials from members, uncover new market niches using Google Adwords, and quickly determine winning tele-seminar content. **www.InfoMarketersAsk.com**

Easy Follow-Up Messages and E-Zines

With AWeber, info-marketers can configure follow-up and newsletter messages with name personalization click-through and open rate tracking, attachments, RSS, and split testing at no additional cost. Messages can include HTML using our 51-plus predesigned templates, or you can create your own with the integrated easy editor and images or plain text. **www.AWeberEmail.com**

Printing/Mailing Services

Give Your Sales Letters the Best Chance for Success With Dave Brady

When you need a 1,000- to 10,000-piece lead generation mailing printed, stuffed, and sent out the door, call Dave Brady, Datum Direct, at 312/492-8822. Dave can take your letters, customize items inside the envelope, and with an inkjet printer address envelopes with a handwriting font and use live stamps.

Information Resources

The Ultimate Shortcut for Success and Profitability in Information Marketing

Every month, hundreds of startups turn to the Information Marketing Association to get their businesses started quickly. With its two monthly newsletters, Best Practices in Information Marketing monthly call, and a monthly Get Started Quick coaching call for those just starting out, there is no better tool to make your business profitable. And, for a limited time, it's FREE.

Readers of this book can join the Information Marketing Association for FREE by visiting **www.GetIMAFree.com** today. You may cancel your membership at any time. There is no obligation.

Over the next two months you will have the opportunity to enjoy all of the membership benefits that our members already enjoy. Here is a brief summary of the benefits you will receive over the next two months with this opportunity:

Month #1

IMA Insiders' Journal	$197.00
No B.S. Info-Marketing Letter	68.42
Best Practices Tele-Seminar	130.00
Tele-Seminar Transcripts & CD	49.00
Jump Start in Information Marketing	
Business Tele-Seminar	562.50

Month #2

IMA Insiders' Journal	$197.00
Ultimate Information Entrepreneur Special Report	68.42
Best Practices Tele-Seminar	130.00
Tele-Seminar Transcripts and CD	49.00
Jump Start in Information Marketing	
Business Tele-Seminar	562.50

Special Bonuses

9 Info-Marketer Insider Secrets to Simplify Your	
Business and Maximize Profitability	$995.00
IMA Easy-Content CD	95.00
Total Value	**$3,103.84**

Info-Marketers' A–Z Blueprint Seminar

For Anyone Who Is in or Wants to Be in the HIGHLY PROFITABLE Business of Providing Information

Here's a partial list of topics discussed by Bill Glazer at the Information Marketing Business Development Blueprint Seminar:

1. Seven Decisions the New Info-Marketer Needs to Make
2. How to Evaluate a Niche or Subculture Market
3. How to Thoroughly Profile the Prospective Customer

4. How to Leverage the Affinity You Have With a Niche
5. How to Create a Relationship With a Niche You Have NO Affinity With
6. How to Get Testimonials When You Just Start Out in a Niche
7. How to Get GREAT Testimonials From Customers/Members
8. How to Use Your Lead Generation Strategies to Give You a Whole Lot More Information About Your Market Than JUST New Leads
9. A Close Look at a Beginning, Simple Marketing Funnel
10. An Inside Look at the Six-Year Evolution of Bill's Marketing Funnel
11. An Inside Look at Bill's 2004 Marketing Funnel
12. How to Create Joint Ventures That Produce Good Leads at Bargain Cost
13. How to Work Effectively With Trade Journals and Associations
14. How to Systemize and Automate the Entire Marketing Funnel
15. How to Grow Rapidly With Minimum Staff
16. How to Find the Right Staff for an Info-Marketing Business (#1 headache, I hear!)
17. When to Give Up the Front End and Concentrate on the Back End
18. The Easiest Ways to Create Back-End Products
19. Different Coaching Program Models to Consider
20. Outside-the-Box Lead Generation Strategies (like "The Industry Survey")
21. Successful Uses of Audiotapes and CDs as Sales Tools
22. How to Sell via Trade Shows, Seminars, and Speaking Opportunities
23. How to (Legally) Use Broadcast FAX
24. How to Mine Unconverted Leads 12 to 36 Months After Acquisition

25. How to Build the Most Saleable Info-Products/Kits
26. How to Minimize Refunds
27. How to Maximize Referrals
28. THE COMPLETE BUSINESS BLUEPRINT—Used for Bill's BGS Marketing Business
29. How to Maximize Profits AND Customer Value With "Forced Continuity"
30. How to Front-End a Newsletter
31. How an "Offline Guy" Uses the Internet Painlessly and Profitably
32. An Inside Look at the Financial Truths of Info-Businesses: Actual Revenues, Costs, Profits, etc. (Real Case Histories)
33. How to Identify Missed Opportunities in Your Info-Business Plan
34. Seven Most Frequently Made Mistakes to Avoid
35. How to Expand from One Niche to Multiple Niches—How I'm Doing It Now
36. How to Negotiate With Media to Make Sure You Get the Best Deal—Even After They Already Said You've Got the Best Price
37. How to Analyze New Vendors to Avoid a Business Nightmare
38. Copywriting Formulas and Shortcuts—Bill will give you his own copywriting questionnaire that he personally uses before he writes any copy for a client or himself. Frank Discussion on Outsourcing vs. Doing It In-House (the Pros and Cons)
39. When Do You Give Up on a Niche?

For more details visit **www.InfoMarketingBlueprint.com** for a special limited time offer just for buyers of this book.

Champions of the Info-Summit

Who Else Wants to 'Pick-the-Brains' of the Sharpest Information Marketers in the World?

Imagine ... Just ONE IDEA Can Make You Independent for the Rest of Your Life! This program includes:

Big Breakthroughs in the Information Marketing Business

How a Successful Info-Business Was Increased by 500 percent in 12 Months

How Agora Did It

Copywriting Secrets From the Pro

How to Most Successfully Market Your Million-Dollar Seminar or Boot Camp

How to Sell High-Priced Coaching

Integrated Media Magic: How to Crossbreed Online and Offline Marketing for ANY Information Business

How to Sell Information Online ... Even If You're a Total Computer Dunce!

Secrets of Online Copywriting

Tele-Seminar Selling Secrets

How to Turn Unconverted Leads Into a Flood of Extra Profits by Adding Inbound and/or Outbound Telemarketing to Your Marketing Funnel

The Five Gold Rings of Wealth Production From Info-Entrepreneurship

How to Turn Your Info-Products Into a Lot of Extra Cash, Automatically, on EBay

For more details visit **www.InfoMarketingChampions.com** for a special limited time offer just for buyers of this book.

Creating Copy That Sells

A Step-by-Step System That Removes All the Guesswork, Waste, and Frustration From "Creating Copy That Sells" Once and for All ... GUARANTEED!

The info-marketing business requires a lot of salesmanship. Quite frankly, no matter what business you pursue, there is no more important skill you can learn than effective sales copywriting. Today, it's never been easier to learn.

Bill Glazer created a groundbreaking web-assisted product that puts at your fingertips all the tools you need to become an expert copywriter. In addition, it walks you through the entire process step-by-step so by the time you finish the program, you have produced high quality sales letters, just like the marketing pros.

In part, this system includes:

- The "11 Building Blocks" that must be incorporated into just about every piece of copy you write.
- The "20 Critical Copy Concepts" that will take your work to the next level. Many of these are tools that only very successful pros think about. In fact, they are the tools (and tricks) that often separate the good copywriters from the professional copywriters.
- "Kopy Kryptonite." These are the BIGGEST MISTAKES that people make when writing copy that will kill your results the same way that Kryptonite affects Superman. I've identified seven of them, and believe me, you need to know what they are and avoid them like the plague.
- The "Step-by-Step Questionnaire" I use to get me organized before I write copy and also how to get the right "raw material" to mold into great copy.

Visit **www.InfoMarketingCopyThatSells.com** for more information.

Newsletters

Seven Newsletters That Unlock Your Vault to Riches in One Easy Package for Your Convenience

Matt Furey's *Internet Marketing Money-Generator*—Each month, the Zen Master of the Internet® gives you hard-hitting real facts of what works in Internet marketing.

Psycho-Cybernetics—The Newsletter—Monthly teachings of Dr. Maxwell Maltz permeating the subconscious minds of achievement-oriented entrepreneurs worldwide to program yourself for success.

Eddie Baran's Website Critiques—How would you like to get inside the mind of THE MAN who has been responsible for creating ALL of dozens of money-generating web sites since the year 2000?

Pete the Printer's *Client Newsletter With Direct Mail Secrets*—When it comes to anything having to do with print marketing, Pete Lillo, aka "Pete the Printer" is the man top marketers call on time and again.

Pete Lillo's Dynamic *NEW SUCCESSAMERICA Newsletter*—Monthly stories proving that anyone can become a Success in America (or elsewhere) with hard, focused work and a determination to focus.

Matt Furey's *Maximum Health & Fitness*—Matt's international bestseller, Combat Conditioning, continues to give everyone from martial artists to traveling businessmen the keys to getting fit and staying fit.

Dan Kennedy's *Look Over My Shoulder Program*—Dan Kennedy, aka "The Millionaire Maker," and the world's HIGHEST paid copywriter (his typical fees are now $100,000 plus royalties) allows you to see the projects he is working on and how they develop into finished m"Magnetic Marketing."

For a limited time, this collection of newsletters is available on a 2-for-1 Special, limited to 98 people. For the details visit **www.Info MarketingGoldCrown.com** right now.

Future Publications

Look for these future publications by the Information Marketing Association

Information Marketing Association Official Guide to Newsletter Profits

In this book, we'll dissect the simple and easy ways to make a great living or side income by publishing newsletters. This book will detail the easy ways to generate content and sign up subscribers.

Information Marketing Association Official Guide to Creating Info-Products Quickly

In this book, we'll outline the easy ways anyone can create products from their existing knowledge, easily acquire knowledge from others, or actually get your customers to create products for you. This book will detail the easy ways info-marketers create million-dollar products that sell for 10 times their production costs.

Information Marketing Association Official Guide to Building Super-Profitable Info-Businesses

In this book, we'll detail the techniques and business models top info-marketers use to provide their existing customers with additional value for maximum profits. This book will detail the easy ways to generate additional revenue from your existing customers.

Information Marketing Association Official Guide to Building Profitable Coaching Businesses

In this book, we'll detail the profitable models to use to build coaching programs, including the benefits and drawbacks of individual coaching and small-group and large-group coaching models. This book will detail the easy ways info-marketers sell and deliver coaching services for maximum returns.

Information Marketing Association Official Guide to Building Seminars and Speaking

In this book, we'll detail the methods the most successful seminar promoters use to fill seminar rooms and make maximum profits from their events. This book will detail the marketing, arrangements, and on-site logistics to make it easy to create events that attendees love to attend and that are profitable for you.

Information Marketing Association Official Guide to Internet Marketing

In this book, we'll outline the ways to make big money selling information products over the Internet. This book will detail the easy ways to generate products, the marketing techniques, and the specifications for your web developers to implement.

Index